3rd Edition

An Introduction to the
SOCIOLOGY
of HEALTH
and ILLNESS

KEVIN WHITE

Los Angeles | London | New Delhi
Singapore | Washington DC | Melbourne

Los Angeles | London | New Delhi
Singapore | Washington DC | Melbourne

SAGE Publications Ltd
1 Oliver's Yard
55 City Road
London EC1Y 1SP

SAGE Publications Inc.
2455 Teller Road
Thousand Oaks, California 91320

SAGE Publications India Pvt Ltd
B 1/I 1 Mohan Cooperative Industrial Area
Mathura Road
New Delhi 110 044

SAGE Publications Asia-Pacific Pte Ltd
3 Church Street
#10-04 Samsung Hub
Singapore 049483

© Kevin White 2017

This edition first published 2017

First edition published 2007, reprinted 2007, 2008
Second edition published in 2010, reprinted 2011, 2013
(twice), 2015, 2016

Editor: Natalie Aguilera
Editorial assistant: Delayna Spencer
Production editor: Katherine Haw
Copyeditor: Jane Fricker
Indexer: Bill Farrington
Marketing manager: Sally Ransom
Cover design: Shaun Mercier
Typeset by: C&M Digitals (P) Ltd, Chennai, India
Printed by: CPI Group (UK) Ltd, Croydon, CR0 4YY

Library of Congress Control Number: 2016944806

British Library Cataloguing in Publication data

A catalogue record for this book is available from
the British Library

ISBN 978-1-4739-8207-9
ISBN 978-1-4739-8208-6 (pbk)

CONTENTS

LIST OF BOXES, CASE STUDIES AND TABLES

Boxes

Case Studies

Tables

ABOUT THE AUTHOR

 Kevin White is Reader in Sociology at the Australian National University, Canberra. He has held appointments at Flinders University, Wollongong University and Victoria University, Wellington, New Zealand. He has published widely in the sociology of health and in the social history of medicine. At ANU he lectures the large introductory class, Introduction to Social Psychology; the Sociology of Health and Illness; Classical Social Theory; and Qualitative Methods.

ACKNOWLEDGEMENTS

In preparing this third edition I am indebted to our postgraduate student Ms Miranda Bruce for research assistance.

I am grateful to the following publishers for granting permission to draw on parts of previously published work: Baywood Publishing Company for parts of 'The State, the Market and General Practice: The Australian Case', *International Journal of Health Services*, 2000, 30 (2): 285–308; David Lamb and Susan Easton for permission to use parts of 'Ludwik Fleck and the Foundations of the Sociology of Medical Knowledge', *Explorations in Knowledge*, 1993, 10 (2) 1–21; and to the International Sociological Association for allowing me to draw on 'The Sociology of Health and Illness', *Current Sociology*, 1991, 39 (2): 1–145.

1

INTRODUCTION

o   Diseases are socially produced and distributed – they are not just a part of
    nature or biology.

o   The key variables shaping the production and distribution of diseases are
    class, gender and ethnicity, and the ways in which professional groups
    define conditions as diseases.

o   Medical knowledge is not purely scientific, but shapes and is shaped by the
    society in which it develops.

o   Sociologists, depending on their model of society, develop different
    explanations of the social shaping and production of disease. Marxists
    emphasize the role of class; feminists the role of patriarchy; Foucauldians
    the way society is administered by professionals; and those focusing on
    ethnicity, the impact of racism.

Sociologists study health and illness not only because they are intrinsically interesting,
and go to issues at the centre of human existence – pain, suffering and death – but also
because they help us to understand how society works. For sociologists the experience
of sickness and disease is an outcome of the organization of society. For example, poor
living and working conditions make people sicker, and poorer people die earlier, than
their counterparts at the top of the social system. Even when there are improved living
conditions and medical practices, but inequalities based on class, gender and ethnicity are not tackled, the differences between the rich and the poor persist and widen.
Disease and inequality are intimately linked. The outcome of the unequal distribution
of political, economic and social resources necessary for a healthy life is the social
gradient of health. Those at the top of the social system are healthier and live longer
while those at the bottom are sicker, do not live as long, and die more from preventable
disease and accidents. These links between social factors and health and disease are the
focus of this book.

   This book demonstrates the relationship between social structures and the
production and distribution of health and disease in modern society. Specifically,
it examines the impact of class and the role of the medical profession, gender and

ethnicity on the production and distribution of disease. It argues that there is no simple relationship between biological and individualistic explanations of what causes sickness and disease. Furthermore it demonstrates that medical knowledge is not disinterested, objective, scientific knowledge, but is both shaped by and shapes the social structures within which it is embedded. Following some scene setting for the principles of the sociology of health, and of the social and political climate that is shaping our understanding of the causes of health and disease, the book reviews Marxist, Parsonian, feminist and Foucauldian approaches to health, as well as examining the data on the impact of ethnicity on health.

In modern Western societies it is usually assumed that health differences are biologically caused or that individual lifestyles result in people becoming sicker and dying earlier. The argument of this book is that there is little evidence that disease is caused by purely biological factors, operating separately from social organization. It is also the argument that individual lifestyle choices are socially shaped, and that a focus on them as an explanation of the cause of disease misses the social factors involved in producing individual actions. Rather, there are a wide range of mediating social factors that intervene between the biology of disease, individual lifestyle, and the social experience shaping and producing disease. These range from standards of living and occupational conditions, to socio-psychological experiences at work and at home, of men's and women's social roles, and of hierarchical status groups based on ethnicity. These factors, in turn, have to be seen against the background of the overall patterns of inequality that exist within specific societies. This includes whether or not there is a political commitment to reducing inequality and providing a social environment that prevents sickness and disease – of guaranteeing housing standards, food standards and conditions of employment, as well as enhancing lifestyles that increase health and longevity. Put simply, the impact of income inequality now appears to be central to the continued existence of inequalities in health. As Wilkinson (1996) has shown, countries with low relative differences between the richest and the poorest are the healthiest.

Sociology, Genetics, Social Mobility and Lifestyle

Sociologists argue that our understanding of the social production of disease is not helped by explanations:

- that focus solely on genetics at the expense of the social environment;
- that claim that the sick are poor because they experience downward social mobility;
- that fail to recognize that lifestyle choices are shaped by social factors.

In our daily life, three dominant representations of the causes of disease, especially in the media (the newspapers, medical docudramas and TV soaps), stand out. The first of these is the genetic explanation. Genetic explanations regularly feature in articles and programmes in which claims are made that there is a genetic cause for obesity, drug addiction, alcoholism, divorce and homosexuality, to mention just the most common. There is, however, no evidence for a genetic contribution to what are cultural practices, nor any scientific justification for the negative moral evaluations of them that are couched in the language of medical science. These conditions are clearly culturally specific and professionally defined – not 'facts' of nature. Furthermore, there is little that can be done about even those diseases for which there *is* genetic evidence for their origins. Short of undertaking a eugenicist or genetic planning experiment, the knowledge of genetic predisposition does not help either individuals or policy makers to deal with disease. In fact, by reducing the explanation of the individual's condition back to a lowest common denominator of biology, the genetic explanation systematically excludes a sociological explanation, and functions to deflect our attention from the ways in which social life shapes our experience of disease. Between the genetic predisposition for a specific disease and its development lie the intervening variables of politics, economics, gender and ethnicity. It is these variables that must be taken into account in explaining the transformation of a 'genetic risk' into a social reality.

A second common assumption is that the sick experience downward social mobility, while the healthy experience upward social mobility. This is an extension of what is presumed to be Darwin's argument about the survival of the fittest. There is no support for this argument in the literature. The sickest are certainly in the poorest sections of society, but they are sick because they are poor, not poor because they are sick. Where sickness and downward social mobility intersect, it is in those conditions where political, cultural and social practices already discriminate against the individual – the single mother, the disabled, the differently coloured and those with AIDS.

The third dominant explanation for the existence of disease, in what should otherwise be healthier societies, is that people adopt a lifestyle that makes them sick, and are therefore individually responsible for their condition. The lifestyles explanation claims that freely made bad choices about diet, smoking and exercise make people sick. Again, there is very little evidence that individual effort at this level will achieve much in the way of a healthier society. Moreover, all the major studies, brought together in this book, show that good lifestyle choices are overwhelmed by wider structural variables in determining health and illness. Lifestyle actions do not account for more than a minor part of the variation in health status. Even if they did, since they are unevenly socially structured rather than individually chosen, they are the outcome of inequality rather than the cause of it.

For sociologists of health these three explanations have two common features. They make the claim that when individuals become diseased it is a problem of the individual's own body and of their unique biology. Put another way, these explanations individualize and biologize the explanation of disease. Often they are combined into explanations that blame individuals for lifestyle choices that they are biologically incapable of coping with, because of their genetic make-up. This 'over-determined' individual and biological explanation is very common in societies based on racialized status groups.

─BOX 1.1─

ABORIGINALITY, LIFESTYLE AND GENETICS – OBSCURING SOCIAL PROCESSES

In Australia, it is claimed that Aboriginal people have higher rates of diabetes because they freely choose bad Western foods such as potato chips, soft drinks and alcohol, for which they are genetically not 'programmed'. Thus their health problems read as the following equation. They choose poor foods (therefore it is their fault) + they are genetically not capable of processing Western food (the fault of their individual biology) + they are lazy or indifferent about their health (the fault of their culture). The conclusion, which policy makers informed by this way of approaching the problem then reach, is that it is the Aborigines' problem that they are sicker and die sooner, and that there is little or indeed nothing that can be done about it.

A sociological account, on the other hand, directs attention to the political and economic shaping of lifestyles available to subordinate populations, and to the way in which racism systematically destroys the beneficial aspects of an Indigenous population's culture.

The Sociological Perspective

Sociologists, on the basis of empirical research, demonstrate how the interactions of class, of professional interests, of power, of gender and of ethnicity enter into the formation of knowledge about and treatment of a sickness or disease. They demonstrate the social production and distribution of diseases and illnesses. Sociologists show how diseases could be differently understood, treated and experienced by demonstrating how disease is produced out of social organization rather than nature, biology, or individual lifestyle choices. While sociologists make no claim to being biological scientists they do make the claim that biological knowledge can be sociologically explained, to show that our knowledge of health and disease is created in a political, social and cultural environment. There is no pure, value-free scientific knowledge about disease. Our knowledge of health and illness, the organizations of the professions which deal with it, and our own responses to our bodily states are shaped and formed by the history of our society and our place in society.

Since sociologists do not accept the medical model of disease and illness as simply biological events, they then examine the social functions of medical knowledge. That is, they examine the way medical and biological explanations of disease function in our society. Medical knowledge is produced in and reflects structural features of society. It explains as 'natural' what, from a sociological perspective, are social phenomena. Why the working class is sicker and dies earlier, why women are diagnosed sick more than men, and why ethnic groups do not receive the services they need – these require a sociological explanation and not a biological one. Medical explanations obscure and paper over the social shaping and distribution of disease, disease categories and health services.

Postmodernity and Sociology

The arguments of the sociologists of health are particularly important in the current economic and political climate. There has been a major restructuring of the labour market in the Western capitalist economies, with a decline in industry and, associated with this, of trade unions and class-based political movements. There has been a resurgence of the philosophy of liberalism – that the state should not be involved in the provision of welfare services, and that individuals should take more responsibility for their own lives. The economic changes are sometimes summarized in the term 'postmodernity' – that we have moved beyond organized capitalism, and into a new era in which consumption rather than production is the key to social life. Some sociologists have celebrated these changes. The claim is that we now live in a postmodern world, freed of the old structures of industrial capitalism and the bourgeois nuclear family. For Ulrich Beck, these changes mean that people 'will be set free from the social forms of industrial society – class, stratification, family [and] gender status' (Beck, 1992: 87). Identity has become fluid and negotiable, separated from 'social structures', which are now claimed to be just a figment of the sociological imagination. For some theorists the discovery of the body, linked to these weakened structures, has led to the argument that we construct our bodies as we see fit. Anthony Giddens, for example, emphasizes the openness of the body, and of individuals to shape it: 'We have become responsible for the design of our own bodies' (Giddens, 1992: 102). Similarly, Bauman (1992) has argued that both our sociological knowledge and the world that we live in are uncertain, ambivalent, deregulated and insecure. The stable basis of our identity has gone, as have the certainties of social science knowledge. At the core of these changes, according to Bauman (1998), is a transformation from a culture of production, in which hard work, thrift and self-discipline held sway, to a world of hedonistic indulgence. Rather than hard work resulting in savings and social prestige, we are rewarded with 'free sex', designer drugs and 'life in the fast lane'.

─BOX 1.2─

MODERN SOCIETY MAY HAVE CHANGED –
BUT KEY SOCIAL STRUCTURES PERSIST

It is the argument of this book that there is little evidence that social structures of class and gender, of ethnicity and of inequality have stopped shaping people's lives. Industrial capitalism may have changed its appearance, and patriarchy may no longer be the bulwark of women's oppression, but they both still structure health and illness, and distribute disease unequally through the population. In the area of health and illness individuals have not been freed from the structures of patterned inequality, nor have their choices increased. In fact, society has become more unequal, and the poor sicker.

Sociological Approaches to Health and Illness

Different sociological perspectives on society give rise to different accounts of the role of medical knowledge, and of the social causes of disease. They are also based in different sociological models of society, in part complementary, in part contradictory. Marxist approaches emphasize the causal role of economics in the production and distribution of disease, as well as the role that medical knowledge plays in sustaining the class structure. Parsonian sociology emphasizes the role of medicine in maintaining social harmony, pointing to the non-market basis of professional groups. At the same time, its critical sociological edge is maintained by the way it highlights the social control function of medicine in enforcing compliance with social roles in modern society. Parsons' work both contradicts Marxism – by highlighting the importance of the non-economic sphere of society – but also adds to it in providing a description of the sick role as a social role that is shaped by the social strains of modern society. Thus Parsons is both conservative and critical at the same time.

Foucault, too, highlights the social role of medical knowledge in controlling populations, and like Parsons emphasizes the diffuse nature of power relationships in modern society. Also, like Parsons, he sees the professions, especially the helping professions, playing a key role in inducing individuals to comply with 'normal' social roles. For Foucault, modern societies are systems of organized surveillance with the catch being that individuals conduct the surveillance on themselves, having internalized 'professional' models of what is appropriate behaviour. Marxist feminists identify the ways in which class and patriarchy interact to define the subordinate position of women in society and the central role that medical knowledge plays in defining women as childcarers and housewives. Foucauldian feminism, on the other hand, is more alert to the ambiguities of women's roles, and the way that women

TABLE 1.1 *A simplified overview of the sociology of health*

Theory	Model of society	Cause of disease	Role of the medical profession
Marxist	Conflictual and exploitative	Putting profit ahead of health	To discipline and control the working class; and provide individualized explanations of disease
Parsonian	Basically harmonious and stable set of interlinked social roles and structures	Social strain caused by meeting the demands of social roles	Rehabilitate individuals to carry out their social roles
Foucauldian	A net of power relations, with no one dominant source – administered surveillance	'Diseases' are labels used to sort and segregate the population to make it easier to control	To enforce compliance with 'normal' social roles; and to ensure that we internalize these norms
Feminist	Exploitative and repressive of women through patriarchy	Carrying out the social role enforced on women by patriarchal men; the medicalization of a woman around her reproductive life cycle	To enforce conformity with patriarchal norms of femininity and motherhood

can challenge their medicalization. However, on balance, medical knowledge – especially as it is manifest in self-help movements and health self-surveillance – is deeply pervasive. Feminist Foucauldians argue that large parts of the women's health movement have been incorporated into a patriarchal net of self-surveillance. Sociologists who focus on ethnicity present a picture of society as 'racialized', as operating with a scientifically discredited notion of race to justify the exclusion and subordination of people of different skin colour or ethnic identity.

Thus there are competing models of society as harmonious or conflictual, as a set of structures 'doing things', or of individuals voluntarily complying with their social role, and of the sometimes complementary, sometimes competing, role of class, gender and ethnicity in structuring unequal health outcomes in society.

Political Economy and Marxist Approaches

Researchers in the materialist and Marxist traditions have produced one of the most powerful sociological accounts of the production of disease and its social pattern of distribution. These approaches emphasize the determining role of economic interests in both producing disease and in shaping the way it is dealt with. Marxists argue that medicine serves a key function in capitalist societies: it blames the victims of diseases (caused by the capitalists' pursuit of profit) for their own condition. Furthermore, the very way in which disease is treated is itself an aspect of capitalist society. The medical profession acts as an agent of social control of the working class, individualizing and depoliticizing disease, and controlling access to the sick certificate. High-cost, technical 'fixes' are pursued, which do not heal people but do produce enormous profits. Medicine in a capitalist society reflects the characteristics of capitalism: it is profit-oriented, blames the victim, and reproduces the class structure in terms of the people who become doctors (generally male, privately educated upper-middle-class students), or nurses (generally lower-middle-class women). Access to health services also reflects class inequality.

Parsonian Sociology of Health

An alternative analysis of medicine is provided by Talcott Parsons, who argued that modern societies, while having a capitalist economy, have noncapitalist social structures. He argues that the medical profession is one such structure. Medical professionals are motivated by factors other than making money, such as caring for their patients. They perform a key noneconomic function by acting in the interests of the whole community, treating individuals specifically for their disease, without passing judgement on them, and utilizing the best of scientific knowledge. They are, if you like, a balance to the fly-wheel of competitive capitalism in which the market would otherwise run over individuals. At the same time, Parsons goes on to make the important point that medicine is a major institution for controlling deviance in modern societies. It is not just a benign institution based on scientific care, but acts to check the deviant tendencies of individuals, who otherwise might try to escape their social roles. Parsons argues that the strains of modern life may be so great as to drive people into the sick role to escape their normal responsibilities, and this tendency needs to be checked. So while he has a more favourable perspective on medicine than the Marxist, he still sees it as performing a social function that is beyond its claim to be the purely scientific treatment of disease. Parsons' analysis shows how the medical profession acts to control motivated deviance and provides an account of illness as a response to social strain. Parsons' concept of the sick role is a very useful concept for problematizing the idea of disease as natural and biological, but is limited in its focus on acute illness episodes. Overall, Parsons' 'consensus' focus on modern societies as stable is not as true as it appeared to him, writing in the 1950s. Neither is his picture of the altruistic workings of the medical profession as persuasive as it might once have been.

Foucault's Sociology of Health

It is with the development of the category of disease – the product of the professionalization of medicine – that Foucault is concerned. Michel Foucault calls attention to another important aspect of modern society: it is an administered society, in which professional groups define categories of people – the sick, the insane, the criminal, the deviant – on behalf of an administrative state. For Foucault, medicine is a product of the administrative state, policing normal behaviour and using credentialled professionals to enforce compliance with the 'normal'. Modern society is a version of Max Weber's Iron Cage, in which the profession (and its disease categories) provide a totalizing surveillance of citizens. Foucault also makes the important point that most of us, most of the time, have internalized these norms of behaviour and rarely require the services of the helping professionals. As will be seen, his argument raises serious questions for the Marxist and the feminist positions. For feminists, modern society is patriarchal and men wield power over women, who are forced to comply with men's definitions of how they should appear and perform. However, Foucault's theory of power emphasizes its diffuseness and the willingness of most of us – men and women – most of the time to comply with societal norms. Equally, Foucault's argument challenges Marxist accounts that focus on power as centralized in the hands of the capitalist class. For Foucault, power is not the property of any one group, whether based in class relationships or patriarchy. The usefulness of Foucault's position is the way in which he historically locates medical knowledge, especially allowing for the development of the sociology of the body. By showing how the body is historically constructed, Foucault has been appropriated and extended by feminists who show that it is the construction of gender-specific bodies that needs analysis.

Feminist Approaches

It is the case that the Marxists overlook the ways in which contemporary life is not always shaped by economic factors; that Parsons does not go very far in documenting the 'strains' of social life; and that for all his interest in bodies, Foucault does not discuss gender. Feminist sociology seeks to extend and develop especially Marxist and Foucauldian sociology. Feminists' key argument is that the way in which we are socialized into masculine and feminine social roles will have a determining effect on our health and illness. They argue that medicine plays a vital role in enforcing conformity to these social roles, and is especially targeted at women. This is because controlling women's ability to reproduce is central to a patriarchal society. It is no accident, the feminists argue, that almost all the medical attention paid to women is around their reproductive organs and their life cycle as it relates to their ability to have children. In many cases, the diagnoses and treatment of women as diseased are no more than thinly disguised social norms of women's appropriate social roles, especially their role as mother. There have been powerful accounts of the role and function of modern medicine growing out of an intermingling of Marxism and feminism. Marxist feminists have argued that the origins of capitalism, patriarchy and medicine are intertwined. The need to guarantee the legitimacy of offspring to allow for the inheritance of capital meant that the medical profession played a crucial role in the control of women. In contemporary capitalism, the profession performs the function of legitimizing the domestic role of women in the 'private' sphere, converting (into a 'fact' of nature) women's mothering and nurturing roles. It thus guarantees the rearing and nurturing of the next generation of workers at minimum cost to capitalists. It also makes women responsible for a larger part of the health care of the unprofitable sectors of the population – children and the aged.

Feminist reactions to the way in which medicine 'medicalizes' their bodies have raised crucial issues at the centre of sociological explanations of disease. On the one hand, to explain women's experience of a capitalist patriarchy as 'disease' provides them with an explanation of the way in which they are oppressed. For example, arguing for the existence of premenstrual syndrome as a disease provides an account of their stress that has a social legitimacy. On the other, to transform their social experience into a biological explanation leaves them powerless in the face of male medical practitioners' definitions of them as diseased.

Bringing the Approaches Together

There is no definitive cause of inequality in health and in the patterns of disease distribution. Class, patriarchy and bureaucratic and professional surveillance inter-mingle with each other in shaping the contents of medical knowledge and the individual's experience of health and disease. In addition to class and gender, as a result of the massive migratory processes since the end of the Second World War, ethnicity has also become a major variable in the experience and distribution of disease. In some cases being from a migrant ethnic group is a positive factor, while in others it operates negatively. What interests sociologists is how ethnicity intersects with gender and class, so that those who are from low-status ethnic positions find themselves members of the working class, and if they are women, suffer from the triple impact of skin colour, class and gender. The patterning of health inequality is a dynamic one and at different times class, gender and ethnicity will have greater or lesser impact. It is to understanding this constantly changing structuring of inequality in health that sociologists are most interested in making a contribution.

BOX 1.3

SOCIOLOGY, SCIENCE AND MEDICINE

The assumption that unifies sociological accounts of sickness and disease is a rejection of behaviourism, the claim that we passively respond to environmental factors, as a model for human action. Health and disease are cultural products, and individuals as social agents react to, transform and are shaped by the experiences of health and disease. There is no one-way determination from nature and biology through to the individual and society. Rather, for sociologists, it is the structures of society that shape who will get sick, how they experience their condition, how they will be diagnosed and treated, and how they will recover. What looks like 'natural behaviour' is, in fact, the product of social interaction. Ours is a culture that gives privilege to those who claim to be 'scientists'. However, sociologists are sceptical that science – whether of the medical sort or any other sort – exists in any independent sense from the social relationships which produce it. Science is itself a social product, determined in its content and shaped by broader social variables, and in the case of the analysis of medicine in this book, by professional interests and by class, gender and ethnicity.

Integrating the analysis of modern medicine in terms of the different sociological approaches outlined above – the analysis of the Marxists, the Parsonians, the feminists and Foucauldians – we can make a number of statements which lie at the heart of a sociological analysis of medicine. Modern medicine, and the explanations of the individual, the body and our understandings of disease it produces, is the outcome of the development of modern bureaucratic society, and the interplay of the structuring of life chances based on gender, class and ethnicity.

Medical knowledge and medical practices are not distinct from the social: medical knowledge is socially produced knowledge. The boundaries and activities of the medical profession are not defined by natural objects, nor biological realities given independently of social life; they are the outcome of political and economic struggles around the negotiated realities of the body and disease. Consequently, the claim that technological and scientific knowledge underpin medicine's claims to professionalism and autonomy has to be seen as the successful mobilization of resources to become a profession, and not the cause of professionalization. In support of this claim, witness the way in which professional groups redefine knowledge to protect themselves from boundary encroachment. For example, the medical profession has deskilled the use of the stethoscope as it passed into usage by nurses.

Medicine acts as a cosmological system in modern society – historically replacing religion – and provides answers to central questions to do with the relationship of nature to society, of the individual to society, and of the impact of such social variables as class, ethnicity and gender on our individual biographies. It provides in the language of science what are, fundamentally, socially informed and value-laden explanations of our life chances, and acts from a sociological perspective as a system of social control. It makes inequality based on class, gender and ethnicity look natural and inevitable.

From a sociological perspective, biology is not itself the overriding factor in the development of a disease. Rather, it is the prevailing social and economic conditions that allow disease to develop which must be accounted for (Canguilhem, 1988; Stern, 1927; White, 1991a; Zinsser, 1935). Sociological accounts of health and illness have developed against the background of a sociology of knowledge that emphasizes the ways in which 'nature' is socially produced, and the ways in which the claim to understand nature is a political and social process. Furthermore, given that germs do not speak for themselves, it is our interpretation of events that leads some conditions to be categorized as diseases (White, 1992). As Rosenberg puts it: 'Meaning is not necessary but negotiated … disease is constructed not discovered' (Rosenberg, 1989: 2).

In addition to the sociology of knowledge, historical epidemiology has played a large part in the development of health sociology. Thomas McKeown (1979) demonstrated very clearly that medicine and its scientific practices contributed very little to the transformation of the health of the population in the nineteenth century. In fact, he estimated that medicine contributed about 1 per cent to the overall decline in the mortality rates of the nineteenth century. Rather, he argued that what made the difference were the social and political factors of improved housing, nutrition and sanitation (see also White, 1999).

Conclusion

This book presents an overview of the development of the sociology of health, which highlights some of the key conceptual underpinnings of the sociology of health in Chapter 2 developing the work of Émile Durkheim in the sociology of science, and a survey of the development of the sociology of health in Chapter 3. It also reviews recent changes in the social and political environment that have meant a resurgence of the individualistic approach to health and illness, as well as putting individuals and communities more at risk of disease and early death, in Chapter 4. The materialist and Marxist (Chapter 5), the Parsonian (Chapter 6), the Foucauldian (Chapter 7), and the feminist accounts of the social functions of medical knowledge (Chapter 8) are presented, while Chapter 9 provides an analysis of the intervening role of ethnicity in the experience of sickness and disease. In Chapter 10, the conclusion, I draw these perspectives together in the context of the suggestions of the World Health Organization about the social requirements for a healthy society. It also draws together the theme of the book: that social structures cause sickness and disease and that individualistic explanations or solutions to health inequalities are of limited value. Indeed, individualistic and lifestyle explanations contribute to the ongoing inequality of society and to the unequal distribution of sickness and disease down the social system.

Summary

- The 'commonsense' understandings of the cause of disease portrayed in our culture – especially the idea that lifestyles are freely chosen – individualizes and obscures the way in which disease is socially produced.

- The commonsense understanding of medicine as the application of 'objective' 'scientific' knowledge to a purely biological body obscures how diseases are produced in structures of inequality that are social – be they based on class, gender or ethnicity.

- At the centre of all sociological accounts of medicine is the argument that medical knowledge performs social functions independently of whether it cures and heals – to discipline the working class, to enforce compliance with social roles, to administer and categorize individuals, or to ensure that women conform to their feminine roles.

- Medical knowledge and practices are social accomplishments, and not the inevitable outcome of science or nature.

Discussion Questions

1. Different theories of society produce different accounts of the role of medicine in modern society. Compare and contrast two of the theories outlined in this chapter.

2. What does it mean when sociologists argue that diseases are social products and not just biological facts?

3. Can you think of conditions that were once thought of as normal but now require medical intervention?

Further Reading

Conrad, P. (ed.) (2001) *The Sociology of Health and Illness: Critical Perspectives.* New York: Worth. A very good collection of articles which highlight the sociological, political, economic and gendered relations of modern medicine.

Freund, P. and McGuire, M. (1999) *Health, Illness and the Social Body.* Englewood Cliffs, NJ: Prentice Hall. A very good textbook, using mainly American data, overviewing the social relations of disease.

Germov, J. (ed.) (2005) *Second Opinion: An Introduction to Health Sociology.* Melbourne: Oxford University Press. A collection of articles covering a range of health topics and issues related to the class, gender and age dimensions of health and wellbeing, with a chapter dedicated to nursing and sociology.

Marmot, M. (2004) *Status Syndrome: How Your Social Standing Directly Affects Your Health and Life Expectancy.* Oxford: Bloomsbury. A detailed exploration of factors contributing to the social gradient of health.

Turner, B. S. (1995) *Medical Power and Social Knowledge.* London: Sage. Explores the sociology of health in a way that advances sociological arguments about changes in contemporary society.

Turner, B. S. (2004) *The New Medical Sociology: Social Forms of Health and Illness.* New York: Norton. Explores how society makes us sick, examining macro-processes such as globalization, risk, economic deregulation and technological change.

2

THE SOCIAL CONSTRUCTION OF MEDICAL KNOWLEDGE

- o Underpinning the sociology of health is an argument that scientific knowledge is a social product. The sociology of knowledge was developed in classical sociology by Émile Durkheim.

- o In the contemporary sociology of health this has led to the development of 'social constructionism', which argues that medical knowledge can be explained in social terms, as the product of specific societies. I illustrate this argument in a range of examples, including masturbatory insanity and hysteria.

- o One of the earliest developments of this argument is in the works of Ludwik Fleck, who demonstrated the way in which medical knowledge of disease, of infection, and of the body can be shown to be the product of politics, economics and cultural factors.

- o The chapter presents his work on syphilis, and of the ways that skeletons are represented, as case studies of the constructionist approach. It also shows the lasting impact of both Durkheim and Fleck's approaches to the formation of the sociology of health.

Each of the sociological approaches reviewed in this book implicitly questions the 'objectivity' and 'factualness' of medical knowledge. In this chapter, I review the origins of these approaches in the explicit critiques of medical knowledge developed from a sociology-of-knowledge perspective (White, 1988). In this perspective, the sociology of health and illness can be seen as a subset of the sociology of knowledge. The Marxist approach demonstrates how capitalist social relations shape medical knowledge; the feminist approach shows how patriarchal assumptions constitute the medical knowledge of women's bodies; while the Foucauldian approach argues that medical knowledge is constituted in the administrative apparatus of the state and in professional disciplines. Medical knowledge is also shaped and produced out of racist social practices.

The sociology of knowledge is developed in classical sociology in the work of Émile Durkheim. Durkheim argued in his book *The Elementary Forms of the Religious Life* (Durkheim, 1915), and in *Primitive Classifications* (Durkheim and Mauss, 1963), that the concepts that we use to think with – space, weight, force, time and mass – are not reflections of nature, but of the social organization of society. This insight was developed in a largely overlooked book by Ludwik Fleck (1935 [1979]), *The Genesis and Development of a Scientific Fact*. The chapter starts with a discussion of the way in which the sociology of health has developed the social constructionist approach based on a sociology of medical knowledge.

Generally speaking, medical sociology has not concerned itself with the knowledge claims of medicine. Mechanic's (1981) textbook, for example, specifies 15 research areas in the sociology of medicine, not one of which refers to medical knowledge. This absence is characteristic, both of the sociology of health and of medical history, and has four general presuppositions (Wright and Treacher, 1982). First, since medicine and medical knowledge were taken for granted by sociologists, research tended to focus on the achievements of medicine, institutional developments such as hospitals and clinics, and proposed individualistic explanations of social change. In short: great advances, great hospitals and great men (White, 1996). Second, medicine was seen to be part of the natural sciences and granted an epistemologically privileged position. Thus its knowledge claims were not open to sociological enquiry in the same way as those of other professions. As such, both for medicine and the sociologists of it, a key conceptual component followed: namely that diseases were natural objects, and the social contribution to understanding disease was limited to epidemiology. This led to the fourth proposition, that for medicine to advance it had to distance itself from the social. The more abstracted from human relations it became, the more 'scientific', then the better it would perform.

These four claims have been seriously challenged in recent times. In the first place, it has been argued that medicine is not distinct from the social. Detailed studies of the sociology of professions have shown that the boundaries of medicine are not defined by natural objects, but are rather the outcome of struggles with, for example, other paramedical groups (Willis, 1989), or with other professional groups such as lawyers, over areas of competence – particularly the right to define insanity (Smith, 1981). The domain of medical knowledge is a negotiated one. In the second place, medicine's claim to study natural objects has been disputed by studies that show how groups claiming technical knowledge can redefine knowledge, thus enhancing their power – and their power in turn enhancing their knowledge. As Nietzsche put it, 'knowledge works as a tool of power. Hence it is plain that it increases with every increase of power.' Furthermore, as Jamous and Pelloile (1970) have shown, a key aspect to a profession's claims to a knowledge base is not the technical content of the knowledge, but the indeterminacy surrounding its implementation. Third, anthropological works, such as Mary Douglas's (1973) *Natural Symbols*, have illustrated that, like other areas of human thought that are essentially cosmological, medicine is a set of categories that filters and constructs experience. Finally, the impact of Foucault's work in general, and *The Birth of the Clinic* (1973) in particular – that medicine is a discourse which produces its own objects – has shown how medical practice is as open to sociological analysis as any other social institution.

─BOX 2.1─

THE SOCIAL CONSTRUCTIONIST THEORY OF MEDICAL KNOWLEDGE

The social constructionist theory of medical knowledge has three major aims:

1. to demonstrate that medical knowledge parallels other forms of knowledge, through either analogy or isomorphism, and thus to show the social nature of medical thought;

2. to introduce the contextual elements that influence the development of medical thought, and by emphasizing the relativistic implications of both historical and anthropological research into medicine, highlight its contextual qualities;

3. to examine medicine as social practice and ask the more general question of how medical knowledge comes to be constituted as an abstract entity, and the implications of this for examining the process whereby medical concepts are transferred into social life (Wright and Treacher, 1982).

As Elias (1971) has argued, the programme for contemporary sociology (when applied to knowledge) is to break down the assumption that 'nature' is separate from 'society'. Studies of the professionalization process of dentists at the beginning of the twentieth century have illustrated quite clearly that there is a relationship between knowledge claims and the successful professionalization of the occupation. It is not one in which knowledge of 'nature' leads to greater 'scientific' cogency and then to social recognition (Nettleton, 1985). Rather, the acceptance of a theory depends on the objectives of the social group mobilizing the knowledge, and their social characteristics (Lawrence, 1985).

---BOX 2.2---

MEDICAL AND DENTAL KNOWLEDGE AS SOCIALLY LOCATED

Dussault and Sheiham (1982) argue, convincingly, that the acceptance by British dentists of Hunter's theory of oral sepsis at the beginning of the twentieth century – that bad teeth were the source of all other bodily ailments – occurred within a social and political context rather than one in which 'science' was at work. The professional dental bodies were weak, had difficulty attracting members and were not publicly recognized. At the same time, in the broader social context, there was a growing awareness of the need for a fit population if national efficiency was to be achieved. Dental sepsis offered a focus for the profession and a leverage on the state, for a profession in pursuit of an occupational monopoly. The theory of oral sepsis improved the self-image of the profession, and linked the health of the nation to qualified and registered practitioners. The appeal of oral sepsis lay not in its scientificness – it was largely rejected in the USA (for reasons to do with professional and social factors) – but because it satisfied the needs of the actors involved. Thus, not nature, not science, but a social and political context guaranteed its success.

The impact of the constructionist approach can be examined under three headings:

1. It problematizes reality, particularly the claim that we understand nature through an objective natural science.

2. It demonstrates how scientific medical knowledge mediates social relations.

3. It shows how the technical realm of medical practice is not neutral with respect to social processes.

Making Reality Problematic: The Problem of the Medical Model of Disease

The most important application of this argument is to be found in the sociology of disease. Within the medical model, disease is presented as a fact within the context of a natural science methodology. In this perspective, disease is essentially the absence of health. This biological determinism holds that disease and manifestations of it are recognizable by a natural science methodology. This approach can vary, with disease being defined as any entity or condition that deviates from the norm of the species, thus placing the organism at a biological disadvantage. The most popular contemporary analyses of 'biological disadvantage' are socio-biological accounts of the lowering of inclusive fitness. But this premise leads those in this position to argue for absurdities from within their own framework.

For example, the concept of inclusive fitness is both too broad and too narrow when it comes to defining disease. It is too narrow insofar as any 'disease', such as an infection, which does not affect genetic fitness, is not regarded as a disease. It is too broad insofar as voluntary celibacy and a lifestyle away from genetic relatives (and hence having no impact on their inclusive fitness) becomes a disease. The second problem with such approaches is with the concept of normality. There are at least seven distinct senses of the term 'normality'. Of these the two most important that medical thought operates with are: (1) Commonness/usualness, in a statistical sense of lying within the range of variability of a double standard of deviation on either side of a normal Gaussian curve; and (2) Averageness, i.e. that which has the highest frequency of occurrence.

The major difficulty with definitions of disease which use statistical concepts of normality is that they are difficult to operationalize. For example, consider whole populations affected by epidemics of the plague or parasitic infections. Using the statistical concept of normality it is now logically impossible to classify the population as diseased. Similar difficulties are met in utilizing an explanatory framework of normal function. These are concepts of disease that are based on the identification of the failure of the parts contributing to the goal of the whole organism. On this account of disease it is not possible for an organ to be non-diseased and yet lose its function. As Margolis has pointed out, this is quite possible. For example, with increasing technological innovation in artificial reproduction, human sexual organs may completely lose their function of reproduction (Margolis, 1976).

These logical problems in a positivist account of disease, combined with an awareness that concepts of disease are inextricably linked with judgements of a moral and ethical nature, have produced their own response in turn. That diseases are the product of the social rather than the biological is clear in the literature – especially when the subject of discussion is sexual behaviour, gender identity, ethnicity, addiction or gender preference. Authors such as Toon (1981) seek to take into account the findings of this type of research, arguing that a distinction must be made between those disease categories which value judgements enter into, and those which they do not. In other words, the attempt is to distinguish problematic social action, which may be falsely classified as disease, from 'real' diseases.

Within contemporary medical philosophy, however, it has become almost impossible to distinguish disease from non-disease. Such an attempt to distinguish between disease and subjective psychological or social factors has been made by Taylor and Scadding (1980). They suggest that disease in general – that which separates the class of patients from non-patients – is distinguished by (1) a desire for therapy by the patient; (2) a recognition by others in the individual's environment that aid should be administered; and (3) a concern expressed by a medical practitioner. However, as they point out, these characteristics embody those very social and cultural influences that they think should be excluded from any definition of disease. They conclude:

> The dilemma is insoluble at present as there are as yet no hard and fast rules which are satisfactory enough to put the diagnosis of disease in general on an objective unassailable basis. (Taylor and Scadding, 1980: 423)

—BOX 2.3—

DISEASES CHANGE INDEPENDENTLY OF THEIR BIOLOGY – THE CASE OF TUBERCULOSIS

Attempts like these to distinguish diseases from social circumstances lead to other problems. Thus Bollet is taken aback by the fact that tuberculosis steadily declined after 1855 in the UK – that is to say, prior to the discovery of the tubercle bacillus. By attempting to explain disease as a biological phenomenon, Bollet is led to the (for him) puzzling conclusion, that 'many changes have occurred in the nature, frequency and distribution of major diseases, beyond those which can be attributed to improved medical understanding and use of diagnostic terms' (Bollet, 1981: 15). Similarly Klepinger can only conclude, 'Some diseases change their expression; new diseases arise and some die out' (Klepinger, 1980: 481). This inability to theorize diseases only arises if they are given a privileged epistemological position, and not seen to be socially constructed. The problem does not arise if diseases are seen as actions. More fully, if the self-understanding of an epoch's illnesses, the action surrounding a disease and the social structure within which they exist are interrelated, as for example in Zinsser's classic study of typhoid, then these paradoxes do not arise (Zinsser, 1935). As Rosenberg has summarized it: 'Disease does not exist as a social phenomenon until it is somehow perceived as existing' (Rosenberg, 1989). Even more pithily, as another sociologist put it, 'Disease does not exist; what exists is social practices' (Delaporte, 1986: 131).

Sociologically, then, we can circumscribe the problems of a positivist medical theory by suggesting that the category of disease will come into play in those situations in which the boundary between 'nature' and 'culture' is problematic; and where agency and structure (or individual and society) are contested issues. A good example of this in the literature is the contested nature of repetitive strain injury (RSI) (Hopkins, 1989).

BOX 2.4

DISEASES PRODUCED IN A SOCIAL ENVIRONMENT – RSI

Whether or not RSI is a disease is a contested issue. To some commentators – generally employers – it is the outcome of a general lack of tone, poor posture and unfitness. Others – generally representatives of the unions involved – focus on equipment and work processes, suggesting that the conditions of employment in modern offices, with the lack of control experienced by the worker and the drudgery of the work, inevitably give rise to the complaint. For yet others – the psychiatrists – it is a form of compensation neurosis and/or a form of hysterical conversion syndrome, or the product of the medico-legal system. Thus, whether or not RSI is a disease, or will become a disease, is a political issue and the outcome, not of biological factors, but social relationships (Arksey, 1994; Tesh, 1988). Furthermore, sociologists who enter the debate, particularly those who utilize a constructionist perspective, will themselves become actors in the definitional process as their work is appropriated by representatives of different positions to suit their own interests (Martin and Richards, 1995). Similar analyses have been conducted on the development of Alzheimer's disease (Fox, 1989), hypoglycaemia (Singer, 1984), hypertension (Blumhagen, 1980), dyslexia (Erchak and Rosenfeld, 1989), endometriosis (Capek, 2000), Gulf War Syndrome (Brown et al., 2003; Zavestoski et al., 2002), chronic fatigue syndrome (Clarke and James, 2003) and the category of psychosomatic disorder (Helman, 1985).

Medical Knowledge Mediates Social Relations

Rather than diseases being the simple working of nature, the constructionist approach suggests that they are deeply embedded in social relations. Foucault, for example, can be understood to argue that the core of social life is twofold. In the first place the population needs to be regulated; and in the second, the individuals have to be disciplined. As Turner (1984) has argued, bodies need to be internally restrained and externally represented. Both of these requirements can be met in the socially produced categories of disease. Since the stable reproduction of the population, and the relationship of the individual to these structures, are central social problems, they will work themselves out in particular forms of action. Thus, as Turner shows, masturbatory insanity, hysteria and agoraphobia can be seen, not as bizarre episodes in medical history, but as the product of specific socio-historical conditions.

Masturbatory Insanity

Masturbatory insanity was a major disease of men in the eighteenth and nineteenth centuries. However, it can be explained in terms of the need to control populations, and to produce individuals with internal controls. Thomas Malthus argued that human beings were driven by the urge to eat and to reproduce, and further, that reproduction would always outrun the production of food. Thus there was a perceived need to control people's desires, and to internalize moral actions such as the delay of gratification and self-denial. It was in this context that medical thought developed with a focus on reproduction and sexuality. The concern with sexual promiscuity had a parallel in economic theory: one should save one's money and not be a spendthrift. These two social concerns were brought together in the idea that one should save one's sexual abilities in the same way that one should save money. The disease of masturbatory insanity had physical symptoms – baldness, stammering, blindness, skin diseases, to name a few – but it provided a means of social control over the activities of men (Englehardt, 1981). It illustrates the way in which medical thought is structured and sustained by the social, political and economic concerns of the social groups producing it. Analysing diseases as social products allows us to see changes in the social structure which give rise to changed forms of behaviour, and to new labels for controlling people.

—BOX 2.5—

POST-TRAUMATIC STRESS DISORDER

Following the First World War and the documentation of the experience of shell shock, Kardiner posited the existence of a traumatic neuroses, laying the basis for post traumatic stress disorder (PTSD) (Kardiner, 1941). PTSD was first listed in the American Psychiatric Association's *Diagnostic and Statistical Manual* in 1980. Early attempts to formulate a diagnosis appeared in DSM-I (1952) as gross stress reaction. According to DSM-IV, the memory of a past traumatic incident relives itself in the present. Individuals diagnosed with PTSD persistently re-experience the trauma, make persistent efforts to avoid stimuli associated with the trauma, and have persistent increased arousal and high levels of anxiety. The condition is of considerable interest to sociologists of psychiatry because its inclusion as a disease was highly contentious, representing the rejection of prevailing Freudian and psychodynamic-based explanations of anxiety, and their replacement with the medical model, and it was intricately linked to reactions to the Vietnam War (Young, 1995).

Hysteria

The disease of hysteria operated in a similar way in the nineteenth century to constrain women. As the nineteenth century developed, it produced enormous social upheaval, as new structural options for participating in the division of labour developed. Women, in particular, experienced new options as school teaching, nursing and voluntary reform work developed. Men, on the other hand, were concerned to restrain women in their traditional roles within the household. In this a medical system developed that insisted emphatically on the differences between men and women. It was argued that in men the brain predominated, and in women the nervous and reproductive systems, and in particular the ovaries and uterus. Women who went to work, or attempted to, put themselves at risk of hysteria by denying the biological imperative of reproduction. Furthermore, education would lead to sickness, since the brain and the ovaries could not develop simultaneously. So the disease of hysteria worked on a number of levels. It allowed men to classify women who attempted to participate in the workforce as diseased. In turn, this provided an active and hostile role for women to react against their social role. In this it must be noted that disease categories are simultaneously categories of subjugation and rebellion. Similar analysis has been carried out on chlorosis in the nineteenth century (Figlio, 1978), and agoraphobia in the early twentieth century (de Swaan, 1981).

Disease works not only with patriarchy but also with class and age, in mediating social relationships. In analysing miners' nystagmus, an epidemic disease between the wars in the UK, Figlio shows how medical knowledge and its definition of psychosomatic illness was bounded by the social, political and economic situation (Figlio, 1982). Studies by Silverman illustrate the ways in which apparently straightforward biological facts – Down's syndrome, cleft-palate surgery and paediatric cardiac catheterization – are the product of discourse within the clinical setting that depend on the wider socially accepted definitions of a 'normal' child. In fact, figures showing that 'normal' children were more than three times as likely to receive surgery for atrial-ventricular caval defect could only be explained if social variables played a more important role than 'medical' variables in these children (Silverman, 1981, 1983, 1987).

By corollary, the non-treatment of some conditions can be shown to depend not on the medical characteristics of the patient, but their racially ascribed characteristics. It would appear on the surface that, given a biological condition and a treatment procedure, social factors should play a minimal role in the treatment of the condition. This however is not the case, as can be demonstrated in the next section.

The Technical Realm of Medical Practice

The argument that the technical is not distinct from social relations has probably been one of the most recent challenges for sociology (Bijker et al., 1987; Callon et al., 1986), but one of the earliest for the sociology of health. In 1927, Bernhard Stern demonstrated that every one of the taken-for-granted practices of modern medicine was contested at its time of discovery. He documents the opposition to dissection, to Harvey's theory of the circulation of the blood, to Auenbrugger's theory of percussion, of opposition to vaccination, to Holmes and Semmelweis, to Pasteur, and to asepsis and antisepsis. His argument was that if the technology did not fit in with its prevailing culture then it did not count as a technical advance. Thus dissection, and Harvey's theory, challenged the religious understandings of the body which infused medical theory. Vaccination was opposed by the medical profession because it was a folk practice which required no special skill, and thus threatened their economic wellbeing since no one would pay a fee for a vaccination. Ideas about infection being spread by doctors were rejected because they were an insult to the gentlemanly status of medical practitioners.

Thus what counts as the technical, scientific and accepted practice of medicine is primarily shaped by cultural, economic and professional factors, with scientific considerations only secondary. The technical and the scientific are not given in themselves, but are socially moulded and formed.

Medical Technology and Social Relations

The application of the technical is also socially formed. In cultures in which there is inequality based on ethnicity, this is clear. The treatment of coronary artery disease is a well-established surgical procedure, with recognized benefits for the patient. It is a procedure which can be determined as nearly as possible on 'objective' clinical grounds. Yet in New Zealand in 1983, when 822 coronary bypass operations were performed, only 10 were carried out on members of the minority Indigenous population, the Maori, despite the fact that age-specific death rates for the Maori from heart attack are significantly higher (Pomare, 1988). A more recent study reached similar conclusions, finding that although Pacific and Maori people had higher rates of coronary artery disease, rates of coronary artery revascularization procedures (the main surgical procedures used to overcome the blockages in the arteries) were much lower in both groups than among Caucasians (Tukuitonga and Bindman, 2002). An Australian study also found that Indigenous Australians who experience an episode of acute myocardial infarction (a heart attack) are less likely than non-Indigenous Australians to receive percutaneous coronary intervention (Coory and Walsh, 2005). Similarly, a study of cancer treatment in the United States showed that ethnic minorities are less likely to receive immediate extractive surgery, and are also less likely to receive ongoing therapy following invasive procedures (Brown and Shavers, 2002). The diagnosis of diseases among subjugated groups in racialized societies – those where different groups are ascribed different characteristics putatively on the grounds that they are of a different race – is similarly a product of the social structures of those societies. The technical and scientific practices of medicine are not the value-free workings of a disinterested science, but the product of social relations.

Similar dynamics can be illustrated with controversies in twentieth-century medicine (McKinlay, 1981), notably in cancer research around the efficacy of non-orthodox treatment (Behar, 1983), the legitimacy of 'alternative medicine' (Hirschkorn, 2006), the ongoing debate about the benefits and dangers of water fluoridation (Martin and Richards, 1995), concerns about over-diagnosis of Attention Deficit Hyperactivity Disorder (ADHD) in children and adults (Conrad and Potter, 2000), and medical consensus on liver transplant therapy (Markle and Chubin, 1987). The debate over the efficacy of drugs and of vitamin C in the treatment of cancer has shown that the ways in which medical therapies are assessed is dependent on the political, economic and social powers of those involved, that the gold-standard clinical trials of new drugs have built into them the biases of their assessors, and that this is not something that can be overcome by methodological reform, but is what in fact constitutes professional medicine (Richards, 1991).

The critique of technological determinism has also been used to examine the development of the medical profession. The medical profession has risen to its position of dominance in the health sphere not because of its scientific-ness, nor because of its technical advances, but because it has organized itself as an occupational group to exclude or control other workers in the field. Willis (1989), for example, illustrates this argument by showing how medical practitioners subordinate some practices (e.g. midwifery), limit the practices of other health practitioners (e.g. optometrists, who are not allowed to deal with diseases of the eye) and exclude certain other occupations from legitimate health practice (e.g. chiropractors). Willis's three case studies, illustrating the dominance of medical practitioners over other health practitioners, are written against the background of the major paradox of the development of modern medicine. That is: the medical profession organized itself and achieved high social, political and economic status in the late nineteenth and early twentieth centuries before it had developed a coherent knowledge base (McKeown, 1979). By fully applying this insight Willis escapes the technological determinism of other accounts of the historical processes surrounding the development of medicine (for example Youngson, 1979). The point is that while technology does change and develop, both the way in which it is applied, and the organization of the labour force administering it, are always the outcome of social and political struggles.

The Sociology of Medical Knowledge

Robert Merton, one of the most influential sociologists of science, argued that the scientific method epitomizes communal sharing of results, the search for universal truth, disinterested objectivity, unflinching originality and a scepticism of what has gone before (Merton, 1973). Indeed this is the image of science taken for granted in our society. For Ludwik Fleck, writing in the 1920s through to the 1940s, all of these were beside the point for a sociological understanding of medical science.

─BOX 2.6─

LUDWIK FLECK AND THE FOUNDATIONS OF THE SOCIOLOGY OF MEDICAL KNOWLEDGE

The work of Ludwik Fleck has been overlooked in most accounts of the development of the sociology of medical knowledge. Our understanding of the origins of the sociology of medical knowledge, and the sociology of health and illness in general, is poorer because of this (White, 2015). This is on two counts. In the first instance, it is suggested that it has led to an oversight of the Durkheimian basis of the sociology of medical knowledge. In the second, Fleck's work pre-dated both Kuhn and Foucault, and the former in particular drew on his work in formulating his account of the formation of scientific knowledge. The latter, on the other hand, is indebted, like Fleck, to Durkheim's sociology, though drawing very different conclusions about the nature of modern social life.

Fleck was born in 1896 in L'viv, Ukraine. He studied medicine and specialized in bacteriology and infectious disease. Between 1943 and 1945 he was incarcerated in Auschwitz and Buchenwald. He became Professor of Medicine at the University of Lublin and in 1957 moved to Israel. He died in 1961.

For Fleck, medical knowledge was a social product (see Cohen and Schnelle, 1986, for his essays; and Fleck, 1935 [1979]). He was profoundly influenced by the relativistic turn in physics and by reading Niels Bohr on the nature of physics in 1928. Bohr concluded that 'an independent physical reality in the ordinary sense can be ascribed neither to the phenomena nor to the medium of observation' (Fleck, 1935 [1981]: 240). That is to say, what was observed and the observer existed in relation to one another. The object of enquiry is not distinct from the enquiring subject.

What physics calls nature is the product of the physicist's laboratory, and Fleck argued that a similar case could be made for medical knowledge. Fleck argues that the view of the world that the individual scientist or medical researcher will have is dependent on the group that they are trained and socialized into.

Fleck and Representations

The lesson Fleck took from quantum physics was that objective reality could not be the basis of our knowledge. Rather, what we have is representations of our knowledge of reality. Durkheim had sought to make sociology the study of moral facts – of ideas – and Fleck sought to extend this analysis to encompass the study of scientific ideas. Further, he did this in a way that extended the formulations of the Durkheimians. As Fleck wryly noted, the Durkheimians were fine when discussing the representations of primitive peoples but less able to analyse Western scientific thought from the same perspective: 'All these thinkers trained in sociology and classics, however, no matter how productive their ideas, commit a characteristic error. They exhibit an excessive respect, bordering on pious reverence, for scientific facts' (Fleck, 1935 [1979]: 47). Fleck set out to show that the knowledge of the natural medical sciences was also a representation, a product of the social.

Fleck's Sociology of Medical Knowledge

Fleck unflinchingly attempted to provide an account of how the fundamental categories of scientific medicine were produced. To do this, he combined the relativism of the physics of the 1920s with a sociology of scientific knowledge. In this, his concept of thought style was critical.

In the concept of a thought style Fleck develops a philosophical analysis of science – that the discovery of scientific facts depends not upon the discovery of a pre-existing nature, but the theories we have about that nature. He also develops a sociological analysis of science, demonstrating that the discovery of scientific facts depends on non-scientific factors, such as religious, political or economic considerations. For Fleck, scientific knowledge is collective knowledge, historically located and the product of interactions between competing groups with alternative definitions of reality. Thomas Kuhn (1962 [1970]) in *The Structure of Scientific Revolutions* was to develop Fleck's insights into the concept of paradigm.

—BOX 2.7—

FLECK'S CONCEPT OF THOUGHT STYLE

- Knowledge is only possible on the basis of a tradition of shared assumptions, which do not exist to be challenged, but to be supported by scientific investigation.

- Theories act to produce the questions we ask, and predispose the answers we give. They are a 'world view' producing the possible realities open to us, and limiting them.

- There is no Archimedean point from which to assess competing thought styles, which may be incommensurable.

- For Fleck, learning medicine and science is about socialization into the community of scientists and practitioners, of developing the appropriate thought style. What will count as a fact is a product of the thought style we are educated into.

Fleck illustrates how thought styles operate by reference to two unrelated areas of medical knowledge: syphilis and anatomical drawings.

Syphilis

In his study of syphilis, Fleck demonstrates that our understanding of syphilis has a history that reflects the political, economic and cultural organization of society. Radically, rather than tracing the history of syphilis as a progressive development out of a dark past, he suggests that even current understandings of it are based on cultural factors. He proposes a historical typology of our knowledge of the condition, all of which is interrelated. Historically, the first understanding was that syphilis was linked to fornication and to the position of the stars, which he calls a mystical-ethical idea. Second, syphilis was linked, with other venereal diseases, to its reactions to heavy metals such as mercury. This he identifies as an empirical-therapeutic notion. Third, there is a pathogenic concept, that syphilis is related to perverted blood. Fourth, there is the idea of a specific cause of syphilis, an aetiological notion.

The discovery of the Wassermann reaction – the test for syphilis – in 1906 (which Fleck worked on) provides Fleck with an empirical case study with which to advance the argument that progress in medicine is a social and political event, dependent upon thought collectives, rather than a rational, scientific event. The Wassermann reaction was the resolution of these four thought styles and, as Fleck points out, the post-Wassermann understanding of syphilis reflects aspects of each of them. Fleck argues that research into syphilis was motivated by moral outrage about sexual promiscuity, instigated for political reasons by civil authorities, within the context of nation-state rivalries around biochemical discovery. Thus social, political and moral factors, binding scientists into a thought collective, both generate research topics and guide their outcome.

Fleck is concerned to show that the way in which medicine and its practitioners conceptualized disease depended on their culture. Indeed, he wanted to show how bacteriology itself was a social product. He draws attention to two aspects of our thinking about disease and syphilis. The first is that our thinking about illness reflects its origins in nineteenth-century imperial expansion. Thus it is full of military metaphor, with invading micro-organisms doing battle with the body. This underlying motif of medicine is a direct reflection of its historical and cultural origins. The second aspect is the role of Christian thought in concepts of disease. Disease is seen as a demon that infects the person. This means that diseases are always moral categories and that they always carry social meaning (see Sontag, 1978). They are not morally neutral. Indeed, we could say that diseases are normative judgements about what is good, dressed up as facts. So what Fleck is suggesting is that all scientific studies depend upon non-scientific elements. These factors are the product of group membership, and the participants may be unaware of them.

Anatomical Drawings

Fleck provides another example of thought styles of medical knowledge. In analysing the development of anatomical drawings, he argues that they originally had a primitive and symbolic character. In the Middle Ages, in the drawings of Vesalius, they are pervaded with an emotional content. For example, drawings represent the skeleton but at the same time they are also symbols of death. Fleck (1935 [1981]) argues that anatomical drawings in the Middle Ages portrayed the world view of that period – they are about religion, death, God's organization of nature, and the place of humans in the cosmos. Anatomical drawings most commonly expressed death and are used to remind people of their mortality. In the modern period, we presume that they represent nature, but Fleck argues that, in fact, they reflect modern cultural predispositions. They have two characteristics which are immediately apparent. First, presentations of the body are mechanical. Modern medicine developed at the same time as Descartes was describing the human being in terms of clockwork. People were no longer regarded as whole organisms (vitalism). This image was replaced by a mechanical image that complemented the Industrial Revolution (mechanism). This, Fleck argues, accounts for the highly technical nature of these drawings. Fleck concludes that anatomical drawings are 'ideograms' corresponding to current ideas. We do not see better or more clearly; rather our way of seeing changes. Thus the content of anatomical observation has changed according to changes in thought style. The knee joint of today is a mechanical device and has nothing in common with the genu of the ancient anatomists, who conceptualized the knee as the site of mercy: 'What we find we are faced with in anatomical drawings are ideograms corresponding to current ideas, not the form which is true to nature as we construe it' (Fleck, 1935 [1981]: 246).

The content of anatomical drawings depends on the thought style to which we belong. As Fleck puts it:

> in the last resort what is, and how it is observed therefore depends on our entire culture and its development. It must be assumed that the observation of distinct objects is possible only on the basis of preconceived opinions. An empty mind cannot see at all. There are no observations that are true to nature except those that are true to culture. (Fleck, 1935 [1979]: 247)

Thought Styles After Fleck

Thought styles have continued to be influential as a way of analysing scientific and medical knowledge production as well as scientific controversies. In the brief examples which follow I am not concerned with exploring the tensions and problems in these studies, but rather just with providing evidence of the heuristic value of the concept of thought style.

The philosopher Ian Hacking has worked extensively on thought styles. For him, they define 'what it is to be objective (truths of certain sorts are just what we obtain by conducting certain sorts of investigations answering to certain standards)' (1992a: 4) for a scientific group or area of research. That is, they perform both ontological functions (defining the reality that is to be investigated) and epistemological functions (how to study and report on that definition of reality). Scientific thought styles 'become not the uncoverers of objective truth but rather standards of objectivity' (1992a: 19). Truth and objectivity are the consequences of a specific style, and thus truth and objectivity will vary from style to style. Over time, Hacking argues, a style becomes increasingly secure and social factors are decreasingly relevant to its status: 'The style ends as an autonomous way of being objective about a wide class of facts, armed with its own authority and available as a neutral tool for any project or ideology that seeks to deploy it' (Hacking, 1992b: 133). Clearly, there is much to be discussed about Hacking's argument; for example, how does one style come to this position of dominance, and once dominant how is it freed from social determinants? Historians too have found great utility in utilizing the concept of thought style. In his magisterial three-volume study of Western science, Crombie (1994) uses thought styles to marshal his data. Thought styles are based on ideas of nature, of science and the way scientific enquiry should be organized, a triumvirate Crombie refers to as 'commitments'. These commitments 'regulate the problems seen, the questions put to nature and the acceptability of both questions and answers' (Crombie, 1994: 4).

The historian of biology Maienschein (1988) has documented rival schools of biology in the United States, and in embryology between Germany and the United States (Maienschein, 1991a). Under the umbrella of epistemic styles she defines 'a biological style [as] characterised by a shared set of problems regarded as appropriate, techniques regarded as useful and approaches regarded as productive' (Maienschein, 1988: 173), thus allowing her to develop an analysis of a 'Chicago style' of biology developing around 1900. In *Transforming Traditions in American Biology, 1880–1915* (Maienschein, 1991b) she demonstrates a shift in style of doing biology. The shift was from a focus on development to a focus on heredity, and to factors internal rather than external to the organism. This new focus led to epistemological shifts – in the way questions were asked, in how they were to be answered, and what counted as an adequate answer: in short to a new thought collective. In her work on comparing American and German embryology between 1880 and 1915, she argues that the American thought style developed as a pragmatic, focused approach, while the Germans retained historical, evolutionary perspectives. The Germans 'sought causal mechanical explanations of as many phenomena as possible, guided by strong theories which achieved confirmation when they fit with as much of the available data as possible', while in the American case the search was for 'definitive facts, as many as possible, which might be quite specific or narrowly based' (Maienschein, 1991a: 407). The two epistemic styles 'emphasized different goals, processes of investigation and standards of evidence' (1991a: 407). As she says in another work on 'epistemological styles', which she adapts to biology: 'a biological style is characterized by a shared set of problems regarded as appropriate, techniques regarded as useful, and approaches regarded as productive' (Maienschein, 1988: 173). In short they function as Fleckian thought collectives, creating the conditions for knowledge production, methods of determining facts, and methods for determining what counts as adequate knowledge. The difference between thought styles and traditions for her is that traditions are historically bound, whereas styles can be independent of their historical period – as in Fleck's case study of syphilis – intermingling with each other over time.

Similarly Harwood (1993) has identified differences in thought style in German and American genetics in the period 1900–1930. Harwood argues that two different thought styles developed in German genetics, each with different methods, approaches and understandings of genetics.

As a sociologist Harwood sets out to demonstrate that these different thought styles are carried out by different social groups. In Mannheim's original formulation of the sociology of knowledge he argued that membership of specific social groups – classes or generations for example – led to a shared world view and to ways of seeing, acting and understanding based on the membership of that social group. The group specifies 'how fruitful thinking can be carried out' (Mannheim, 1936 [1972]: 276). Thus science is not based on the 'nature of things' or on 'pure logical possibilities' (Mannheim, 1936 [1972]: 267) but on the group's shared world view. In the same way, Harwood elaborates of his book that it is 'not only [a contribution to] the history of genetics, but to the historiography of science more generally. I hope to persuade others that "style of thought" is a useful analytical (rather than merely descriptive) concept in the history of science' (1993: xvii). Hence he argues that in one thought style – which he labels the comprehensives – the social group came from the upper middle classes, saw themselves as the carriers of a high German culture, rejected the developing industrial society and resisted modernization. The pragmatic thought style was carried by a social group from lower down the social hierarchy, who were less worried about tradition and had a very different thought style about the role and place of science in the transformation of German culture. In documenting this social basis of the competing views, Harwood demonstrates the presence of a thought style 'when particular ontological and or epistemological assumptions recur in a variety of scientific domains and these assumptions differ from one group to another' (1993: iv).

Fleck's work has also been used in micro-sociological studies of medical practices. For example Arksey (1994) uses it to explore the contested definitions of RSI; de Carnargo (2002) has developed it in the context of physicians' ongoing self-education, Pena (2011) has demonstrated the changes in thought style of renal allograft pathology; and Aronowitz (1998) examines the impact of thought collectives on the classification and diagnoses of conditions as diseases. It has also been applied in an ethnographic study of a brain imaging laboratory (Roepstorff, 2002). Thus we see that contemporary work reflects Fleck's original concerns with changes in thought collectives over time and at the level of the classification and definition of diseases.

Fleck, Foucault and Kuhn

The link between thought collectives and their power to form and coerce the individual scientific practitioner is not fully developed by Fleck, though he does emphasize 'thought coercion'. Rather he presents an empirical argument showing how knowledge develops its status as truth as it moves through the social networks of scientists and researchers. This transformation of conjecture into fact can be shown in the process by which knowledge moves out from an esoteric enclave of practitioners who communicate via journals, to an exoteric circle of consumers of textbook knowledge. It was not until the work of Foucault that the coercive aspect of knowledge was theorized, with his concept of knowledge/power.

Between Kuhn's paradigms, Fleck's thought collectives and Foucault's epistemes there are similarities and differences (see Kimsma [1990] for a fuller discussion). For Kuhn, there are rational aspects to paradigms. Scientists adhere to them because they solve puzzles better, though there is no rational basis to their transformation. For Kuhn, existing paradigms are rational, though changes in paradigms are not. The reasons paradigms change in the Kuhnian framework is to do with the structure of professional practice, which for him is the irrational aspect, and through the development of objective knowledge, which allows the basis of science's claims to objectivity. For Fleck, thought collectives are irrational. They owe their existence to social factors, and act in such a way as to coerce (unconsciously) practitioners' activities. Furthermore, there is continuity in thought collectives over spans of time, and components of earlier thought collectives are incorporated in current ones. Foucault's epistemes represent a higher level of analytic and empirical abstraction, shaping the general orientation of all sciences of a historical period. Where Fleck and Foucault depart company from Kuhn most is in their claim that there is no way to assess the relative merits of competing thought collectives or epistemes. Where Foucault goes beyond Fleck is with his analysis of the impact of modern medicine on the individual.

Foucault is concerned with the processes whereby the human is turned into the subject of scientific investigation and control (Foucault, 1982). Central to this process was the development of modern positivistic medicine, as he demonstrated in *The Birth of the Clinic* (1973). Medical standards of normalcy spread into the human sciences, individualizing the self, producing subjectivity and, at the same time, providing the basis for social control. In other words, for Foucault, the discipline of medicine provided the tools whereby subjectivity could be experienced and enforced. The modern period produces individualization but not individual autonomy. In this Foucault departs from Durkheim's cautious approval of the cult of the individual. While the forced division of labour led to anomie, it also freed individuals from the constraints of social bonds. Sociology could aid in the development of a free division of labour, allowing for the full development of the individual. For Foucault, sociology was deeply implicated in the very episteme which had given rise to medicine. While it might transform relations of power/knowledge, it could not step outside of them.

Fleck, however, was operating empirically at a lesser level of analysis. He was more concerned to document the mediating structure between the individual as shaped by the thought collective and the social shaping of medical knowledge.

Applying Fleck

We can use a Fleckian analysis to examine current thought collectives in medicine. A contemporary example of Fleck's position can be developed out of Nicolson and McLaughlin's (1988) study of accounts of multiple sclerosis (MS). Whether MS is conceptualized as a vascular disease, or one in which the body's immune system is implicated, depends upon the previous training and background of the medical researchers involved. Their competing perceptions of what counts as the problem to be investigated is a product of their socialization into a particular scientific community, and is a product of their training and education. Thought collectives work not only at the level of professionalization, but also at the level of what counts as knowledge.

A major plank in biomedicine is the claim that chemically active agents will have an impact on the body – that specific drugs will cure specific ailments. The strength of this thought collective leads to surprising results. Because pharmacological substances are the only ones that are supposed to have an impact, the corollary is that inert substances will have no impact. In Fleckian terms, this thought collective is the result of the effect of Cartesianism, in particular the mind–body dichotomy, on modern medicine (Romanucci-Ross and Moerman, 1988). This means that the well-established placebo effect is considered an anomaly, even though it can account for up to 90 per cent of ulcer cures (Moerman, 1981).

Likewise, a Fleckian analysis can provide an explanation for cases such as the Tuskegee syphilis experiment (Jones, 1981). In this experiment, conducted by the US Department of Public Health, tertiary syphilis was allowed to develop in poor, homeless black men. Treatment was withheld so that the natural history of the disease could be documented. Such an experiment is possible in a thought collective that conceptualizes disease as existing independently of human agents, and divorces the experiencing subject from the 'biological reality' of the disease.

Another example of the social shaping of medicine through the working of thought collectives is the 'Unfortunate Experiment' at the National Women's Hospital, Auckland (Cartwright, 1988). In this, cervical cancer was allowed to go untreated. The defence by the clinician involved was that since the treatment threatened the fertility of the women it was better that they be left untreated and remain fertile. From his perspective, inside patriarchal medicine, it was better that the women remain capable of bearing children than to be cured at the risk of their fertility. From a Fleckian perspective, these examples of racist and patriarchal medicine are not aberrations on the way to true knowledge, but are the logical outcome of societies structured on ethnic and gender ascriptions. Medicine cannot do anything other than to reflect these structural and cultural thought collectives at the core of modern society. As these principles, these thought collectives, change, then so too will the technical content of medicine. These examples move in levels of generality from the thought collectives of specific groups of doctors, to biomedicine's lack of understanding of the mind–body dichotomy, to medicine's mediation of structural variables in modern societies.

It is at this point that we approach the limits of Fleck's sociological analysis of medicine. He is on firm ground in documenting the cultural and political factors which shape medical knowledge. At the micro level of scientific discovery, his participant observation of the rational reconstruction of the irrational Wassermann studies is exemplary. At the macro level of the shaping of the contents of medical knowledge, in his studies of anatomical drawings, his analysis has great purchase. But at the level of the structures of power/knowledge as they form in societies that are structurally divided on class, gender and ethnic lines, we need specifically Marxist, feminist and sociological accounts of the particularities of social inequality.

Conclusion

It is easy to assume that medical knowledge is a natural science, and presume that it is not open to sociological analysis. In other words, medical knowledge is scientific in the sense of being unaffected by social and political variables. Disease can also be thought of as a product of nature that exists independently of society, and as such is not contaminated by social variables. Fleck's understanding of medical knowledge is one that emphasizes the social nature of its contents. As he puts it 'In science, just as in art and in life, only that which is true to culture is true to nature' (Fleck, 1935 [1979]: 35).

The full implication of this position is that there are only historically specific classificatory schemes, which are the product of human interaction. To summarize Fleck's work we can make three major points. First, he provides a sociological theory of medical knowledge. This is characterized by two arguments: ideas only exist in cooperative exchange, that is, he provides a radically anti-individualistic account of knowledge formation; and two, by corollary, it is only as members of thought collectives that we can have knowledge. Second, he historicizes the theory of knowledge. There is no linear progression of knowledge, only a changing in thought styles, as some problems lose their salience and become irrelevant. Third, he reformulates the idea of a scientific fact as the product of thought collectives imposed upon us, and not the product of nature.

Fleck's understanding of medical knowledge, then, is one that emphasizes the social nature of its contents. For Fleck there are no natural facts, only social categories, some of which have power because they are marketed by the groups in their thought collectives as science. In this Fleck provides a strong check on the tendency of the sociology of health to slip into the epistemology of medical positivism. He provides a rich stock of empirical studies showing how medical categories are socially constituted, and are a check to the argument that the contents of medical knowledge are determined by nature.

Fleck's contribution deserves to be more recognized, both historically and contemporarily. Historically, he is owed an important place in the antecedents of the sociology of medical knowledge and medical sociology generally. Without doubt Fleck's work is an outstanding application of Durkheimian sociology to the study of medical knowledge. But his work also has a contemporary relevance for its foresight both methodologically and conceptually. Methodologically, the use of participant observation in the laboratory, which forms the core of his analysis of the Wassermann reaction, is an approach still under-utilized by sociologists of health. Conceptually, the argument and analysis of professional groups as carriers of thought styles provide a bridge between the level of individual action and macro concepts of social structure such as class and patriarchy. In fact, by adopting a Fleckian perspective the sociologist is all the time forced to look at the interaction of politics, knowledge and vested interests in producing knowledge of our bodies and our health. It is meeting this challenge that the rest of this book deals with.

Summary

- In this chapter I have laid out the principles of the social constructionist account of medical knowledge.

- Constructionists argue that medical knowledge is produced by and reflects the society that it is formed in. It is not knowledge of an independent nature, but the outcome of competing groups defining nature and its contents.

- Fundamentally, the core of medical knowledge will reflect the key assumptions of the society that produces it. In Fleck's examples we can see how military metaphors, mechanical metaphors and religious thinking imbue medicine.

- These arguments, based in the classical sociology of knowledge of Émile Durkheim, are essential to problematize medical knowledge, which in our society appears to be part of the natural sciences, dealing with an independently existing nature.

Discussion Questions

1. What does Fleck mean when he says that only that which is true to culture is true to nature?

2. In what ways are diseases shaped by historical, economic and religious factors?

3. Are all diseases socially constructed?

Further Reading

Fleck, L. (1935 [1979]) *The Genesis and Development of a Scientific Fact*. Chicago: University of Chicago Press. Fleck's book is very readable, and one of the classics in the field.

White, K. (2015) 'Ludwik Fleck, the Sociology of Knowledge and the Sociology of Medical Knowledge.' In *The Palgrave Handbook of Social Theory in Health, Illness and Medicine*, edited by F. Collyer. Basingstoke: Palgrave Macmillan.

Wright, P. and Treacher, A. (eds) (1982) *The Problem of Medical Knowledge: Examining the Social Construction of Medicine*. Edinburgh: Edinburgh University Press. A good collection of constructionist analyses of medicine, and a good starting point for this area of health sociology.

3

THE DEVELOPMENT OF THE SOCIOLOGY OF HEALTH

o   This chapter provides an overview of the relationship between sociology and medicine as disciplines from the 1950s onwards.

o   This is a history of the development of an increasingly critical assessment of medicine by sociologists. The process can be captured in the distinction between a sociology *in* medicine and a sociology *of* medicine.

o   It also continues to advance the argument that disease is a social process, and through the concept of medicalization, demonstrates how gambling, alcoholism and learning disabilities have become diseases.

The relationship between sociology and medicine as disciplines and practices has always had a major impact on the field of the sociology of health and illness. This chapter reviews this changing relationship before moving on to discuss some key characteristics of a sociological account of modern medicine and the social functions of medical knowledge. In particular, it explores the concept of medicalization: the transformation of actions into diseases. It argues that while there may be benefits in medicalizing some conditions – it makes sufferers eligible for compensation for example, and removes blame from the individual for their condition – it also means that we hand over areas of our social life to professional control and definition.

The Relationship Between Sociology and Medicine

The relationship between sociology and medicine can be broadly schematized as having three phases. In the first, the discipline established a disciplinary base within the universities of the USA. Though it had found expression in the works of Henderson (1935, 1936) and Wirth (1931), it was only in the 1950s, following Parsons' work on the medical profession in his book *The Social System* (1950), that the field started to develop a clear identity. Parsons was not the only theorist working in this area but his work, by situating the study of health in the broader concerns of sociology, gave the field a clear definition (Fox, 1979; Turner, 1986b).

Notwithstanding the elements of Parsons' work which were critical particularly of the medical model of disease, and of the organization and professional structure of medicine, this period was characterized by the subordination of sociology to medicine. This is the period of sociology *in* medicine (Twaddle, 1982).

Throughout the 1950s, sociology applied to the field of medicine was used to assist the dissemination of medical knowledge and to encourage patient compliance with medical directives. In this relationship medicine was the senior partner, and the interaction occurred within a broader cultural context that saw medicine as the paragon of science and of the rational application of scientific principles and technology to human beings. Sociology attached itself to medicine to gain prestige. Within sociology, this was the period of dominance of the structural–functionalist perspective.

BOX 3.1

STRUCTURAL FUNCTIONALISM IN SOCIOLOGY

The basis of this perspective is that society, like the parts of an organism, is a harmonious, balanced set of interacting institutions. Each institution (structure) serves a particular set of social needs (functions) to ensure a stable society. For example, the religious, educational and medical institutions of our society all interact to socialize, train and repair individuals to ensure their smooth integration into society. Medicine, in the works of Talcott Parsons (1958), who was the major theorist of this position, served as a key illustration of the way in which an institution functioned through the harmonious interrelationship of the social roles people played within it. He identified a shared set of expectations between the patient and the doctor. The doctor was a highly skilled professional who applied scientific knowledge to the patient's trouble, without regard to factors such as race, gender or religion. The patient, on the other hand, sought out the doctor and complied with the doctor's directives so as to get better. It should be emphasized that Parsons was constructing a model of this situation or, as sociologists would say, an 'ideal type'.

In this period then, medical knowledge and practice held sway, shaping health sociologists' views of the field and setting their research agendas for them. The main task of applied sociological research was to increase patient compliance with the doctor's commands. The tone of this period can in part be caught in the title of a book by one of Parsons' students. This is the study *The Student Physician: Studies in the Sociology of Medical Education* by Robert Merton (1957). This conveys a sense of power and authority deriving from specialist training in a scientific specialty. It also serves to set the medical trainee apart from trainees in other fields, putting them on a pedestal of their own.

Medical Bias in the Sociology of Health

Medicine incorporated many sociological insights without problem, and schools of behavioural medicine, community medicine and primary care medicine were established throughout the late 1960s and 1970s. Medicine and sociology may have had different emphases, and sociology may even have been making some very challenging propositions about the medical model, but basically they shared the same outlook, and sociology saw itself working with medicine. To put it quite clearly, sociology had a medical bias – or rather, biases. There are four that are self-evident, and three others that are more hidden (Gold, 1977).

First, inherited from Parsons and congruent with the medical profession's self-image, while sociology could accept illness as a form of deviance, it nevertheless took for granted that the doctors were the appropriate group to deal with it. What this rules out is that illness may be a source of political protest or a valid social response to other societal factors. It followed from this, second, that complex social problems such as alcoholism, gender identity, or depression were defined individualistically – as the product of a deviant or uncoping individual – and were treated medically, usually by drugs rather than by attempting to modify the social environment. Third, sociological research was geared towards ensuring patient compliance with the doctor's orders. Of the articles published in the leading American journal on the sociology of health and illness, the *Journal of Health and Behavior*, between 1960 and 1976, 60 per cent were on the attitudes and behaviour of patients (Gold, 1977). 'Noncompliant patients' have become an important topic again, following the development of the 'evidence-based medicine' movement in the 1990s, which claims that medical practitioners should use the most 'proven' forms of practice. If what the doctor uses fails, then it is a consequence not of poor medicine, but of deviant patients not following the doctor's orders (Lerner, 1997). Fourth, only those problems defined by medicine as problems, e.g. illicit drug use, were studied. Others, which from a different perspective were problematic, for example, doctors' prescribing habits of addictive drugs, were ignored.

These four more-or-less obvious characteristics of medical sociology in this period are built on three more fundamental propositions. First that disease and mortality are, *ipso facto*, problematic and require medical intervention. The focus on disease deflects attention from the wider environment. Nowhere is this clearer than in the approach to the 'disease' of cancer. The huge amount of money poured into cancer research is at the cellular level, that is, at the intra-individual level. And it is focused on the outcome of the disease process. The condition itself, we know, or at least the US National Cancer Advisory Board tells us, is in 80 per cent of its occurrences the product of environmental factors (Doyal and Pennell, 1979: 61; see also Doll, 1988). The disease model systematically obscures the social conditions of sickness and disability. Second, this focus on disease is problematic from another perspective, in that it has embedded in it a premise about the right of professionals to make decisions on behalf of individuals on the basis of technical criteria. Take, for example, the problem of euthanasia. Medical control makes it difficult for the ethical and moral problems to be discussed in their own right. The presumption of the inviolability of human life is not self-evident and needs to be politically and morally established. Medicine blocks this discussion by turning it into an apparently technical problem of types of death − be it brain, respiratory or electrical. The third deep assumption of this medico-centric approach is that, if things are not working, it is the patient's fault, and not that of the medical practitioners or the health institutions.

Challenging Medicine

In the 1960s and 1970s, the second phase of sociology's relationship to medicine, the sociology *of* medicine, the argument was made that some of the problems in the health-care system − of access, equity and efficiency − could best be explained by the way in which medicine was organized, both institutionally and professionally. Sociologists started to argue that the real social role of medicine was to control sectors of the society; they developed a critical perspective on the organization and practice of medicine. The practice of medicine was not just the application of scientifically factual and value-free techniques. Erving Goffman's book *Asylums* (1961) opened up the critique of medicine as a value-loaded system of social control operating under the guise of science. He was followed by what is now called the anti-psychiatry movement (Cooper, 1967), particularly identified with the works of Thomas Szasz (1971) and R. D. Laing (1961). They argued that the categories that medicine uses to label a person, that is, the disease labels, do not necessarily have an underlying biological reality but reflect the social values and prejudices of the medical professionals. They held that this was particularly the case when the diseases were mental and no physical basis for them could be established. As R. D. Laing put it: 'I do not myself believe that there is any such "condition" as "schizophrenia". Yet the label is a social fact. Indeed this label as a social fact is a political event' (Laing, 1964: 64). At their most critical, sociologists challenged the very distinction between sanity and madness that psychiatry rests on.

This in turn raised questions about the neutrality of, or even the necessity to use, technological interventions in treating patients. The therapeutic techniques of psychiatry − surgical interventions such as frontal lobotomies, electroconvulsion therapy and mind-altering drugs − came to be questioned. It was argued that technology and science were connected to professional interests in experimentation and the bureaucratic requirements of a smoothly functioning institution, whether the hospital or the asylum. The tone of this period, a critical and sceptical stance towards the claims of medicine, is conveyed by the title of Howard Becker's (1961) book *Boys in White: Student Culture in the Medical School*. The emphasis is on training and schooling, and the implication is that medical professionalization is just like any other on-the-job training. Furthermore, anyone can undertake it – even boys.

┤BOX 3.2├

CHANGING ASSESSMENTS OF MEDICINE – CHANGING EXPLANATIONS IN SOCIOLOGY

In this double movement – the critique of psychiatry and the demystification of medical training – sociology started to distance itself from medicine. This process also marked a movement away from Parsons' 'grand theory'. Parsons had attempted to work out a complete theory of society and then to establish its validity by looking for empirical evidence of it. His critics called for a reversal of this process: theory should be grounded in the study of empirical social reality and develop out of social life as it is lived (Glaser and Strauss, 1968a). This gave rise in the sociology of health to a series of studies based on participant observation in hospitals and clinics (Glaser and Strauss, 1968b; Roth, 1963).

The publication of Eliot Freidson's *Profession of Medicine: A Study of the Sociology of Applied Knowledge* and *Professional Dominance*, both in 1970, marks a consolidation of the sociology of medicine into an examination of medicine, medical knowledge and medical practices. Freidson argued that the medical profession dominated the health sector, not because it was the humanitarian, scientific elite that it portrays itself as, but because it was politically well organized. It has a monopoly of practice guaranteed it by the state, enjoys autonomy over its own work, and defines for the wider society the issues that medicine has control over. It maintains its aura of high standing, despite the often-degrading aspects of its work, by passing the worst of the 'dirty work' off onto subordinate occupations such as nursing. The work of Ivan Illich (1975) continued a strong critique of orthodox medicine, demonstrating the ways in which medicine actually causes sickness, a process for which he coined the word 'iatrogenesis'. And as contemporary sociologists like Fox (2008) point out, iatrogenesis has been, and continues to be, a necessary part of Western medicine's adherence to 'scientific progress' – another fundamental aspect of medicine's claim to legitimacy and power.

──BOX 3.3──

THE CRITIQUE OF MEDICINE – IATROGENESIS

Ivan Illich demonstrated the ways in which modern medicine actually causes sickness and disease, a process for which he coined the word 'iatrogenesis', which comes from the Greek, meaning 'physician-caused'. Clinical iatrogenesis is the damage done to the patient by the practices of medical practitioners. Social iatrogenesis is when the health-care system actually supports those features of industrialized capitalist societies that cause disease and death. Structural iatrogenesis is the increasing dependence of the population on professional health care for what used to be 'normal' experiences of the human condition, especially suffering and death (Illich, 1975).

Social Aspects of Disease – The Critique of the Medical Model

The 1970s and 1980s saw the development of a new confidence – the third phase of the relationship between medicine and sociology – among sociologists working in the area of health and illness. Rather than taking for granted the medical model, they started to question it. The medical model explained disease and illness as the outcome of the invasion of a germ or virus into the individual's body. The cure was the administration of drugs or the application of technologically based treatments (Engel, 1981). That individuals became sick because of the invasion of a germ or virus, and could be cured by the application of medically prescribed regimens, overlooked the fact that individuals also lived in social groups that may have had as much to do with their illnesses and diseases as germs or viruses. It is quite possible to be infected with a germ or a virus and not be diseased (Open University, 1985). This finding is particularly well established in the case of tuberculosis, where occupation and living conditions play a large part in whether or not the disease develops. We can put this point the other way round. Many people have high levels of what are taken to be indices of disease – high blood pressure for example – without suffering any ill effects. Furthermore, large-scale community studies have shown that significant proportions of the population have symptoms of diseases but report no subjective awareness of them. It is these sorts of findings that show that there is no one-way relationship between a biological base and the person's social experience of health or illness that interests sociologists.

Indeed, a key aspect of the sociology of health is to go further and carry out research that shows that it is your social characteristics which actually play a predominant role in determining your sickness and health status. Your occupation is clearly related to your health. The lower your occupation on the British Registrar General's scale, the poorer your overall standard of health, and the shorter your lifespan. Similar correlations have been established in relation to your social position as a man or as a woman, that is to say, your gender. The generation you belong to also appears to play a large part in your health, as does your marital status (Macintyre, 1986).

Sociologists are interested in the finding that diseases and feelings of sickness are far from being determined by some underlying biological reality. Further, they are interested in exploring the relationship between social conditions as either causes or facilitators of disease. Lest it be presumed that these findings reflect the lack of knowledgeability of the patients, that is to say, that it is because lay people do not understand the workings of their own bodies, it should be pointed out that variations in diagnosis and treatment of conditions are well established among the medical profession. Even those who are trained in the science and biology of medicine carry out their tasks as social beings, rather than as value-free scientists.

BOX 3.4

SOCIAL FACTORS SHAPING MEDICAL PRACTICE

- The number of operations performed in an area is, in part, a function of the number of surgeons in the area. A study of coronary artery bypass grafting in the UK found that intervention rates were an outcome of the number of cardiologists, not clinical need in the population in an area (Bunker, 1970).

- The USA, with a fee-for-service system and twice the ratio of surgeons to population as the UK, has twice the surgical intervention rates (Bunker, 1970).

- It is also well demonstrated that rates for elective surgery vary in relationship to the medical profession's income level (Bloor, 1976). Similarly, the diagnostic habits of doctors are open to the sway of fashion.

- Lastly, doctors treat patients in ways that reflect the social standing of the patients. Those of lower class or status are seen for a much shorter period of time than those of high social status. This may even extend to death, with dead-on-arrival patients of apparent high social standing subject to more attempts to revive them in Accident and Emergency wards (Glaser and Strauss, 1968b; Sudnow, 1967). The socio-economic status of a patient may also influence the quality of surgery they receive. A study of women being treated for breast cancer in Western Australia found that women in lower socio-economic groups were less likely to receive breast-conserving surgery instead of a mastectomy than women in higher SES groups (Hall et al., 2004).

Sociologists demonstrate the social processes that underlie the feeling of being sick, the diagnoses of being diseased, and the treatment of those who are held to be diseased. Sociologists argue that germs or viruses may be necessary for a disease to occur, but that they are not sufficient in themselves. The social environment comes between the germ and the individual, and it is responsible for whether or not a disease develops (Twaddle, 1982). Following the work of social historians, sociologists demonstrated that the prevailing social conditions had to be conducive before a germ developed into a disease (McKeown, 1979). By corollary they argued that good social environments – and not more medicine – would produce healthier populations.

Take for example the distribution of cancers. Medicine argues for, and obtains, enormous resources to search for the cause of cancer at the level of laboratory studies. But, as Box 3.5 shows, cancer is socially produced on the level of politics, class and economics.

BOX 3.5

THE SOCIAL PRODUCTION OF CANCER

The causes of cancer lie in environmental pollutants and the way their use is unrestricted to increase productivity and profitability.

- A study in the Western Health Board of Ireland (Galway, Mayo and Roscommon) found that between 1980 and 1990 all cancers increased, with significant increases among semi-skilled farm workers of testicular cancers, non-Hodgkin's lymphoma and leukaemias. Farmers who used protective clothing and were less likely to be exposed to tractor-based crop spraying techniques had a lower incidence and were also less likely to have experienced the increase in cancer (Kelleher et al., 1998).

- As if to add insult to injury, socio-economic status is a protective factor in the survival rates for a range of common cancers: the higher your socio-economic status, the more you survive the cancer (Schrijvers and Mackenbach, 1994).

- In a study of 22,458 children who developed leukaemia between 1953 and 1980, proximity to industrial pollution, especially combustion products and volatile organic compounds, was causative in the later development of cancer (Know and Gilman, 1998).

Class patterns of disease are laid down from conception. Additionally, it appears to be the case that for the most socio-economically disadvantaged children, later improvement in socio-economic status, or avoiding lifestyle risk factors as adults, does not reduce their risk of heart disease (Glikman et al., 1995).

Key Concepts in the Sociology of Health

The sociology of health ranges over a wide territory: how some conditions come to be called diseases; the experience of being sick or ill; the organization of the medical profession; the ways in which health policies are produced; and the workings of hospitals. In all these areas, sociological studies of health and disease provide microcosms of the working of the wider society. Thus sociologists are interested in health and disease, not as health practitioners, but as students of society. This point is important to make for a number of reasons.

The first is that sociologists are not trying to tell health practitioners how to do their job, though some of their findings can tell us interesting things about how medicine and nursing are practised. For example, studies of the daily work lives of general practitioners can alert us to patterns of treatment, diagnoses and prescribing that are common to all practitioners who share a range of social characteristics – such as, for example, the length of their training, whether or not they are in a rural or urban setting, a solo or multiple practice, and whether they are male or female (White, 1994).

This brings us to the second important point that characterizes a sociological perspective: the focus is not on the individual as such but on the group of which the individual is a member. So when a sociologist is confronted with a sick individual the question is not 'Why is this individual sick?' but rather 'What is it about the group to which the individual belongs which puts them at risk of being sick?' The sociologist thinks of society not as individuals who conglomerate into groups, which is the psychologist's perspective, but as a set of structures that will produce certain life chances for the individuals within groups. We are born into these groups – male or female, black or white, members of this or that class, this or that ethnic group – and by and large, no matter what our intentions are, we will not change our position in them. In other words, the sociologist's perspective is not on the individual as such but on the group to which they belong. For a sociologist, what people get sick of, how they are treated, and what they die of are a product not of their personality or, primarily, of their biology, but of their position in a set of power relationships that are formed out of access to those social goods which guarantee the quality of life. Key intermediary variables which facilitate or block access to goods and services are class, gender and ethnicity.

A third point is this: a key element in a sociological perspective on disease is to see the very ways in which we label and treat illnesses as a form of social control. What gets defined as a sickness and how it is treated is not always a product of biological necessity, but may be an aspect of wider social assumptions about what is appropriate behaviour. Take, for example, the 'Unfortunate Experiment' at the Auckland Women's Hospital in New Zealand. Professor Herbert Green thought that it was better to have fertile women who may have a foreshortened lifespan than healthy but sterile women. He therefore did not treat cancer in situ of the cervix. The women remained fertile, but many of them died. His non-treatment was as much a product of the view of women as child-bearers as it was of clinical medicine.

Let me now highlight another characteristic of a sociological approach to health. What will count as medical knowledge, and the role of the medical profession, is the outcome of political and social factors. The argument is that the development of the medical profession is not the outcome solely of scientific factors, but is dependent on cultural beliefs about the nature and meaning of disease.

The Concept of Medicalization

The taken-for-granted way of thinking about sickness and disease in our society is called the medical model (Engel, 1981). That is, most of us usually believe that being sick or diseased is a straightforwardly physical event. It is the consequence of a germ or a virus or bacterium entering the body and causing it to malfunction. The cure or the solution to the problem lies in taking professional medical advice and, usually, some form of drug that wipes out the offending organism and restores our body to a stable physical state. So for most of us, being sick is a biochemical process that is natural and not anything really to do with our social life.

This medical model, however, applies to a very limited range of acute medical conditions. Yet medical explanations of behaviour are all around us, in TV shows, 'medical wonder' breakthrough stories in newspapers, and in the self-help section of the bookshop. How is it that medicine, with a relatively narrow area of practice, has become so pervasive? What other functions does it fulfil in social life than simply the technical repair of the body?

The key element in a sociological perspective on medicine is to see the ways in which diseases are labelled and treated as a form of social control, and that what is labelled a disease may only tangentially be linked to a biological occurrence in the body (Wainwright, 2008; Zola, 1972). Put another way, what gets defined as a disease and how it is treated are not simply a product of biological imperative but are an aspect of wider social expectations about what is appropriate social behaviour. Our failure to conform to those expectations may lead to us being labelled diseased and sick. And this may easily lead to legally sanctioned chemical, surgical or electrical treatments to enforce our conformity with social roles.

Therefore we must think of disease as being as much a social process as a biological product of nature. Sickness and disease are the product of social arrangements, both in terms of what it is we get sick from, as well as in terms of who it is that gets sick. Thus sickness and disease are not static categories of nature, but are part of the ongoing social processes of life. Let me start with a brief historical example of how sickness is a product of social relationships, both in what counts as a disease and in terms of who suffers from it. The example also illustrates the role the medical profession plays in providing a scientific justification for forcing individuals into their 'normal' social roles.

Disease: Nature or Society?

The example I have in mind is a disease called drapetomania. This was a disease that American plantation blacks suffered from in the American South in the nineteenth century. The diagnosis of drapetomania meant that a slave had a tendency to run away from his or her master. It was written up in medical textbooks, and could only be treated and diagnosed by doctors. It was thought to be a real condition, requiring professional medical treatment to cure it (Cartwright, 1851).

BOX 3.6

DRAPETOMANIA

Running away from the plantation owner becomes a disease because of specific social and political circumstances of a racist society in which whites dominated and subjugated blacks in an economic system of slavery. Its existence was a product of that society and it helped to reinforce the power relations of that society. It could only come into existence in circumstances of the subjugation of one group of people by another, with the dominant group defining the activities of the subordinate group as being so far beyond the pale that they must be sick and in need of treatment. In other words, the existence of the disease reflected the social organization of the society in which it existed.

The treatment for the condition also reflected the ethos of the time. The nineteenth century was a period in which professional medicine was developing on the basis of a claim to technical and scientific skills. Medicine indeed was developing as the dominant way of looking at the world, a position it has consolidated today. Furthermore, it was replacing the church as the social institution delegated the task of admonishing wayward individuals and bringing them back into the realms of normal society. So rather than explain the activities of the blacks in religious terms - that they were possessed, or that they ran away because they were heathens - and then call in the priest to exorcise them, or convert them, the white plantation owners called in the doctors. And the doctors, as skilled practitioners of a technical and scientific practice, diagnosed the condition as a disease and prescribed a remedy: the removal of both big toes, thereby making running a physical impossibility.

This example may appear far-fetched, occurring in a different century, and before medicine properly became a science. However, a brief examination of the way in which women are 'diseased' and 'treated' in the twentieth century reveals similar social processes as the basis of diagnosis and treatment. The examples that follow make it clear that 'scientific' medical explanations are used to enforce compliance with expected social roles. Sociologists have developed the concept of medicalization to explain the way in which the apparently scientific knowledge of medicine is applied to a range of behaviours that are not self-evidently biological, or even medical, but over which medicine has control (Conrad, 1992).

Medicalization and Women

'Medicalization' is particularly useful for explaining the experience of women in Western medicine. Feminist sociologists of health have examined medicalization at a number of levels. Medical textbooks and journals have been criticized for their sexist attitudes (Koutroulis, 1990). Analysis of doctor–female-patient interactions in the surgery has revealed the daily workings of sexism (Foster, 1989). Barrett and Roberts analysed the interactions between male doctors and middle-aged female patients and found that 'women were remorselessly confirmed in traditional family and domestic roles and more than one instance of a woman's refusal to do housework resulted eventually in hospitalization and electro-convulsive therapy' (Barrett and Roberts, 1978: 46). Further, the higher the status of the doctor, the more sexist and unequal the doctor–patient relationship became. Other studies have shown that stereotypes which suggest women are less emotionally stable than men can influence clinical diagnosis. *The Diagnostic and Statistical Manual of Mental Disorders*, first published by the American Psychiatric Association in 1980, is a set of standards with relation to psychiatric symptoms and diagnosis. A study by Loring and Powell showed that, despite the introduction of these presumably objective standards, male clinicians were still more likely to diagnose female patients as having emotional disorders, and overestimate the prevalence of depressive and histrionic disorders in women (Loring and Powell, 1988). A more recent Australian study into the detection and treatment of psychological disturbance by primary care physicians revealed that doctors were more inclined to diagnose female patients with psychological disturbance than male patients. The study compared the results of a patient-completed standardized questionnaire measuring non-psychotic psychological disturbance with the physician's assessment of the patient. Overall, the study showed that a higher proportion of non-disturbed women were classified by their physician as disturbed than non-disturbed men (Redman et al., 1991).

The monopolization of the technology that the medical profession exercises has also been examined (Gabe and Calnan, 1989). In these studies the general medicalization thesis is given sharper focus by arguing that it is women, in particular, who are the object of patriarchal medical control over drugs, and medical and surgical techniques. This is particularly related to the prescription of tranquillizers, and to the medicalization of childbirth. The claim that technological innovations represent improvements in the area of childbirth has been challenged (Williams et al., 1998).

In general, feminist health sociologists argue that medicine controls women by enforcing passivity, dependence and submission as appropriate feminine traits. By focusing on the individual rather than their social location, doctors reproduce the situations that lead the women to the surgery in the first place. Treating suburban neurosis with Valium, for instance, reinforces the traditional role of women that they are seeking to escape.

The Social Functions of Medical Knowledge and Practice

The above illustrations provide the basis for some of the central explanations provided by sociologists of the social functions of medicine. First, they alert us to the fact that medicine is an institution of social control. Medicine in modern society is a mechanism for controlling what are, from the perspective of the powerful group, deviant activities of other groups and individuals. Second, what gets diagnosed as a disease is often the product of social and political circumstances, and especially of the interplay between class, gender and ethnicity. Third, the seemingly purely technical and scientific practices of medicine – surgery to remove big toes in the example of drapetomania, or psychosurgery in others, or the prescription of sedatives in yet others – are all explicitly directed at enforcing compliance with social roles. The technical and the scientific practices of medicine are not the value-free workings of a disinterested science but the product of social relationships. It should be remembered that medicine's right to define normal behaviour and its control over surgical technology can come together in its treatment of those defined as 'not coping' or 'depressed': between 40,000 and 50,000 Americans had frontal lobotomies performed on them in the 1950s and 1960s (Shuman, 1977).

The Development of Medicalization

Medicine did not arrive fully developed as an institution of social control, but has risen to its current position over the past 150 years. Over this period there has been a change from religious, to legal, to medical institutions as the main locus of social control. In this development, activities that were once thought of as immoral and the domain of the Church (gluttony, for example) or the law (e.g. suicide) are now seen as medical issues. Medicine rose to dominance by first mounting an effective claim to be a science, and second by making an effective claim that its knowledge was not restricted just to the biological arena.

When medicine was developing in the eighteenth and early nineteenth centuries it focused on the individual's body and the biology of disease. Disease was understood primarily as an aspect of the sick person's body. As a new science, medicine was attempting to mimic the natural sciences and to produce objective explanations of disease. In the twentieth century, medicine redefined its area of competence to include the individual's psychological, economic and social circumstances. This development of the 'bio-psychosocial' model of disease reflects the increasing development of individualization in modern societies (Arney and Bergen, 1984). With it, both individuals and medicine become more concerned with the workings of the whole person, and the need for individuals to develop internal mechanisms of social control, rather than externally administered ones. This is an important development which, as we shall see, Foucault analyses in depth. The outcome was an all-encompassing definition of disease covering all aspects of an individual's existence. In the following section, two case studies of this process are developed – the medicalization of gambling, and alcoholism.

GAMBLING

To illustrate the process of medicalization we can look at the process whereby gambling became a disease in the USA (Conrad and Schneider, 1980). Pay particular attention to the changing definitions of gambling – from immorality in the nineteenth century to a disease in the twentieth century. At the same time, notice the way that we can analytically study the problem.

First, there has to be something about the behaviour that makes it problematic to powerful groups and to broadly accepted cultural beliefs about the right way to live life. Gambling, in nineteenth-century America, was at odds with the Puritan culture of the capitalist work ethic. It undermined the idea that one should work hard and save. So in the first place, there is a broad cultural definition of the behaviour as deviant.

Second, there is a process of 'prospecting', of making the 'medical discovery' of the problem. Thus in 1943, Edmund Bergler published the first paper in a medical journal which discussed the neurotic gambler as a medical problem. In sociological analysis, this is 'staking a claim' to the topic as a medical subject. However, because the behaviour has struck a general chord as a problem in the culture, other interest groups will be forming at the same time.

Third, then, there is likely to be a 'contest' between medical definitions and non-medical definitions and interests in the behaviour. So while Bergler published the first medical book on the topic in 1957, at the same time Gamblers Anonymous, a self-help, non-medically based group, was formed. This leads, in turn, to 'claims making' between the groups. Is gambling a problem of the psyche, of compulsive behaviour, of weak-willed people? Is it genetically inherited, or a biologically based malfunction of the brain? At this stage, the medicalization process may stop – the competition from lay, legal or religious groups for control of the problem may be too strong and medicine withdraws from the competition.

Alternatively, the medical turf may be 'secured' and legitimacy of the medical definition of the problem advanced. This usually happens with the successful setting up of a hospital treatment programme, followed by a legislative enactment that

(Continued)

CASE STUDY

(Continued)

the condition is a medical problem, in need of medical treatment, as occurred for gambling in Maryland in 1978, with the establishment of the first hospital-based therapy team. With this development we have the institutionalization of the claim that the behaviour is a medical problem, for which medical solutions must be found. The final stage of the process is the recognition by the rest of the medical community that this indeed is a medical problem. In the case of gambling, this occurred in 1980, when the American Association of Psychiatrists included a new entry in their handbook, *The Diagnostic and Statistical Manual*, of the disease of pathological gambling.

BOX 3.7

THE PROCESS OF MEDICALIZING
A SOCIAL PROBLEM – GAMBLING

- Nineteenth century – gambling at odds with Puritan culture of capitalist work ethic: definition of behaviour as deviant.

- 1943 – Edmund Bergler publishes a paper which discusses the neurotic gambler: prospecting – the claim of a medical discovery.

- 1957 – Bergler publishes first book on the topic. Gamblers Anonymous founded: claims making – medical and non-medical interests.

- 1978 – First hospital-based therapy team, Maryland, USA: legitimacy – securing the medical definition of a social problem in need of medical treatment.

- 1980 – DSM-III (pathological gambling): institutionalization of a medical definition.

- Conclusion: a medical condition is created by defining action as a disease in need of professional medical help.

This case study is a good example of the historical process by which a behaviour becomes a medical problem requiring professional help. From a sociological perspective a medical condition is created when the medical profession defines the actions of a group as to be so outside the ordinary that it must be a disease, and then successfully maintains this claim.

ALCOHOLISM

The concept of alcoholism as a disease has emerged over two hundred years, and is the outcome of a long historical process and of political dispute over the status of alcohol as a problem drug (Meyer, 1996). From a sociologist's perspective, the definition of a behaviour as a disease is the outcome of debates over complex social and political situations (Acker, 1993).

In Britain and the colonies alcohol was the staple drink, since it was safer and cleaner than polluted water. It was also used in medical treatments. For example, in 1882, 350 gallons of wines and spirits and about 3000 gallons of porter were prescribed for patients at the Melbourne Hospital. The general public also consumed a large amount of alcohol. In the 1830s, Australians drank an average of 680 bottles of beer per capita per year (Lewis, 1988). So in the not-too-distant past a great deal of alcohol was consumed without it being considered either a social or a medical problem.

However, by the turn of the century, drinking became viewed as a threat to the functioning of the working class. With growing urbanization and industrialization, a stable, predictable and compliant workforce was necessary (Baggot, 1990). Two competing professional groups, with different knowledge claims and different solutions to the 'drink problem', competed for control over drunkenness. Medicine and the temperance movement were allies in the sense of actively constructing drunkenness as a problematic behaviour. The temperance movement took the position that any alcohol consumption was a sin, that the working class needed protection from its own sinful tendencies, and that it needed to learn the values of hard work and thriftiness. The medical profession argued that alcoholism was a disease of people unbalanced in mind or body, and who were at risk of addiction. On the one hand, there is an explanation of the behaviour in terms of individual morality, and the proposed solution is one of moral reform. On the other, there is a biological explanation of individuals who are drunks, but little or no focus on the behaviour as a moral problem.

In the early medical texts of William Osler, a pre-eminent nineteenth-century physician and medical theorist, drinking is classified as a habit (Arney and Bergen, 1984). In his texts there is no role for moral outrage or reforming zeal. The person should be under medical treatment to protect her/himself from getting hurt while drunk. The advice of abstinence was given in the context of addiction and damage that might occur while drunk. Only the body was the concern of the medical practitioner, not the morality of the drunk's actions. In a sense, doctors were indifferent to their patients and conducted themselves with what might be called a professional disinterest. This did not prevent them from feeling compassion for the sick and suffering, but they did not see themselves as having a pastoral role in their dealings with their patients.

(Continued)

(Continued)

Fundamentally, to be sick was an accident, and medicine assessed the scope and impact of that accident; that is, it focused on the body and disease. Compassion was exercised to protect victims from the social consequences of the accidents of their disease. This strictly biological focus was transformed through the twentieth century, as medicine developed a more powerful position in modern society. By the mid-twentieth century, medicine had developed into a blend of scientific claims and moral prescription and, in a neatly circular fashion, claimed that there was a biological basis to that morality.

This found institutional expression in the development of psychosomatic medicine, with medical training curricula changing to take into account the psychosocial background of the person. The social backgrounds of patients were becoming technical matters that doctors had to take into account if they were to be successful in treating patients. From a sociological perspective, the psychosomatic movement meant that medical explanations of disease intersected with a moral discourse. In the case of alcoholism, by 1942, this meant that the 'condition' had acquired a psychological dimension in both its diagnosis and treatment. Thus, what had been a physical condition became associated with psychological characteristics.

Through the 1940s and 1950s the patient's social situation became the prime consideration in the diagnosis of alcoholism. Marital problems and maladjustments in the patient's social life became the focus of diagnosis. The balance between psychological and physical factors continued to see-saw, and in the 1960s alcoholism was considered to be a disease of the liver with psychological consequences, which were manifested in dressing and personal appearance.

By the 1970s, alcoholism was explained explicitly as a social condition, being a disease of the liver as a consequence of a way of dealing with stress. The synthesis of a medical/biological model with the moral/social model was now complete, and in the 1980s alcoholism became a behavioural disorder as a consequence of psychological and physical dependence on the drug. Alcoholism is currently three-dimensional: biophysical, psychological and social. The medical net is all-encompassing, and captures all aspects of the person's existence, as illustrated in this medical definition of alcoholism:

> Alcoholism is a primary, chronic disease with genetic, psychosocial, and environmental factors influencing its development and manifestations. The disease is often progressive and fatal. It is characterised by impaired control over drinking, preoccupation with the drug alcohol, use of alcohol despite adverse consequences, and distortions in thinking, mostly denial. Each of these symptoms may be continuous or periodic. (Meyer, 1996: 163)

Medical discourse and moral discourse have blended so much that they are now taken for granted, to the extent that definitions such as the one given above can be taken as unproblematic by both the medical profession and the public. With this development the historical origins of the problem of drunkenness have been reunited – the idea that drinking is morally problematic, from the temperance movement, and that it is a disease, from the medical profession. Medicine has become a socio-moral discourse based on a claimed scientific foundation: it defines correct behaviour and transforms transgressors into diseased individuals in need of treatment.

Developments in the Medical Profession

The processes of the medicalization of gambling and alcoholism are microcosms of developments in medicine. Medicine now blends, in a seamless fashion, value-loaded assertions of what a 'normal' life is, backed up by its claim to be a science, and in turn to be the scientific arbiter of normality. This is particularly true of the specialist practices of paediatrics, psychiatry, the development of general practice and of gerontology. These medical specialties take social relations as their focus, and see them as problematic, rather than as disease in the body. In contemporary medicine, disease may manifest itself in the body, but is seen by medicine as a product of our social relations (Armstrong, 1983).

Paediatrics

Paediatrics presumes that children are inherently at risk of disease or dysfunctional social relations. Medical intervention involves child, parent, siblings, teachers and other significant people in discussions of what are termed developmental problems. These don't necessarily have a biological basis, but require medical intervention and control.

Psychiatry

This locates disease in early socialization, the structure of the modern family, or even the relationships produced by modern industrial society. This is not to deny that a good deal of psychiatry aims to identify a biological basis for mental disorders. But equally, a good deal of it is to do with what can only be called deviance or behavioural disorders. Since we are all at risk of these, we are always potentially diseased or sick, and in need of monitoring and surveillance.

Gerontology

Gerontology defines old age as a disease. The elderly face a triple jeopardy of a decline in social location: death of spouse, loss of income and shrinking of social networks. These social risk factors are translated into medical problems of poor diet, alcoholism (if they are male) and depression (if they are female). Each of these conditions, or the three in tandem, is in need of medical care and monitoring.

General Practice

Medicine extended its reach from the patient's body and into the person's community through the 1970s and 1980s. Community medicine – taking into account all facets of the individual's life – medicalizes all aspects of our daily lives, such that most of us are, most of the time, members of a group called the 'worried well'. Is our cholesterol level all right? Are we going to have a heart attack? Are we eating the right sort of fats? How is our blood pressure? What about our weight? Are we doing enough exercise? We are in constant need of medical check-ups and monitoring – most of which we participate in voluntarily.

The outcome of these developments is that disease is now located in the social relations between bodies, and not just in bodies. It is in our social networks and our patterns of interaction with others – what we eat, who we sleep with, how much we drink, whether we get enough exercise, and on and on. Armstrong suggests that there has been a shift from biological anatomy of disease to the political anatomy of disease. By this he means that rather than focusing on our biology, modern medicine focuses on our social life, and sees it as problematic. We are all constantly in need of professional monitoring, and participate in our own self-monitoring to make sure that we are 'normal'.

Characteristics of the Medicalization of Society

We live in a medicalized society, one in which we explain problems in medical terms. For example, responding to social encounters with heavy drinking is explained as alcoholism. Inappropriate behaviour in the classroom is labelled hyperactive disorder, or, if it involves learning difficulties, dyslexia. The American Centers for Disease Control and Prevention reported that in 2003 an estimated 4.3 per cent of children in America aged 4 to 17 years had been diagnosed with Attention Deficit Hyperactivity Disorder (ADHD) and were taking medication for it (CDC, 2005). Suicide is explained in medical psychiatric terms, as is gambling. Often people's gender preferences, especially if they are homosexual ones, are explained as the outcome of medical abnormalities. The examples could be multiplied endlessly, but let us stop here and make three points about them.

These examples demonstrate the way in which medicine has become a central institution of social control in our society.

- It sorts, labels and treats the deviant, the nonconformist, the malingerer and the sick. In this role it has replaced the Church as the guardian of social values and of correct behaviour. It defines the limits of normal behaviour and defines people as sick if they fall outside these limits. Thus the way in which medical problems are produced, conceptualized and treated is the outcome of specific social and historical situations.

- The second point to note is that the way that we conceptualize some social factors as medical problems has immense significance. Overall it makes the events the problem of the individual – suicide, alcoholism and drug abuse are all laid at the door of the individual. It is their individual problem and it is the outcome of their individual biological or psychological malfunctioning. Thus medicalization treats the problems that people have independently of their existence in a wider social environment.

- The third point is that medicalization makes these problems appear to be the product of nature – of genetics, or biological dysfunction, or of an innate characteristic of the individual. This is a major paradox in modern medicine. It brings into existence our social relationships as problematic, and brings them into the orbit of surveillance, but ultimately suggests solutions that are biological. In other words, the problems are understood in such a way as to make the social environment that produced them disappear.

From a sociological perspective, this chapter suggests that the way social problems are conceptualized as medical problems does us all a disservice. It turns into technical problems the issues that are problems of politics and values, and of the social, structural organization of society. A brief case study of learning disabilities helps to illustrate this point.

LEARNING DISABILITIES, DYSLEXIA AND THE MEDICALIZATION OF THE CLASSROOM

The twentieth century has seen the development of a compulsory, age-graded school system. Children are expected to proceed equally through the school hierarchy, starting from a chronological base. Prior to the twentieth century, the school system (to the extent that it existed) was much more flexible, and progress through school was dependent on mastery of skills. Age was not, in itself, a measure of where a student should be in the system. At the same time, a lack of schooling beyond a rudimentary level was not a barrier to employment and lifetime earnings.

With the development of the middle classes, education was transformed. First, it became a prerequisite for non-manual jobs as the requirements of the labour market became more technically based; and second, the success of one's children at school became a status symbol – an indication of one's worth as a parent (Erchak and Rosenfeld, 1989). This double movement made education a site for dispute when the individual failed. Educational reformers argued that otherwise good students failed because of the 'factory'-style system of educational production, with forced progress

(Continued)

CASE STUDY

(Continued)

through the grades based on age. The policy implications of this explanation would have meant a substantial restructuring of the educational system, and would have amounted to disengaging the schooling system from the labour market – education would have been an end in itself rather than a means towards the end of getting a job. It was a policy, in the context of state-provided education, that was not acceptable either to capital or the state.

On the other hand, what if it could be shown that it was not the fault of any particular individual that they did not thrive at school? What if it could be argued that individual failure was not the result of huge schools with large classes? What if a child's failure at school was not a reflection on the parent, but an unfortunate outcome of biological factors, of a disease? This is, in fact, the solution that has been largely accepted by parents, children, school teachers and the professionals who have developed around this problem: the psychologists, the psychiatrists, the general practitioners and the school counsellors. The explanation of a child's failure, particularly children of professional parents, as being dyslexic, having a specific learning disorder, or suffering from attention deficit disorder, meets a great deal of social need. But even the beneficial aspect of medicalization is socially stratified. Whereas higher-income families are more likely to seek and receive external professional treatment for a child's learning disorder (Curry and Stabile, 2004), parents – and especially mothers – of lower-income families are more likely to be personally blamed for their child's under-performance, and be expected to do additional unpaid work to compensate (Reay, 2006).

In terms of the argument that this chapter has developed, sociologists would see these 'diseases' as the outcome of structural features of a society in which education is a status symbol, in the context of a shrinking labour market. Doctors may treat the 'diseases', and they are usually treated biochemically, but their origins are in the social structure and not in the biological individual.

Assessing Medicalization

Thinking about learning disabilities also allows us to reflect on the implications of medicalization. On the positive side, a number of factors stand out. Labelling a condition a disease has the appeal, at least on the surface, of being humanitarian. Diseases, in the medical model, being 'facts' of nature, do not elicit retribution or punitive sanctions against the sufferer. As will be discussed in the chapter on Parsons (Chapter 6), one of the characteristics of the sick role is that individuals are not blamed for their condition. Medicalization potentially leads to an optimistic outlook, since 'disease' can be treated. This is a great advance in terms of earlier ideas of an individual being marked for life by their condition. Lastly, given the individualistic focus of the medical model, medical social control is potentially more flexible, in that it responds to the individual case, rather than stigmatizing the behaviour.

Equally, though, the negative consequences of medicalization bear considerable thought. By definition, individual responsibility is diminished. Whatever is wrong is not your fault, but the fault of your biology. This may be appealing as a solution to some problems, but not to others. Second, despite the claim to being based on the facts of nature, medicine is not morally neutral. As this chapter has been at pains to point out, the description of something as a disease is covering and overlaying structural problems in society, whether of race, gender or age. Medicalizing an issue also automatically leads to domination by experts. This may be alright in some situations – we do want a surgeon to operate when we have ruptured an internal organ. But do we want to medicalize our love life, our personalities, our marriages or our children, and give a blank cheque to 'professionals' to treat them or us?

Conclusion

For sociologists, labelling a phenomenon as a disease may, in some cases, be unexceptional. But what a sociologist will always be alert to is the hidden moral evaluation embedded in the label, the blend of moral evaluation and the claimed scientific neutrality of the diagnosis. Further, they are always alert to the implicit power structure that the label 'disease' covers. For sociologists, diseases are the intersection between biography, biology and the social structure. Our body is the surface on which contradictory role requirements are inscribed, and it is the surface on which agents of social control inscribe our roles. Medicine plays a key role in this process, defining the 'normal', and enforcing that normality through the legitimate application of its armoury of chemical, electrical and surgical instruments.

The medicalization of behaviour eliminates alternative sociological explanations of why people act the way they do, or respond to social demands the way they do. Running away from white plantation owners is a political act, not the behaviour of a diseased person; resisting the enforcement of 'feminine' roles, as mediated in a patriarchal society by medicine, is a political act, not the behaviour of a diseased person. Constructing actions such as gambling and drinking as medical problems individualizes them, and obscures the reasons why people might see these actions as entirely rational responses to their life circumstances – circumstances which are the product of social forces outside their control. Transforming into diseases the problems of resourcing schools, of training individuals for the labour market, and of large classes is to depoliticize issues and hand control of debates over these issues to a professional elite, who may well be pursuing the interests of their profession, and not those of the children.

Over the twentieth century, medicine has developed from a claimed base in science to becoming a sophisticated system of social control. It transforms what are political evaluations of 'proper' behaviour into apparently scientific claims, which are beyond dispute. It transforms economic and political issues into individual issues, with individualistic solutions designed to maintain the status quo – whether of ethnic relations or of gender, generation or class.

Summary

- This chapter has shown how, over the second half of the twentieth century, sociology has become more critical of medicine, and more sceptical of its claims to be about caring and curing.

- It has raised the paradox that the more medicine takes into account the social basis of individuals' existence, the more it medicalizes areas of life.

- Using a wide range of examples, I have sought to illustrate how disease labels function in the context of specific political, economic, gender and class-based situations.

Discussion Questions

1. What is medicalization? Can you think of any examples of conditions that have been medicalized?

2. What are the benefits of medicalization?

3. Can behaviours that have been medicalized be de-medicalized?

Further Reading

Conrad, P. (2007) *The Medicalization of Society: On the Transformation of Human Conditions into Treatable Disorders.* Baltimore, MD: Johns Hopkins University Press. This is a great overview of the medicalization thesis, applied to a range of case studies including social anxiety, adult ADHD and sexual orientation.

Gerhardt, U. (1989) *Ideas About Illness: An Intellectual and Political History of Medical Sociology.* London: Macmillan. A good overview of the developments and paradigms in the sociology of health.

4

POSTMODERNITY, EPIDEMIOLOGY AND NEO-LIBERALISM

o   How we explain and understand disease is a product of political and economic life. Changes in the economic structure of society – called postmodernity – are having a significant effect on our explanations of the cause of disease.

o   While in the mid-twentieth century the emphasis was on the role of the state to protect individuals from the market, there is now a resurgence of liberalism, with an emphasis on the individual as responsible for their own health.

o   Current explanations in epidemiology reflect these new political and economic circumstances, focusing on individual lifestyles and risk factors, and moving away from a focus on structural features of society.

o   One consequence has been the development of analysis of the psychosocial supports open to individuals to help them prevent disease; another has been the development of the social capital approach – the claim that strong local communities will act as a protective mechanism against disease.

o   Whether or not strong communities, or economic equality, will best protect individuals is now a big debate in the sociology of health.

The current economic climate and associated structural changes in the political sphere have implications for the medical profession, the patient and the role of the state in the provision of health care. As the Welfare State has been transformed by the economic policies of the new right, the medical profession has had one of its major power bases threatened: the right to free (or at least heavily subsidized) health services, especially in the UK and Australia. The process of commodification means that the profession and the patient are more and more turned into objects for exchange on the market. These changes raise profound questions about the organization of social relationships and their impact on an individual's health. These changes will be examined against the background of the development of epidemiology. While epidemiology was originally part of public health, literally meaning the people's health, with a focus on collectivity, it has become increasingly individualistic and 'lifestyle' and 'risk' focused. This change in epidemiology reflects changes in the political and economic structures of modern societies, in which there has been a move away from the provision of services by a centralized state, and a remobilization of liberal arguments for individual responsibility and the need for a 'small' state.

In this chapter I examine the limitations of an epidemiological approach based on individual 'lifestyles' or 'risk factors', drawing on research that demonstrates the very limited impact of these on a population's health. The change to a focus on individuals has also had the effect of causing sociologists to examine more closely the effect of socio-psychological aspects of an individual's health status and vulnerability to disease, particularly their social networks and social support systems. Overall, I suggest that strong social support, and a strong sense of self-efficacy – of being in control of your life – are subsumed by wider socio-economic variables; that is, they reflect economic power rather than existing separately from it.

One other consequence of the growth of neo-liberalism and its drive towards a smaller state sector has been the resurrection of the claim that the 'community' is the basis for an individual's health. This has been particularly forcefully argued by 'social capital' theorists. Their argument is that strong communities, built around resilient sets of social relationships (and, by implication, self-help groups), will both produce a healthier population and cost the state less. The conservative and neo-liberal implications can be clearly shown in this turn to the 'community', and while the evidence is that strong communities are also healthier, it is equally clear that strong communities do not form in the context of economic inequality.

─BOX 4.1─

NEO-LIBERALISM AND POSTMODERNITY

Neo-liberalism is the term used to describe the resurgence of the political doctrine that individuals are best left to look after themselves – reflecting the dismantling of the Welfare State and the modification of the idea of citizenship by conservative governments, since the mid-1980s. Under the imperative of the World Bank and the International Monetary Fund loan and credit arrangements, both developing and developed countries are dismantling their health-care services and the public education sector, as well as privatizing – that is, selling off – public utilities such as electricity, water, rail and port services. The consequence has been the re-emergence of the infectious diseases thought to have been brought under control by the mid-twentieth century (Longbottom, 1997).

Postmodernity is a term used in sociology to describe the changes in modern society. Broadly, these are the decline of the industrial sector; the associated decline of the working class; the decline in unionization and the decline in occupation as a source of identity; and the weakening of the rigid distinction between public and private sectors, with their associated gender division of labour. Some sociologists argue that these transformations have freed individuals from the old constraints of occupation and class, and that we are moving out of capitalism, while others point to the growth in part-time, service sector jobs as new forms of capitalist exploitation.

Postmodernity

While the political philosophy of liberalism has been used to resurrect the individual as responsible for him- or herself, there have also been developments in society and social theory reflecting this change. From a sociological point of view, 'postmodernity' refers to changes in capitalist society over the past 30 years. Broadly, these are the decline of the industrial sector, the associated decline in the working class, the decline in unionization and the decline in occupation as a source of identity, and the weakening of the rigid distinction between the public and the private sectors, with their associated gender division of labour. It is often argued that the consequences of these transformations are increased freedom for the individual, who has been liberated from the old social structures of occupation and class and from the household and gender. We now live in a set of social organizations that allow us to be reflexive about our social identity and, in a sense, to construct our own biographies. Ulrich Beck has argued that we 'will be set free from the social forms of industrial society – class, stratification, family [and] gender status' (Beck, 1992: 87).

Generally speaking, we have seen the reversal of some previous long-term social trends. While globalization and commodification, for example, have continued apace, the centralization and increase in size and scope of nation-state governments has halted. Instead, nation-state governments have been shrinking and shedding functions.

The long-term implications of these large-scale changes are still a matter of debate. Some authors, such as Wagner (1994), understand the pattern of change as a swing back towards liberalism, or more accurately, the emergence of neo-liberalism. Others, such as Crook et al. (1992) understand the change as being a phase shift from modernity to postmodernity, that is, a distinctive move out of capitalism.

There are common themes, though, in the postmodernist account of contemporary social structure. These elements are summarized in Table 4.1, which offers a contrast between two abstract societal 'types' – that of the industrial modern society and that of the post–industrial postmodern society.

The changes postmodern theorists point to have significant implications for the organization and delivery of health care. An increasingly decentralized state sheds its collective functions, especially those around health, either back onto a notional 'community', or, as in the Australian case, it attempts to drive more and more people into private health insurance. The paradox, of course, is that in attempting to devolve its responsibilities, the state makes huge transfers of subsidies to the private sector to make it more appealing to capitalist investors. The Howard government in Australia spent over AUD $2.5 billion in subsidies to private insurers (Leeder and McAuley, 2005), and introduced penalty clauses into

TABLE 4.1 *Industrial modern (IM) society versus post-industrial, postmodern (PM) society*

Characteristics of IM	Characteristics of PM
1. The form of the state:	
Centralized, corporate, welfarist Aggregates power and functions	Decentralized, cross-linked, brokering. Sheds functions: upwards (to the UN/EU), downwards (to local government, community), sideways (to quangos) and out (to the market)
2. The form of inequality:	
Three large groups – the blue-collar working class; male boss; the housewife	'Mosaic' of status groups with complex links between work, gender, the public and private
3. The form of economic production and consumption:	
'Fordist' mass production, mass marketing and consumption	Flexible specialization, niche marketing/consumption
4. The form of politics:	
Mass, class-based parties with a 'machine' character	Social movements with extra-parliamentary existence
5. The contents of politics:	
Domestic: concentrates on 'entitlements', wages	Domestic: concentrates on mixture of 'entitlements' and wages, plus non-material issues
Internationally: concentrates on national interests	Internationally: concentrates on treaties, clusters
6. The form of policy:	
'One size fits all' Solve problems	Local variation Manage problems

With thanks to Dr Stephen Mugford, ANU

private health insurance legislation, making it more expensive for individuals the longer they delay taking it up (McAuley, 2005). So, notwithstanding the rhetoric of the appeal to the market, the state continues to guarantee the conditions for the accumulation of capital.

In this there is not a transition out of capitalism, but a resurgence of what has always been a key characteristic of state activities: the socialization of the costs of production and the privatization of profit (O'Connor, 1984). There is evidence for changing structures of inequality with the move from mass employment to the development of a significant minority of an underclass, of intergenerational un-employment and of welfare dependence (Bauman, 1998). If we are moving out of 'modern capitalism' into 'postmodern capitalism', it is certainly not the case that inequality has decreased under postmodern forms of capitalism. As the evidence cited throughout this book documents, inequality in Britain, America and Australia is growing faster than at any other time in the twentieth century, and the range of inequality between the poorest and the richest is now greater than in the nineteenth century. The consequence is the resurgence of patterns of infectious and chronic disease, and the increasing mortality rates of the poorest. If we were dying of the diseases of affluence for a brief period in the middle of the twentieth century, it is certainly not the case now. Current mortality and morbidity patterns owe their origins to poverty.

A significant aspect of postmodernist thought is that we are all 'agents' who make choices, rather than dupes of a society that rigidly lays down our roles. At one level, this 'reflexive turn' in sociology is part of the cross-generational re-actions of sociologists to their elders. The development of symbolic interactionism and phenomenology in the USA in the 1960s was a clear response to Talcott Parsons' structural functionalism, which, as one of his critics put it, made us all 'dupes' of the social system (Garfinkel, 1972). So is the current crop of theory from Europe a reaction to the structuralist Marxism of the 1970s of Poulantzas (1975) and Althusser (1971), in which individuals were conceptualized as 'trägers', on predetermined paths throughout their lives in the social system? At this level, the focus on the individual is to be welcomed as a corrective to the excesses of what has gone before.

Postmodernist theory emphasizes the increasing options open to individuals to shape their own lives. The argument is that social structures of modernity, espe-cially class and, to a lesser extent, gender, are no longer as important in individual biographies. This can be captured in the claim that there is increasing individual-ization and reflexivity. In terms of health, this has meant an increased focus on the options for individuals to choose their lifestyles and 'risk' behaviour. Put in socio-logical terms, the shift is to agency rather than structure. However, the choices that are open to individuals – of constructing their identity through smoking, drinking, drug taking, etc. – are structured for them in terms of their access to a variety of scripts that fit their lives.

Indeed, it is the case that the way in which 'risk' is presented in current epidemiology and health circles is one that challenges the very health-giving aspects of social life. The focus on risk behaviour is individualizing, rationalizing and implicitly destructive of explanations that use concepts such as community, sociability and conviviality (Forde, 1998). Put in a nutshell, what we can see in current epidemics of risk and the solutions to them is a drive towards individual responses. It is better to exercise in a solitary fashion in a gym on an exercise machine than it is to participate in a community-based group sport.

Liberalism and the Development of Neo-Liberalism in Health Policy

Historically, philosophic liberalism has its origins in the eighteenth century, and became influential in the political sphere in the nineteenth century. It was the political arm of the new capitalist class that developed out of the Industrial Revolution. Its major implication for policy was as little government intervention in the market as possible. Society was to be the outcome of individuals striving on their own, pursuing their own interest, and in this way achieving the greatest happiness of the greatest number. Quite clearly, though, there are problems with liberalism from the point of view of the vast majority of society. We do not all start equally, and once we have started, different groups have more power than others. This is particularly so in a capitalist society, where you must sell your labour power to survive, and the ownership of the means of production is concentrated in a small, dominant class. The policy does, however, benefit those in the capitalist class, since it allows the uncontrolled pursuit of profit and exploitation of the workers.

The Nineteenth and Early Twentieth Centuries

It was against the outcomes of liberalism that the great social reformers of health railed in the nineteenth century. Booth's 17-volume study of the London poor, Henry Mayhew's social journalism on the poor, and Engels' *The Condition of the Working Class in England* (1974) are only the better known of a huge literature linking poverty and inequality to disease and death (White, 2001). What they all had in common was the argument that the pursuit of profit produces sickness and disease, and that in such a social system, individuals on their own were powerless to protect themselves. It was only through reform of the government and collective action through the unions that better food, water and housing, as well as controls over factories and places of work, would be effected (Szreter, 1988). At the centre of the research carried out by the reformers was the discovery of the social patterning of disease. Disease was not randomly distributed throughout society. Rather, disease clearly went with concentrations of poverty, slum dwellings and industrial occupations. Thus epidemiology – the study of the people's health and the distribution of disease – was central to the development of public health.

It provided overwhelming evidence that individuals could not be left to their own devices when it came to their health. One other factor played a large part in motivating health reforms in Britain at the turn of the nineteenth century. When the government built up the army for the Boer War, and then the First World War, it found that the working classes were so weak they could barely lift the heavy Lee-Enfield rifle then in use. The men of the working class were starved, toothless and sick (Dussault and Sheiham, 1982).

This mixture of political activism, social reform and national interest combined, following the Great Depression of the 1930s, to produce the beginnings of the Welfare State. John Maynard Keynes argued for a strong role for the state to control productivity and wages, so as to control the tendency of capitalism to 'boom and bust'. Between the end of the Second World War and the late 1970s, interventionist governments ameliorated the impact of the market, protected working and living conditions, and controlled the economy to prevent large swings in unemployment. However, the costs to capitalists on their profits were always an issue – for example, in terms of the provision of safe working conditions, or of controls over the minimum wage, or the eight-hour working day – and it is these costs that today they are fighting to reclaim.

The Dismantling of Welfare and the Resurgence of Neo-Liberalism

Now, under the imperative of World Bank and International Monetary Fund loan and credit arrangements, both developed and underdeveloped countries are dismantling their health-care services and the public education sector, as well as privatizing – that is, selling off – electricity, water, rail and port services (Labonte, 1998; Terris, 1998).

—BOX 4.2—

CONSEQUENCES OF NEO-LIBERALISM ON DISEASE PATTERNS

Today we are seeing a resurgence of the infectious diseases in the Americas that were lethal in the nineteenth century. In the early 1990s, 941,805 cases of epidemic cholera occurred in the Americas, with 8662 deaths. The resurgence is a product of the same causes of diseases in the nineteenth century – lack of controls over water supplies and contamination of drinking water with sewage – and putting the pursuit of profit ahead of any other concerns (Pan American Health Organization, 1994: 164).

In Australia, the deregulation of legislation controlling the preparation of food has led to a steady increase in the reporting of food poisoning (Thomson et al., 1998).

(Continued)

(Continued)

In South Australia in 1995, for example, following changes in food preparation processes, 18 children required dialysis and one died (Cameron et al., 1995).

Similarly, the 2014 outbreak of Ebola in Africa has been largely blamed on an insufficient, unstable and poorly supported health-care system, which has developed in response to global pressures on countries on the continent to 'modernize' with 'the rest of the world', but also to repay their foreign loans at untenable rates (Kentikelenis et al., 2015).

Overall, infectious diseases once thought specific to the nineteenth century are on the increase (Longbottom, 1997).

The withdrawal of the state from the public realm was enshrined in the infamous statement by the then British Prime Minister, Margaret Thatcher: 'Society does not exist, only the individual.' The full implication of this statement for disease prevention came out in the 1988 British policy document 'Our Healthier Nation: A Contract for Health'. In this paper the Secretary of State dismissed attempts to secure the social environment in which individuals could pursue healthy lifestyles as 'Nanny state social engineering' (Secretary of State for Health, 1988: 28).

The impact of neo-liberalism on public health and the subsequent change in disease rates is likely to result in one of the biggest reversals of health status in the modern world. It is increasingly clear that the burden of disease in countries like Australia is on the poor – people are suffering not from diseases of affluence but diseases of poverty – with an ever-increasing gap in health status between those at the bottom and those at the top of the social system (White, 2000b). As Beaglehole and Bonita have argued, 'Public health is the collective action taken by society to protect and promote the health of entire populations' (Beaglehole and Bonita, 1997: xiii). In their analysis, good public health depends upon health education and general education, female autonomy (especially of control over fertility), adequate nutrition and accessible, adequate preventative health services – all factors threatened by neo-liberal policies.

BOX 4.3

THE WORLD HEALTH ORGANIZATION AND
THE SOCIAL BASIS OF DISEASE

In extensive studies the WHO has reported that the health of populations depends upon collective action to control unemployment and work environments; the provision of adequate public transport to the elderly, to the psychologically at risk and the impoverished; and the provision of structures that provide support and lead to social cohesion and tight control over food as a political issue (Marmot and Wilkinson, 1999; Wilkinson and Marmot, 1998).

When the WHO focused on individual actions, it was to point out that these actions were at the end of the chain of social causation, and not the beginning. Individuals' health-related behaviour is shaped by their social position and not freely chosen. For example, young men who were unemployed in the year before being studied were significantly more likely to be smokers, to drink heavily and to have a drinking problem than those who had not experienced unemployment (Montgomery et al., 1998). Unemployment is bad for your health.

Good health depends on prosperity, redistributive economic policies and the integration of health and welfare sectors of government.

Epidemiology: The Early Foundations

Sociologists and epidemiologists were close allies, developing arguments for the social base for a healthy population. In the nineteenth century, the social investigators into disease and social conditions, the early statisticians and epidemiologists, were mainly qualitative researchers. In the words of one historian of sociology, they were 'social explorers' (Kent, 1981). Engels, Mayhew and Booth, for example, all went out and looked at the conditions of the poor (White, 2001). Friedrich Engels, Marx's co-author, in fact lived with them. Their reports on their findings used statistical information on the patterning of disease in the slums, and were complemented by their account of living conditions, which, in turn, were used to elaborate explanations of why it was that poverty and disease were linked. They suggested explanations involving overarching social factors such as the social relations of the factory, or the maintenance of wages at subsistence levels by employers, or that the pursuit of profit would always be at the expense of the workers' health. The early epidemiologists provided rich qualitative data, backed up with statistical evidence of the way social life caused sickness and disease and how the poor experienced it. However, epidemiology has undergone significant transformations in what it researches and in how it reports its research since the nineteenth century.

It is often argued that the origins of epidemiology are in the search for the single cause of infectious diseases, especially of diseases such as cholera. Today, it is suggested that, due to the complexity of diseases, epidemiology must search out the 'multiple causes', and as such lose some of its power to predict and control disease, or to inform policy debates. This is a construction of the history of epidemiology that suits the current focus of epidemiologists. Classical epidemiology did not focus on the search for micro-organisms, nor did its practitioners attempt to separate their findings from the social and political environment in which disease flourished. The famous case of John Snow, who showed the transmission of cholera through the faecal contamination of water supplies, is usually related as an example of a single mechanical intervention – removing the Broad Street pump handle that controlled water supply for the area. The implication is that a simple technical solution eliminated the specific cause of an infectious disease, i.e. preventing the consumption of contaminated water. However, this is not what Snow reported. Rather, he pointed out that while the presence of cholera would cause disease, it was specific social conditions that would allow it to spread and which would determine its virulence:

> It is amongst the poor, where a whole family live, sleep, cook, eat, and work in a single room that cholera has been found to spread when once introduced, and still more in those places termed lodging houses, in which several families were crowded into a single room. It was amongst the vagrant classes who lived in this crowded state, that cholera was most fatal in 1832, but the Act of Parliament for the regulation of common lodging houses has caused the disease to be much less fatal amongst these people in the late epidemics. (Snow, 1936: 36)

Limitations of the Risk Factor and Lifestyle Explanations

Clinical epidemiology has moved away from these social origins. First, it has moved to a focus on individual behaviour, and the so-called risk factors of individual behaviour; second, it has moved almost to purely statistical ways of communicating its findings. These developments have significant implications for the contribution epidemiologists can make to explaining patterns of health and disease.

Epidemiology now reflects the core assumptions of neo-liberalism: it is individualistic, and makes little or no reference to 'social factors', focusing rather on individual risk behaviour. However, the pursuit of unidimensional 'risk' factors cannot accommodate the complexities of social life, while the focus on individual risk factors has replaced a focus on the structural factors that produced the social environment that sustained health. This is despite the now-overwhelming evidence that 'risk factors' do not account for the patterning of disease. As Terris states:

> The evidence is clear that the currently recognised risk factors for cardiovascular disease are responsible for only a small part of the differences in mortality by social class. These differences continue to widen, and the prospects are that this process will become intensified with time. (Terris, 1996: 434)

Furthermore, Yen (1995) argues, the reliance on risk factors reflects a shift towards 'managerial' health practices. Under this scheme, GPs are encouraged to think of the individual's health as a matter of identifying and 'containing' a variety of risks, which effectively 'reduces the integrated person to a highly limited set of behaviours and characteristics' and implies a system of care based on a patient's ability to 'perform' the necessary risk factors (1995: 34). The more that so-called risk factors are examined, the more difficult it seems to be to conclude what role they play in determining health.

—BOX 4.4—

EMPIRICAL LACK OF SUPPORT FOR
RISK FACTOR APPROACHES

A large-scale study of ischaemic heart disease in Finland found that those in the top socio-economic groups were dying of fewer heart attacks, but that an analysis of risk factors in their lifestyles accounted for less than half of this improvement (Vertianen et al., 1998).

Similarly, a study of Gerona in Spain, which has very low heart attack rates, actually found that the 2404 people in the sample had very high risk factors – a prevalence of hypertension, number of smokers, increased high-density cholesterol, and high lipoprotein and mean cholesterol levels (Masia et al., 1998).

Even if it were lifestyle risk behaviours that were the cause of disease, extensive studies have shown that it is almost impossible for people to change their lifestyle on their own and in isolation from their social circumstances. In the Multiple Risk Factor Intervention Trial (1982) conducted in the USA, a group of highly motivated men, in the top 10 per cent risk group for coronary heart disease, were supported by counsellors and psychologists over a six-year period to change their eating and smoking behaviour. However, the trial showed that only modest changes to behaviour could be sustained. The trial also alerted researchers to the problem of intervening at the individual level. For every one of the men who did modify their behaviour, nothing was being done to prevent others from adopting the same lifestyles. That is, the factors which predispose people to adopt unhealthy lifestyles – of work stress for example – are ignored in interventions trying to treat the individuals who have already adopted them. When epidemiologists focus on the proximate causes of disease (diet, cholesterol and hypertension, for example), they individualize the causes of disease and miss the distal social causes. As Link and Phelan (1995) argue, we need to contextualize risk factors to see how individuals are exposed to them and have limited access to resources to respond to them. It is the lack of resources to respond to risks that is the fundamental cause of disease patterns. If we want to change the patterns of disease then we must change the distal – not the proximate – causes.

Developing a Sociological Model of Disease: Disease Classified by Social Cause

One way of doing this is to develop a sociological model of the causes of disease, in contrast to the medical and epidemiological explanations of disease as inherently individual occurrences. Sociologists argue that rather than classifying diseases as they work themselves out at the individual level, they should be classified by their social causes. Such an approach alerts us to those environmental factors that can be changed and thus prevent diseases from developing, rather than trying to change individuals (Syme, 1996). It also addresses the issue, pointed out by Cassell (1976), that similar social circumstances lead to a wide range of diseases. That is to say, specific social, environmental, political and economic environments lead to a wide range of diseases, and the predictive value of these circumstances is stronger than a focus on lifestyle factors.

─BOX 4.5─

A SOCIOLOGICAL MODEL OF DISEASE

One sociologist who has developed such a model of disease, focusing on social causes rather than disease processes, is Peter Davis, Professor of Public Health at the University of Canterbury in Christchurch New Zealand (Davis, 1994). Davis's argument is that rather than focusing on individual diseases and individual bodies, health research and health policy should be directed to the economic, political and cultural institutions that produce disease. Thus he proposes classifications of disease based on the economic, social, cultural and political determinants of ill health and disease.

- In the economic sphere, the institution of the labour market, inside an economic framework of capitalism, which results in profit being placed before safety, would be shown to be the cause of industrial death and accident.

- The social shaping of disease, through the institutions of family and kinship, working themselves out in the context of urbanization and social mobility, would be targeted as contributory or causative in hypertension and mental illness.

- Cultural factors of beliefs, practices and lifestyles, usually manifest in different consumption patterns, especially of diet and alcohol, would be seen as key factors in obesity, bowel cancer and lung cancer.

- At the political level are those diseases which are a product of the structures of power and the different participation rates of different groups in an unequal society, which result in diseases due to problems of access to services and equity in the distribution of services.

Davis's work allows us to develop a social model of the determinants of disease. The focus on social causes allows us to break with the sense of biological inevitability that the medical model of disease leads to. His sociological approach captures the social dynamics of an individual's actions. People's lifestyles and actions are seen in terms of the context of the social groups they live in, the economic imperatives that place them in specific working conditions (exposing them to risk), and the political and economic context that shapes access to treatment. While it may not help individual sufferers in the short term, it prevents individuals from suffering in the long term. Davis's model is supported by considerable evidence of the social determinants of disease and of the need to reorient our approach to disease to one in which the focus is on social institutions rather than individual actions.

Epidemiology and Statistics

Epidemiology also reflects the rise to dominance of statistics in the social sciences since the Second World War. While epidemiological knowledge has far-reaching implications, its usefulness is restricted by the language of positivism and of its presentation as computational data. It has a statistically reductionist understanding of truth, which, by definition, excludes narrative and situational, qualitative accounts of truth. The positivist method is tied to an approach that evades the impact of structural factors on individuals' health. Thus, social class has not been a priority for epidemiologists. In fact, epidemiologists usually actively exclude measures of class in their attempt to identify risk factors, since class, by any measurement, is overwhelmingly the causative factor in the production and distribution of disease.

Keith Paterson (1981) is critical of positivist epidemiology because it replicates the 'facts' of capitalist society. It takes diseases at face value, as existing independently of social structures. Following from this it takes for granted the import of positivistic statistics: 'By its focus on disease as a problem of incidence, conceived of as a product of a number of mechanically related risk factors, epidemiology denies that the structure of social relations in society also had a primary determining role in the shaping of diseases' (Paterson, 1981: 23). Positivist epidemiology systematically obscures the social forces that produce and reproduce the poverty and inequality which give rise to disease. In contrast, he proposes a materialist epidemiology, which examines:

> underlying structures and relationships and considers that the purpose of theory is to describe the fundamental processes that actually explain the observable regularities. Thus the aim of a materialist epidemiology would not be to deny the observed relationships between various diseases and different facets of the host agent and environment, but rather to penetrate beneath the surface appearances described in statistical associations to the underlying socio-economic and historical context in which these associations are located. (Paterson, 1981: 27)

The flight to statistics has meant a flight from analysis and any attempt to produce an argument about why patterns of disease exist as they do. As Smith has put it, epidemiologists have produced 'a vast stockpile of almost surgically clean data untouched by human thought' (Smith, 1985). The statistical information is a blizzard of unrelated findings and correlations about risk factors. Yet they do serve a social function in our society: the knowledge provided by epidemiologists has an enormous impact on us as individuals in our daily lives. Epidemiologists construct categories of risk that we as individuals are then alerted to. In particular, epidemiology, interlinked with media representations (Markova and Farr, 1995) and backed up by professional health groups, now produces 'risk epidemics'. As Forde points out,

> by increasing anxiety regarding disease, accidents and other adverse events, the risk epidemic enhances both health care dependence and health care consumption. More profoundly, and perhaps even more seriously, it changes the way people think about their health, disease and death. ... The message of the odds ratio from epidemiological research advocates a rationalistic, individualistic, prospective life perspective where maximising control and minimising uncertainty is seen as a superior goal. (Forde, 1998: 1155)

The epidemiological structuring of risk is part of the neo-liberal society in which we live: risks are constructed as individual events that we are responsible for. Yet they are also fabricated and not amenable to intervention at the individual level. The whirlwind of risks – of cholesterol levels, of coffee, salt, sugar and many others constructed on a regular basis in the newspapers – depoliticizes the wider causes of sickness and disease, and leaves us blaming ourselves for conditions that are outside our control (Crawford, 1980; Frohlich et al., 2001).

Constructing categories of risk is a complex situational, political and ethical process and not simply a statistical exercise performed with objective tools on an 'objective' reality. Probability statistics depend on the choice of the numerator and the denominator and, depending on these choices, 'risks' can be constructed in virtually any way the researchers like (Heyman et al., 1998). Constructing them in such a way as to blame the victim and hide the environmental, the social and the political causes of disease is a political act. That they are constructed in such a way as to turn solutions to them into profit for the medical–industrial complex, to make us agents of our own social control, and lead to a focus on individuals in already subordinated groups, is no accident. It reflects how medicine is both shaped by and shapes the social, political and economic structures of contemporary political and economic life.

Psychosocial Perspectives on Social Inequalities in Health

Durkheim provided the first argument with empirical data that the quality of social life has a serious impact on the mental health of people. He argued that those with the weakest social ties were at risk of egoistic suicide because, unconstrained by social life, they overvalued their own existence and came to see themselves as existing independently from, and without obligation to, the community. Equally, and importantly (since it is much overlooked), he argued that too strong a set of social ties placed the individual at risk of altruistic suicide – of sacrificing themselves, overzealously, on behalf of the group. Too much integration, or role demand, is as bad as too little integration.

It is in this Durkheimian tradition that sociologists focus on the impact of social networks, social stress and the role of the community in preventing or causing ill health (Durkheim, 1966). Stressful social events cause us to modify our behaviour patterns and are usually accompanied by physiological and emotional reactions. Stress has been conceptualized as working its way out in three major areas: life events, chronic strain and daily existence. If these stressors accumulate, the argument goes, we lose our ability to cope, and disease and illness follow – usually through the impact of depression and anxiety (Cohen and Williamson, 1991). It seems to be clear that major negative life events – the sudden need to adapt quickly to major life occurrences such as death, divorce or unemployment – will, in the six weeks following, result in physical symptoms, psychological distress and psychiatric symptoms. Chronic stress is also implicated in poor health (Brown, 1989). Elstad (1998) has provided a valuable overview of this area. He points out that the psychosocial perspective is based on three core assumptions. First, psychological stress is an important cause of health inequalities in affluent societies. Second, psychological stress is socially produced and distributed, and is a product of the strength of social and interpersonal relationships. Third, social and personal interrelationships are mediated by inequality.

Stress

Stressful life events have been linked to heart disease, diabetes, cancers, stroke, foetal death, major depression and low birth weight (Link and Phelan, 1995). The social-stress approach originally conceptualized any socio-environmental change as challenging to the individual. Births as well as deaths, marriages as well as divorce, and the good experiences and the bad were analytically placed together (Holmes and Rahe, 1967). However, it has become clear that there was a social gradient linking poor health and negative stressors. Those who are unemployed and homeless, those at most risk of losing their jobs, and those who are living in poverty face more ongoing, seriously negative stressful events and experience more sickness. The focus of contemporary stress research has come to be on subjectively perceived, long-term stressors, which are distributed unevenly throughout society and reflect wider patterns of inequality (Lantz et al., 2005; Pearlin et al., 2005). The development of a concern for the subjective appreciation of stress is important, since we know that people make different sense out of stressful experiences. It is not just the factual existence of stress that is of concern. It is also how, or indeed whether, individuals experience events as stress. This raises the very important link between the individual and society and shows one way that sociologists attempt to explain it. How we make sense of the impact that social structures have on us is important to their effects on us. The focus on the subjective experience of stress also opens up the very important insight that stressors impact differently on members of different social groups. For example, women are more vulnerable to changes in their social networks, while men are more vulnerable to changes in their work status. Thus there are clear differences on how individuals experience stress based on their socialization into specific groups (Conger et al., 1993).

It must also be kept in mind that from a sociological perspective the stresses of life may be hidden from the individual. Disease and stress are socially caused (Link et al., 1993) and may not be open to individual introspection – they are the social system inscribed on the body of the person. Pearlin (1989) is one of the few researchers who have focused on the sociological causes of stress, and who see it as the outcome of social roles in which individuals are constrained by their class, gender or ethnicity. Processes of achieving and maintaining social status, Pearlin argues, are where stress is most likely to arise, and also most likely to lead to long-term ill health – showing that the structural forces of class and health inequality are inextricably linked (Pearlin et al., 2005). Mirowsky and Ross (1989) have argued that structural powerlessness, alienation and lack of control are all features of the individual's position within the social structure. The major structuralist accounts have been conducted by Dooley and Catalano (1984), who have used analysis of macro-level shifts in the economy to show the impact on individual behaviour, especially the increase in health-seeking actions to resolve psychological problems. In contrast to the individualistic accounts of the impact of stress and individuals' reliance on each other, it is important to realize that group exposure to stress may lead to collective social and political action, such as the formation of a trade union, to ameliorate it (Barbalet, 1998).

The development of the idea that stress causes illness has occurred in a political context. While the stress literature has opened up the medical explanations of disease to social and psychological factors, it has displaced other sociological explanations. The number of articles published on the relationship between social class and mental disorder declined between 1965 and 1985, while the literature on stress burgeoned. Thus, an interest in 'stress', a mechanism that facilitates illness and disease, has replaced social class – the well-recognized cause of psychiatric disorder (Angermeyer and Klusman, 1987). The focus on stress has also been used to move attention away from social factors. Link and Phelan (1995: 90) examined 240 articles published in the *American Journal of Epidemiology* between 1992 and 1993. They concluded that of these, only 13.3 per cent focused on risk factors conceptualized as being social in nature. Indeed, they found that even though many of the articles used the words 'race', 'ethnicity' or 'gender', they did so without examining the social aspects of these categories.

Social Support

The focus on stressors has led to the postulation of the existence of buffers to stress – of coping resources, of coping strategies and social support networks. Individuals are not passive recipients of social roles or role strain. Individuals may act to make sense

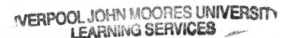

of life stressors and often turn them into positive states, e.g. the experience of divorce, which increase the individual's social resilience. Hall and Lamont (2013) found that, regardless of whether neo-liberalism helped individuals and communities feel 'emancipated' or oppressed, the modern market-dominated ideology requires communities to develop strategies of resilience: finding new methods of identity-formation, creating new measures of self-worth, or forging different communities of belonging, for example. However, it is worth noting that sociology has questioned the popular 'resilience' discourse, often taking the form of self-help books but increasingly prevalent in government publications and policies. Rather than addressing the social conditions that create the need for resilience, they focus on the individual and their lack of 'coping strategies', calling on them to become better moral subjects despite their ill health – which, in the process, can further strengthen the very structures that produce ill health, like patriarchy and racism (see James, 2014, 2015).

But by focusing on the social causes of stressors, individuals may also actively structure their life experiences to gain exposure to positive life events. This self-efficacy approach emphasizes the ways in which individuals make active sense of the stress that they encounter, and takes into account that people may respond to stress in ways that lead to health. An active engagement with stress may lead to a more healthy life.

─BOX 4.6─

MAJOR FINDINGS FROM THE SOCIAL SUPPORT LITERATURE

1. Social integration is positively linked to mental and physical health and lower mortality rates.

2. Perceived emotional support leads to better physical and mental health, and helps to buffer the impact of major life events.

3. The most powerful form of support is an intimate and confiding relationship (Thoits, 1995).

In turn each of these three points are themselves mediated by social structural factors. Those with high social status have an enhanced sense of support, and involvement in social networks is positively correlated with high social status (Turner and Marino, 1994).

The Social Drift Hypothesis

An alternative to a sociological approach is the social drift hypothesis. Peggy Thoits has argued that we still need to keep the social selection or drift hypothesis as an important theoretical alternative to structural explanations. The drift hypothesis is that the sick and depressed and stressed move down the social system and accumulate at the bottom. As she says, 'appreciating the individual as a psychological activist should not be seen as a threat to the social causation perspective, but instead as a challenging opportunity to explore more fully the interplay between personal agency and structural constraints' (Thoits, 1995: 59).

Against the notion of social drift, I would propose the metaphor of social undertow. Thus, rather than conceptualize stressful events as aberrations or unlikely occurrences, it can be argued that it makes more sense to think in terms of the accumulation of risk, of the ongoing effort to keep one's head above water in the face of repeatedly stressful and physically debilitating events (Blane et al., 1993). Coping with stressful events has to be seen within the overall course of a life in which the individual is repeatedly and systematically at risk of health-destroying events, whether narrowly conceived of as lifestyle factors or more broadly as the impact of structural factors such as unemployment, ethnicity, or gender. In short, an individual's health is the outcome of the probability of a whole series of social events, which tend to multiply negatively the further down the social system you go. The individual's experience of either health or disease is a product of the lifetime experience of social events (Blane et al., 1996), and the impact of one set of health disadvantages sets off a descending spiral of other health disadvantages (Kuh et al., 1997; Power and Matthews, 1997). They are not drifting – they are drowning.

Talking About the Diseased Self

The concern for the individual's experience of stress and disease has generated an interest in how individuals talk about their illnesses, how they actively make sense of them in the stories they tell each other of their ailments. Again within this research is the paradox that those with the strongest sense of self-identity, and strongest sense of control over what is happening to them, cope best with stress and illness, but also tend to be placed higher in the social system. It is both the sense of self and the location within the structures of inequality which interact to produce the subjective awareness of the situation. What appears to be central to the experience of sickness, and the distribution of health, is personal identity. As one researcher has put it: 'What resources does each social form make available to individuals from which they may shape an identity they can live with? ... Future research may well set out to discover how action is shaped by the narratives people construct to make sense of their own encounters with inequality' (Bartley et al., 1998: 570).

Narratives are the stories people tell about their illness, sometimes called 'pathographies' (Hawkins, 1990), and they may take a variety of styles. Frank categorizes them as storylines that take the form of explaining the experience and the process of illness, constructed around themes of restitution, chaos and quest (Frank, 1993, 1995).

—BOX 4.7—

FUNCTIONS OF THE ILLNESS NARRATIVE
FOR THE INDIVIDUAL

1. To transform illness events and construct a world of illness.

2. To reconstruct one's life history in the event of a chronic illness.

3. To explain and understand the illness.

4. As a form of strategic interaction in order to assert or project one's identity.

5. To transform illness from an individual into a collective phenomenon (Hyden, 1997: 55).

The development of an interest in narrative has provided an opportunity for a focus on the impact of chronic illness. Bury's concept of 'biographical disruption' is one illustration (Bury, 1982). Bury pointed to three aspects of disruption caused by chronic illness:

1. the disruption of assumptions and behaviours;

2. disruptions in explanatory systems that require a rethinking of biography and self-concept; and

3. the response to disruption.

> My contention is that illness, and especially chronic illness, is precisely that kind of experience where the structures of everyday life and the forms of knowledge which underpin them are disrupted. Chronic illness involves a recognition of the worlds of pain and suffering, possibly even of death, which are normally only seen as distant possibilities or the plight of others. (Bury, 1982: 169)

While this approach adds a good deal to our understanding of the experience of disease, there are limitations. It has been well documented, for example, that patients' attempts to 'tell their story' are overwhelmed in the medical encounter by the doctor's need to translate it into clinical signs and symptoms (Waitzkin, 1991). Furthermore, the linguistic resources that individuals have access to in order to construct their narrative are heavily dependent on educational level. Thus aspects of class and gender will structure narratives. These broader social factors are not much acknowledged in the literature. As Turner and Roszell (1994) argue, control over life circumstances and the perceived ability to control life happenings for oneself – the precise sociological grounds on which one constructs narratives of oneself – are linked to social status. Women, members of ethnic minorities, and those with low education and income have a higher degree of fatalism and less sense of control over life events. A strong sense of self-efficacy (a sense of being in control and triumphing over life's setbacks) is a socially distributed resource. Having a job with flexibility in work routines, having an income sufficient to afford childcare, and having an education that allows one to access state-provided health, welfare and social services, or an accountant to minimize taxes – all of which would enhance one's sense of self and ability to cope with stress – are unequally distributed to start with. Put another way, for effective problem-focused coping actions to work, the situation must be modifiable by the individual (Folkman, 1984).

To sum up, social coping mechanisms, the exposure to life stressors, and participation in social networks are all mediated by structural variables. In addition, there are costs to the participation in social networks and to being socially integrated, which may outweigh any benefits (Rook, 1992). Obligatory social roles can be negative. Those of spouse, parent, relative or carer in the domestic sphere can all be very costly social roles to fulfil. Women are much more likely to be involved in these sorts of wearing and draining relationships (Opie, 1992).

Community, Social Capital and Inequality

Rather than emphasize individuals and their 'choices', sociologists of health argue that the fundamental aspects of our existence – how healthy we are when alive, and whether or not we live as long as the most privileged sectors of society – are dependent on the political and social context and levels of inequality that we live with. So rather than celebrate an individualist account of healthiness, or the operation of the free market, sociologists argue that health is a direct consequence of the health of the community, of the links of reciprocity that bind us together. At the same time there is a political agenda behind the move to the community. A great deal of weight has been placed on 'community participation', much of it intended to shift the costs of health care away from the state and from capital. The concept of community is being reconstructed in the light of the decline of institutionally based services, with the major aim of moving the provision of services from the formal to the informal sector. This has major implications for the gendered delivery of health care, putting even more pressure on women.

For community interventions to work we must understand the structural position of communities. A distinction must be made between community-level intervention, based on transformation of structural features of the community, and those approaches which have as their focus community interventions with changes in individual action as their outcome: As Patrick and Wickizer make the distinction, 'A community level intervention is an intervention organised to modify the entire community through community organisation and activation, as distinct from interventions that are simply community-based, which may attempt to modify individual health behaviors such as smoking, diet or physical activity' (Patrick and Wickizer, 1995: 47).

If we need to be careful when using the term community, we also need a sociologically useful understanding of health needs. For example, one of the major justifications for decentralizing Britain's National Health Service in the 1990s was that individual needs would be better met, and local bureaucracies made more amenable to local needs. However, a study of decentralized health services in Britain found that consumers were not empowered or made more effective in determining local priorities (Milewa et al., 1998).

Needs have usually been conceptualized inside a therapeutic discourse or a rights discourse. However, these are so individualistic in their definitional premises that they cannot incorporate the core of a public health understanding of needs – that of a 'language of need which speaks to the reciprocity and interdependence which characterise community' (Robertson, 1998: 1430). Part of what has been at issue in determining a properly sociological account of need has been the dominance of conventional economic analyses where benefit is understood solely at the level of individual utility. Institutional economics would provide an alternative form of economic rationality, which takes into account that changes at a political, structural or cultural level are a source of value (Jan, 1998). Thus one of the areas where public health has lost out is in a general theory of need and a consolidation of a politics of need. 'Need' is political in its definition, and has to be operationalized in the context of the political understanding of 'community' developed above. It is only when there is a communitarian basis to rights and needs, which allows the community to be involved in establishing what health services should be, that needs are likely to be met (Mooney, 1998).

The relationships between income inequality, social trust and social cohesion are now a significant part of research into the social causes of illness and disease. The social cohesion approach continues the stress model, but accommodates the significant insight that people already live in an unequal society. It starts by asking the question: how does the psychosocial experience of inequality affect health? In part the answer is provided by arguing that there is clear evidence that health policies that increase social support and social cohesion prevent death from heart disease more than individualistic, lifestyle interventions (Eng et al., 2002; Lomas, 1998). As Lomas puts it, when we take an individualistic approach, 'we ignore what our everyday experience tells us, i.e. the way we organise our society, the extent to which we encourage interaction among the citizenry and the degree to which we trust and associate with each other in caring communities is probably the most important determinant of our health' (Lomas, 1998: 1181). It is also argued that the experience of inequality, and the fact of living in unequal societies, lead to feelings of humiliation, shame and a sense of disrespect.

These emotional experiences are linked to low social status and are central to a loop that incorporates violence, inequality and mortality. For example, Wilkinson and his colleagues have established that violent crime rates are closely linked to income inequality, and further, that a central motivation in crimes of violence against people is that the assailants felt that they were not respected (Wilkinson et al., 1998).

This is an important argument linking mortality rates to material conditions, and to providing a sociological link between the individual and society through the mechanism of socially shaped emotions (Barbalet, 1998).

The broader argument is that material deprivation is not the only cause of the social gradient in sickness and disease, and that the experience of inequality is pivotal to our health. The argument is backed up by extensive evidence that inequalities in health status are replicated within class positions, as well as across class boundaries. Put another way: within the lowest sectors of the working class, health is poorer than at the top. But within the middle classes, those in the middle and at the bottom have poorer health than those at the top; and again those at the top of the middle class have poorer health than those in the richest class. This finding has now been established in England and America (Marmot, 1998). The most famous illustrations of this research are the Whitehall studies, which showed a three-fold increase in mortality rates between the bottom and the top of the civil service in Britain. Even more importantly, what these studies established was the limited impact of lifestyle factors on health variations. Marmot and his co-workers controlled for diet, smoking, exercise and blood pressure in their sample, and found that these factors could explain only one-third of the variance in disease between grades (Marmot et al., 1978, 1991). The psychosocial processes around the experience of inequality have an important impact on our sense of control, social affiliations and support, self-esteem, life events and job security, and expose us to chronic psychosocial stress (Marmot, 2004; Wilkinson, 1996).

Social Capital

Social support is not just the product of an individual's interaction with one or more other individuals. If it were, social life would only be the sum of these individual interactions. It is clear that this is not the case. Rather, it is a product of neighbourhoods, associations and organizations, and of institutions that are not just the sum of the individuals participating in them (Felton and Shinn, 1992). Having access to these overarching social organizations goes under the generic name of 'social capital'. The idea of social capital can probably best be understood in terms of the contribution of the 'community' to an individual's health in the form of material (goods, services, shelter) and immaterial resources (trust, norms, identities) (Kawachi et al., 2008; Lomas, 1998). The features of a community relevant to health are, first, its physical structure, which can expose us to risk and make us susceptible to disease. Second is its social structure, that is, the opportunities for interaction that it provides, which may be either extensive or limited, through to political and economic factors such as the redistribution of income. Third, and for social capital theorists the most important, is the quality of social cohesion, of a sense of integration that a community may supply: 'Along with such things as the cultural or social homogeneity of a community, its physical and social structure can either encourage or discourage mutual support and caring, self-esteem, and a sense of belonging, and enriched social relationships' (Lomas, 1998: 1182).

The approach of social capital theorists has some sociologically useful premises (Lomas, 1998). It balances individualistic approaches by directing attention to the impact of social organization, and it challenges the individualizing explanations of disease patterns offered by epidemiology. Epidemiological concerns with screening, immunization, lifestyle and risk-factor change are shown to be beside the point in light of the evidence for structural factors in the production and distribution of disease. Lomas argues in a social capital framework that 'the way we organise our society, the extent to which we encourage interaction among the citizenry and the degree to which we trust and associate with each other in caring communities is probably the most important determinant of our health' (Lomas, 1998: 1181).

Social capital has a close though generally unacknowledged link with Durkheim's concept of organic solidarity. Durkheim argued in his book *The Division of Labor in Society* (1933) that social harmony would come about in industrial society through the formation of communities based on shared occupational interests and a new harmony of the moral individual, whose actions would be guided by a concern for the common good. Contemporary social capital theorists argue that the increased density of social relationships, with improved communication, leads to a revitalized common good and to the alleviation of social conflict. Putnam, the leading American commentator in this area, has defined it thus:

> By 'social capital' I mean features of social life – networks, norms and trust – that enable participants to act together more effectively to pursue shared objectives … To the extent that the norms, networks and trust link substantial sectors of the community and span underlying social cleavages – to the extent that the social capital is of a bridging sort – then enhanced co-operation is likely to serve broader interests and to be widely welcomed. (Putnam, 1995: 664–5)

However, there are problems with the social capital approach. The explanation of poor health in the poorer sections of society as a consequence of their lack of certain attributes – that they do not generate 'good communities', for example – is a continuation of conservative sociological explanations of inequality in general. The theory of social capital continues a tradition in social disorganization theory from criminology, which argued that what socially disorganized communities lacked were forms of social organization – trust and participation in voluntary societies. It was a 'blame the community' approach, which was sociological in not 'blaming the individual', but conservative in its political implications that dysfunctional communities were responsible for their own shortcomings and should solve them on their own. Social capital explanations of the social patterning of disease continue this tradition, since their account does not involve any relationship to economic capital, and by implication suggests not only that are material resources not needed to ameliorate 'underlying social cleavage', but also that 'community building exercises' based around the idea of social capital as an ideologically neutral phenomenon will lower expenditure by capital and the state. This is certainly the way in which social capital has been constructed from the perspective of economic rationalism and neo-liberalism.

Politically, the growth of interest in the concept of social capital has to be seen in the context of the decline of the much older concept – systematically destroyed under President Reagan in the USA, and Prime Ministers Thatcher and Major in the UK in the 1980s and 1990s – of the 'social wage' (Popay et al., 1998). The social wage (the amount of state spending on public health, welfare, education, housing and urban infrastructure of the Welfare State) resulted in the downward redistribution of resources and explains the increase in life improvement over the post-war period (Charlton and Murphy, 1997). While critiques of Welfare State expenditure showed that they benefited the middle class, it is the case that the real material basis of the Welfare State cannot be replaced by idealist appeals to the idea of 'community'. Disease is generally a consequence of poverty. The diseases of inequality, of the perceived insults of an unequal social structure and its limited avenues of dissent, will not be fixed by appeals to community, shared interests, or of looking after oneself. Patterns of health and disease are systematically linked to material structures of inequality in Western societies. Income inequality, social trust and health are related. As Wilkinson has reported, the link between income inequality and population mortality has been independently supported over and over (Wilkinson, 1995; Wilkinson and Pickett, 2006). Improving social cohesion without redressing inequality will not make for a healthier, longer-lived population.

Social Capital or Income Inequality?

Lomas, in his defence of the social capital approach, by and large does not take into account the political economy of the health sector. He notes in passing that the further from individual, technological and drug-based interventions that successful health policy moves, the less opportunity there is for 'entrepreneurship' – that is, for profit making. The implementation of social policies that will foster social cohesion, which Lomas describes as 'radical', are the 'preservation and advancement of social structures such as meeting places, sports leagues, clubs, associations, and all the other elements of a community that allow for the exchange of views and values and engender mutual trust' (Lomas, 1998: 1183). He goes on to suggest:

> A public health that was responsive to this evidence would focus on improving income and power distributions, advocating for increased leisure time to facilitate social interaction, changing planning by-laws to create more public spaces or to encourage verandas on the front of houses rather than patios on the back, or increasing subsidies and support for locally based clubs and associations. In other words, changes in the physical and social structure of communities to create local social capital. (Lomas, 1998: 1184)

Against this statement we can see why sociologists of a critical persuasion are so sceptical of this approach. It blends a naïvety with regard to the institutional, the economic and the political which is breathtaking in its mix of levels of power and interaction, which are not interchangeable. The focus on community is clearly idealistic and ideological.

Kawachi has also argued that lack of 'social capital' is the culprit. He gauged social capital in terms of membership of voluntary organizations and other measures of 'trust' among citizens. Using path analyses he argued that income inequality is focused through poor social capital, and that disease is a product of low social capital (Kawachi et al., 1997). In this approach, social policy interventions need to be at the level of building trust and reciprocal relationships. An approach that takes more account of the realities of economic capital is Wilkinson's work on unequal societies. He argues consistently and coherently that patterns of sickness and disease, and most importantly early death, are a product of the systematic inequalities in specific societies. At the same time, he argues that it is the subjective perception of inequality – that is, relative rather than absolute deprivation – which is the causative factor in disease and death.

Marmot (1998) has examined the link between socio-economic status and health using three measures: self-reported physical health, waist–hip ratio and psychological wellbeing. He and his colleagues found that education level was the strongest predictor of health. The lower the education, the lower the health. This at first would seem to support a social capital approach. Those with higher levels of education would have more resources, information, networks and supports than those at the bottom. But Marmot also found that income had a major impact: 'An alternative measure of socio-economic circumstances, household income, was related to poor health independent of education' (Marmot, 1998: 417). This is an important rider to the socio-psychological and social capital approaches. Material inequality, rather than socio-psychological perceptions of trust and community, is probably more important in explaining the link between inequality and disease rates (Altschuler et al., 2004; Carpiano, 2007). In an argument that links the decline in the Welfare State to the poverty of individuals and their families, Kaplan et al. (1996) and Lynch et al. (1998) have argued that income inequality interacts with, and is exacerbated by, low levels of public expenditure on material infrastructure that shapes our bodily experiences: housing stock, roads and transport, employment conditions, pollution controls and health, and welfare and education spending.

Conclusion

In this chapter I have shown how contemporary epidemiology contributes to an individual lifestyle, risk-factor approach to explain patterns of disease. In this it serves an ideological purpose, obscuring political, economic and social factors that produce the material organization of society, and which have a causal role in ill health.

There is a fine line to be drawn in balancing the relative impacts of the psychological, economic and physical impact of the environment on individuals. Equally, any attempt to improve people's health that does not start with the physical social environment is doomed to failure. Any appeal to social capital that is made in the presence of a community that is experiencing regional economic underdevelopment or recession, is subject to long-term and intergenerational unemployment, and is politically disenfranchised has to be seen as obscuring these structural aspects that impinge on individuals' health. As Whiteis has argued, the 'pathogenic effects of corporatisation, disinvestment, austerity and capital withdrawal [are] an imperative public health issue, essential to any meaningful discussion about health policy or health care reform' (Whiteis, 1998: 795). Appealing to communities to strengthen their social capital, in the context of economic poverty, can only hinder rather than improve people's health. It is the impact of the material organization of society that the next chapter examines.

Summary

- Major changes in the economic, political and social structure of society at the end of the twentieth century have meant a move back to nineteenth-century concepts for explaining disease: that they are the fault of individuals, adopting risky lifestyles.

- The chapter has argued that there is no evidence for this position. Furthermore, those individuals best at helping themselves, as explored by the psychosocial literature, are also economically and politically privileged.

- One other response to the changes has been the claim that 'communities' can provide what was provided by the Welfare State. Again the evidence is that 'healthy' communities cannot exist in the face of economic deprivation.

Discussion Questions

1. How do economic and political policies such as neo-liberalism shape diseases?

2. Unequal societies are unhealthy societies; equal societies are healthy societies. Do you think this is correct?

3. What is the impact of privatization of health services on people's access to health care?

Further Reading

Beaglehole, R. and Bonita, R. (1997) *Public Health at the Crossroads: Achievements and Prospects*. Cambridge: Cambridge University Press. A good review of the development of public health and of the changes in current epidemiology.

Crook, S., Pakulski, J. and Waters, M. (1992) *Postmodernization: Change in Advanced Society*. London: Sage. A good overview of the social, political and economic transformation of contemporary society.

Marmot, M. (2005) 'Social Determinants of Health Inequalities.' *The Lancet* 365: 1099–104. A brief but useful statement of the social determinants argument.

Peterson, C. (1999) *Stress at Work: A Sociological Approach*. New York: Baywood. A thorough overview of the socio-psychological literature on stress.

5

MATERIALIST APPROACHES TO THE SOCIOLOGY OF HEALTH

o   In this chapter I focus on those approaches that emphasize the role of the economic organization of society on the production and distribution of disease.

o   A distinction is made between the British Registrar General's usage of class as based on occupation; the concept of class as one variable among others in the socio-economic distribution of life chances; and the Marxist concept of class as the central feature of modern societies.

o   Evidence is presented to demonstrate the claim that the material organization of social life has an enormous impact on an individual's health, and has more explanatory weight than any lifestyle or medical account of their condition.

o   A restructuring of economic ownership – particularly the rise of corporate investors in the health-care sector – both supports the Marxist analysis of health care as a sector for investment and demonstrates the developing employee status of medical practitioners.

Materialist or structuralist (the terms can be used interchangeably) explanations of disease emphasize those social, political and economic factors beyond the control of individuals and which adversely affect their health. These factors range from the large-scale physical organization of the urban spaces that we live in, and the ways in which the hazards and pollutants of industrial and dockside areas are concentrated, to lead poisoning along industrial highways, and to the more local problems of isolation both socially and from health services because of a lack of access to transport. They also include the outcomes of the material organization of work practices in factories, sweatshops and fast-food chains, where not only may the work kill or harm, but also the experience of repetitive, meaningless tasks makes people vulnerable to disease and early death. As individuals we are born into a society with a material structure that pre-exists us, shapes our aspirations, and limits or enables the pursuit of our goals. A review of materialist evidence for the causes of disease – that is, an account based on social organization rather than the individual or biology – is presented. This is followed by an examination of socio-economic status and then of class analysis as explanatory frameworks for health inequalities.

What Causes Disease: The Materialist Explanation

Not surprisingly, there is a highly charged debate on the impact of social organization and inequality on health. Many commentators argue that the link does not exist at all, but is a product of the statistical techniques used by researchers who want to prove that class position does cause ill health. Those who deny the impact of the social organization of material resources point to individual factors in ill health, and attempt to blame individuals for their situation. This argument takes two forms. The first is that members of the working class get sicker because they adopt unhealthy lifestyles. The second argues that even if there is a class basis to disease, it is because the sicker people move down the social system and therefore are over-represented in the working class.

These explanations have been unsupported by considerable research (Fein, 1995; Feinstein, 1993; Graham, 2009). First, it does not matter what socio-economic measures are used as an indicator of inequality – housing, employment, income or educational level – inequalities of health and disease are significant on all counts. Second, while social mobility is affected by health, its impact on class differentials is small. Even when members of the working class experience upward social mobility, it does not protect them from the impact of their class-based health backgrounds. In a 21-year study of mortality in a cohort of Scottish men, social mobility did not balance out the effect of a working-class background. There continued to be substantial differences between manual and non-manual workers in mortality rates, with cancer being higher for manual workers even though they had moved up the social ladder (Hart et al., 1998).

–BOX 5.1–

STRUCTURAL CHANGES IN EMPLOYMENT CONDITIONS AS A DETERMINANT OF THE HEALTH OF WORKERS

Hamilton compared the health of three groups of workers. The first had been laid off because the factory was closing; the second group were worried that they would be laid off; and the third were not worried and in secure employment.

(Continued)

(Continued)

Those who were laid off experienced higher rates of diagnosed mental health problems. Since their condition did not cause the factory to close, it is clear that the retrenching brought about their health problems. It is social causation that leads to disease, and downward social mobility, not social selection (Hamilton et al., 1990).

Glenn and colleagues found that the health of the residents of the town declined by 7 per cent on a range of measures following industry closure. Following a resurgence in the economy and the opening of new industry, they found that people's health did not recover from the recession level.

For those at the bottom of the social system there is little resilience left, and they do not recover from damage to their health (Glenn et al., 1998).

Third, the claim that it is individual lifestyle factors that cause class differences overlooks the social basis of people's behaviour. The reason that people drink, smoke or eat bad foods has to do with advertising and access to information, rather than individual choice. Furthermore, when studies control for smoking and drinking, a large proportion of the health gap remains. In other words, the gap has more to do with conditions of employment and housing than with specifically individual actions (Whitehead, 1987). This suggests that the explanation for the health inequalities is to be sought in the structural organization of society. Differences in morbidity and mortality are best explained by structural factors such as ownership patterns and the drive to produce a profit at the cost of the workers' health.

Materialist explanations of social inequality attempt to link the biological with the sociological, providing explanatory mechanisms linking individual reactions of stress to patterns of inequality. This is happening in the new disciplines of psycho-neuroimmunology and of psycho-neuroendocrinology (PNI/PNE), which are making advances in tracking exactly which parts of the human organism are affected by stress. Kelly and her associates have brought together the evidence for physiological markers of chronic stress in five areas – glycosylated proteins, the immune system, homeostasis, peripheral benzodiazepine receptors and the waist–hip ratio – showing that all are markers of increased stress and responsible for higher levels of disease in stressed populations (Cohen et al., 2006; Kelly et al., 1997). At a more prosaic level, it has been argued that our susceptibility to the common cold is determined by the strength of our social relationships (Doyle et al., 1997), while the use of and satisfaction with health services are a product of the strength of our social group (Ahern et al., 1996). However, rather than looking for biological pathways between the individual and stress, sociologists have tended to show the correlation between social structures and the socially produced distribution of sickness and disease.

Attempts have been made to disaggregate the contribution of material factors to the cause of specific diseases (Blane et al., 1997). These include the evidence for the causative role of occupation, diet, housing and atmospheric pollution on cancer, coronary heart disease, accidents and chronic obstructive airways disease (COAD). Each of these in turn is related to occupation and income. Better incomes go with better, less hazardous jobs; provide better access to accommodation and increased dietary choices; and determine the locale within a city that the person lives in. Nevertheless, the factors can be separated out empirically.

Occupation

Occupation exposes us to a broad range of physical and psychosocial insults. Take, for example, exposure to cancer-causing agents. Clearly, there are very high-risk industries in which occupation can be easily shown to be the sole cause of cancer, as in the asbestos industry. But beyond this, the prestigious science journal *Nature* reported that 20 per cent of all cancer deaths can be attributed to occupation (Epstein and Swartz, 1981). More recent studies have supported this figure, with the World Health Organization reporting in 2006 that the proportion of all cancer deaths in industrialized countries attributable to occupational exposures is between 4 and 20 per cent (Ivanov and Straif, 2006: 1). Moreover, cancer is one of the leading causes of work-related deaths, contributing to a much higher proportion of fatalities than workplace accidents or injuries (Hamalainen et al., 2007). On top of this, work-related deaths are also distributed according to social factors like gender. For example, in Australia in 2010–2011, serious work-related injuries or deaths were 25 per cent more common in men than in women (Safe Work Australia, 2014). The stress of work environments that combine low autonomy and high workloads in an unsupportive environment has been claimed to be the cause of up to 35 per cent of cardiovascular mortality (Johnson et al., 1996), and has been proven to increase the likelihood of developing mental and physical conditions that lead to type two diabetes, stroke and heart disease (Chandola et al., 2006; Marmot et al., 1997; Rosengren et al., 2004; Szeto and Dobson, 2013).

The data on work-related deaths are chastening, especially as they are likely to be considerably under-reported. For example, deaths in vehicle crashes do not get counted as work accidents. In Australia, recent statistics indicate that between 300 and 700 workers die each year as a result of injuries sustained at work (Australian Safety and Compensation Council, 2006). An estimated 5000 invasive cancers and 34,000 non-melanoma skin cancers per year in Australia are caused by work-related exposure, and approximately 1.5 million people are exposed to known carcinogens (Fritschi and Driscoll, 2006). In the United States, Purdue et al. (2015) found that 5.3 per cent of all cancers were due to occupational exposure. It is increasingly recognized that the health of the individual worker does not necessarily have to be physically at risk for the impact of capitalist employment practices to make itself felt. Lack of autonomy at work, lack of control over the production process and separation from fellow workers – the key components to Marx's account of alienation – are all now supported in empirical research as causes of disease (Benach and Muntaner, 2007; Karasek and Theorell, 1990).

Diet

Though the evidence is sketchy for the impact of diet on mortality, Blane et al. (1997) estimate that diet is responsible for 15 per cent of all deaths. Diet is a material factor, rather than a behavioural one, in the sense that income level defines access to the range of foods available, even if the individual has scope for choice within that range. It is one of the ironies of life in a capitalist society that the unprocessed foods that have been associated with reduced bowel cancer now cost more than the refined and processed sugars and cereals. The regular consumption of 'fast food' and reduction in home-based food preparation across the Western world has also been implicated in rising rates of type two diabetes and an increasing social focus on obesity (Williams and Germov, 2005).

The apparently direct link between eating habits and mortality is always medi-ated by structural forces. For example, a Swedish study of women found that lifestyle factors such as alcohol consumption, obesity, excess abdominal fat and unhealthy diets did not explain raised lipid levels. Rather, the crucial variables were decision latitude at work and annual income. Women with low decision latitude at work, poor incomes and low educational levels, and in blue-collar jobs, had the most unhealthy lipid profile, independently of lifestyle factors (Peter et al., 1998).

Housing

Housing conditions have a well-known impact on health and disease. Blane points to the 12-fold difference in accidental deaths due to falls in the homes of the poor which are caused by overcrowded and unsafe conditions. Poor-quality housing has a large impact on chronic obstructive airways disease (COAD), both in children and subsequently their adult life.

Atmospheric pollution has a major impact on the health of individuals, espe-cially as its effect is often confined to specific areas. These may be proximate to specific industries, such as asbestos plants or nuclear energy plants. It may also be experienced as a consequence of the structure of the city, with heavily used industrial roads running ribbon-like through areas of poor-quality housing and low-income areas. For example, 27 per cent of African-American children living in inner-city slums have elevated blood lead levels, compared with 2 per cent in the suburbs. As the researcher who carried out the work put it, unless something is done, 'we are going to perpetuate a population of poor minority kids whose intellects are eroded by toxins like lead, and who will continue for generations to come to be environmentally, medically and economically disadvantaged' (Freid, 2000: 3055).

Overall then, the case for political and economic factors as causes of disease is overwhelming. Further evidence is provided by the recent changes in the former USSR.

CASE STUDY

TRANSFORMATIONS IN THE SOCIAL STRUCTURE OF EASTERN EUROPE

We can use a materialist approach to examine the impact of the introduction of capitalist social structures to Eastern Europe, demonstrating the impact it is having on people's health. This research demonstrates the very strong causal relations between social disorganization and individual disease and death.

─BOX 5.2─

SOCIAL CHANGE AND INCREASING DISEASE AND DEATH IN EASTERN EUROPE

- In the period 1990–1994, male deaths from accidents declined in Sweden, while in Estonia they doubled. In 1994, the total injury death rate was six times higher in Estonia than Sweden. It has been suggested that the lifestyle 'choices' of Estonian males – the risk factors – are a product of social and political instability of a society in transition (Kaasik et al., 1998).

- The political and social upheaval that occurred in Russia following the collapse of the Soviet Union in the early 1990s and the subsequent major economic collapse in 1998 were followed by a marked decline in life expectancy across the country. Between 1987 and 1994, life expectancy of adult males fell by 7.4 years to 57.5 years. It rose again in 1998 to 61.3 years, before again declining in 2001 by 2.4 years. Female life expectancy followed similar trends, falling by 2.6 years between 1989

(Continued)

(Continued)

and 1994. These significant demographic changes were mainly due to mortality from preventable causes such as non-communicable diseases (including cardiovascular disease and some cancers), alcohol abuse, road traffic accidents and injuries (Levintova and Novotny, 2004).

- Lifestyle factors do not account for these dramatic changes, and Watson has suggested that the changes in the socio-political environment – exclusion from the political process, high levels of frustration with social change, and the increasing relative deprivation compared with Western Europe – are the major explanations (Watson, 1995).

The inequalities of health in Russia are determined by the dysfunction of social structures, socio-economic deprivation and a perceived lack of control over the environment (Bobak et al., 1998). Strong social networks, which are well established in positive self-health evaluations (Molinari et al., 1998), have been weakened in Russia. Along with these weakened support structures, and illustrative of them, is the decline in the relationship between levels of education and morbidity, which has always had a protective effect on people's health (Shkolnikov et al., 1998). Along with economic satisfaction, participation in civic activities has a marked effect on people's positive evaluation of their health, and these two variables appear to account for the massive differences in self-reported health status between Eastern and Western Europe (Carlson, 1998).

More recently, Greece provides a startling example of what may happen when a government drastically severs funding to health care. Following the global financial crisis that began in 2007, the government of Greece attempted to restore the country's faltering economy by adopting austerity measures that have proven controversial and, so far, ineffective. These cost-cutting efforts have also had serious social and health effects on the country's population. The Ministry of Health was downsized by 24 per cent, so health services were cut and many once-free services are no longer available. Meanwhile, unemployment more than tripled from 7.2 per cent in 2008 to 22.6 per cent in 2012.

The cutting of publicly funded health services, coupled with the huge loss of employment in the country, had drastic consequences for the people's experience of health (Kondilis et al., 2013). Between 2007 and 2009, suicide rates rose by 16 per cent, and the murder rate climbed almost 26 per cent, with men over-represented as victims in both cases. Deaths from infectious diseases increased by 13 per cent; there have been outbreaks of malaria and West Nile virus; and rates of HIV infection have increased.

Class as Occupational Position

In 1980, the Black Report distinguished between four different explanations for patterns of inequality in health (Blane et al., 1997). First was that they were statistical artefacts, the outcome of the way in which the measurement tools were used to measure disease and class. Second was that they were the outcome of natural or social selection. This explanation suggests that the healthy experience upward social mobility and the unhealthy downward social mobility. The third explanation is that disease is the outcome of behavioural or cultural practices such as lifestyle factors like diet, exercise, drinking and smoking. The fourth explanation is that class and health are linked by structural factors, such as the way production is organized and the distribution of goods in society. It is with the structuralist explanation that this chapter is concerned, though reference will also be made to the other three explanations.

Critical to this approach is the concept of social class. Medical sociology has not generally operated with complex theoretical definitions of class, and in its simplest usage class is operationalized as corresponding to the British Registrar General's classification of occupations. The great value of this classification system is that it allows occupation to be linked to cause of death, since both are recorded on the death certificate. The classification of occupations is as follows (Leete and Fox, 1977):

Class I: Professional (doctors, lawyers, scientists and professionals).

Class II: Managerial (farmers, teachers, nurses, journalists, managers).

Class III: Skilled manual and non-manual (drivers, plumbers, trades people).

Class IV: Partly skilled (farm labourers, forestry workers, factory process workers).

Class V: Unskilled (cleaners, road workers, labourers).

It is important to note that this way of operationalizing class overlooks women who are not in the workforce, the unemployed, students, the elderly and children.

British studies have found marked differences in health levels between occupational classes, for men and women, and for all ages. The people at the bottom of the social system have a much higher mortality rate than those at the top. This is not restricted to specific diseases, but applies to the majority of diseases. Furthermore, people in the lower classes suffer from more chronic illness, their children weigh less at birth, and they are shorter. There are also marked inequalities in access to health services, and particularly to preventative services (Townsend and Davidson, 1988). These patterns have persisted over the past 100 years, and the lower classes experience a higher death rate than the upper classes. The statistics from the Registrar General's classification show that overall mortality rates had improved between 1921 and 1951. By 1951, classes IV and V achieved the same health rates as classes I and II had in 1921. However, while the mortality rate of classes I and II continued to decline between 1951 and 1981, that of classes IV and V did not, and in fact there was a reversal of the historical trend, with mortality rates increasing in poorer areas (McLoone and Boddy, 1994; Phillimore et al., 1994).

National and international patterns of growing inequalities of wealth and income mean that the inequalities of health are also widening. The USA is now more unequal than at any period since the 1920s (Wolff, 1995). Income inequality is widening sharply, as are socio-economic inequalities in health – especially for deaths attributable to poverty among black men and women (Hahn et al., 1996). In 2001, the top 1 per cent of households in America owned 33.4 per cent of all privately owned wealth, and the top 20 per cent owned 51 per cent. The bottom 80 per cent of Americans, therefore, had a share of only 16 per cent of the nation's private wealth (Domhoff, 2006). By 2012, the bottom 90 per cent of the population owned only 23 per cent of the total wealth in the USA (Saez and Zucman, 2014). Correspondingly, from 1980 to 2003 the difference in life expectancy between the lowest- and highest-class Americans rose to 4.5 years (Singh and Siahpush, 2006). The trend continues. Between 2001 and 2014, the top 5 per cent of men had an increase in life expectancy of 2.34 years, and the top 5 per cent of women, 2.92 years; for the bottom 5 per cent of men, life expectancy increased only 0.32 years and for women, only 0.04 years (Chatty et al., 2016). The rich are getting richer and living longer and the poor are getting poorer and living shorter.

Research in Australia confirms British and American research, and gives an indication of the class basis of Australian society. Age at death and cause of death are linked to social class. The lower classes have a higher mortality rate and live, on average, for a shorter period of time. The lower social classes have mortality rates significantly higher than those of the upper social classes. The mortality rate of the lowest class was approximately twice that of the highest class – a bigger differential than what was found in the British research.

BOX 5.3

SUMMARY: CLASS, INEQUALITY AND DISEASE

The research on this topic can be summarized in the following statements:

- Social class differences in mortality are widening.

- Better measures of socio-economic position show greater inequalities in mortality.

- Health inequalities have been shown in all countries that collect data.

- Social selection and measurement artefacts do not account for mortality differentials.

- Social class differences exist for health during life as well as for length of life.

- Trends in the distribution of income suggest that further widening of differentials may be expected.

The social class gradient of disease also refers to the fact that there are inequalities within the class structure as well as across class boundaries (Blane et al., 1997). In 1978, Michael Marmot reported on the first of what were to become known as the Whitehall studies of skilled white-collar workers in the British civil service (Marmot et al., 1978). He found that those at the bottom of the civil service hierarchy had disease rates four times that of those at the top. Those one step below the top had disease rates twice that of those one step above them. This finding was confirmed over a wide range of diseases, and statistically adjusted rates took into account lifestyle factors such as smoking, high-fat diets, obesity and high blood pressure. Even then the difference between the top and the bottom of the hierarchy was threefold. Some commentators have used the Whitehall studies as proof against materialist explanations of health gradients. The argument is that everyone experiences the impact of social position on their health, not just the poor (Evans and Stoddart, 1990). However, what the data do demonstrate is the nuanced impact of class on health, and its accelerating impact on individuals down the social system.

Untangling Class and Socio-economic Status

Social class must be distinguished from socio-economic status as a measure of socio-economic inequality. These two measures of inequality are derived from two different theoretical traditions in sociology associated with the work of Karl Marx and Max Weber. Socio-economic status is used in epidemiological research and is usually measured in terms of education, income or occupational prestige. Rather than seeing inequality as the product of property ownership, stratification analysis suggests that people may have unequal access to a variety of social resources, and may be high on some but low on others. Within sociology generally, socio-economic and social class explanations are usually taken to be in contradiction with each other. In a classical Marxist sense, class theory works the following way. Classes are interdependent economic relationships, formed around the interplay of property, ownership and labour. Classes reciprocally define each other: the working class exists in relationship to the ruling class. The dissolution of one would result in the dissolution of the other. Class is an objective feature of a society. It is not a personality characteristic or psychological trait of its members. Capitalists are capitalist by virtue of extracting surplus from their workers, not by virtue of acquisitiveness or greed. Workers are workers by virtue of having to sell their labour power to survive. Thus classes are in an exploitative relationship with one another. Whether or not individuals, or classes, are aware of their position is a complicated question in sociology and Marxism. Suffice to say that, under certain circumstances of class consciousness, they may be.

Class analysis provides a unitary theoretical explanation of inequality being produced around the ownership and non-ownership of private property. In this sense, class is not a variable, but constitutive of social relationships. In a capitalist society, the pursuit of profit by the capitalist class means that it will seek to cheapen the cost of labour wherever it can. It will attempt to increase working hours, reduce wages and lobby governments for lower taxes. Each of these has an impact on health. At the level of the workers, the removal of occupational health and safety regulations means increased deaths and injuries at work; the deregulation of environmental controls over pollution means that the rest of society suffers from environmental degradation. The deregulation of the preparation of foodstuffs to reduce the costs of their manufacture means increased food poisoning and death, especially for those most defenceless and most at risk: children and infants. Finally, given the mobility of capital, it will leave nation-states, thereby weakening their tax base, as it seeks to escape taxation.

Structural Position as Socio-economic Status

An individual's position in society can be captured in the short phrase 'socio-economic status'. This refers to our position on the socially valued hierarchy of occupations and income. Low socio-economic status means exposure to a range of material threats that those higher on the scale will not experience and will probably find hard to imagine. As de la Barra (1998) has summarized the insults of poverty, low socio-economic groups are exposed to the worst effects of urbanism: slum dwellings, poor ventilation, garbage and overcrowding. It means exposure to the unregulated labour market, of sweatshops, home-work and piece rates. Fundamentally it means that, as a poor person, you will become poorer. The poor pay higher cash costs, have less access to informal sources of financial assistance, and depend on insecure cash incomes. The poorer you are, the more it costs you to live. These features of low socio-economic status mean that you will have a lower life expectancy, higher overall mortality rates, and higher infant and perinatal rates of death. Low socio-economic status – the combination of unvalued work and low income – is associated with higher rates of death from the 14 major causes of death in the International Classification of Disease. Townsend and Davidson (1988), in an examination of the 78 leading causes of death, found that 65 are more common in manual compared with non-manual male workers. Our socio-economic status shapes our experience of health and disease and largely determines the length of our life and what we will die of. The summary of the Black Report into health inequalities in Britain put it this way 35 years ago:

> The latest evidence shows a markedly higher proportion of the poorer than the richer socio-economic groups among both males and females reporting chronic ill-health. The poorer health experience of the lower occupational groups applies at all stages of life. If the mortality rates of class I (professional workers and

members of their families) had applied to classes IV and V (partly skilled and unskilled manual workers and members of their families) during 1970–1972, 74,000 lives of people aged under 75 would not have been lost. This estimate includes nearly 10,000 children, and 32,000 men aged 15–64. (Department of Health and Social Security, 1980: 3)

The comparison with the statistics for Australia in the mid-1990s are no better. Mathers and colleagues have established that the bottom 5 per cent of the population lost 35 per cent more years of life than the top 5 per cent. Men in the bottom quintile have a 40 per cent higher chance of dying between ages 25 and 65 than men in the top quintile. As the leading researchers in the field put it: 'If it were possible to reduce disease and injury incidence and mortality in all areas to a level equivalent to that of the least disadvantaged quintile, the potential savings in lost years of healthy life would be at least 17% of the total disease burden' (Mathers et al., 1999: 25). Not only are the rich getting richer: the poorer are getting sicker.

─BOX 5.4─

MORTALITY RATES INCREASING AMONG THE POOREST IN AUSTRALIA: 1985–2011

- In 2000, death rates in Australia were highest in the most disadvantaged areas, and across many disease and age categories, mortality rates fell in a continuous gradient from the most to the least disadvantaged.

- In 1985–1987, death rates among men of all ages in the most disadvantaged areas of Australia were approximately 68 per cent higher than in the least disadvantaged. In 1998–2000 this figure had risen to 75 per cent.

- Over the same time period, the relative mortality inequality for females did not increase, but death rates among the most disadvantaged areas were approximately 50 per cent higher than among the least disadvantaged (World Health Organization, 2008).

- Between 1985–1987 and 1995–1997 in Australia, inequalities in death rates between the most- and least-disadvantaged areas increased across a range of disease categories, including sudden infant death syndrome, injury and poisoning, motor vehicle traffic accidents, suicides, coronary heart disease, respiratory diseases and cancer (Turrell and Mathers, 2001).

(Continued)

(Continued)

- Between 1985–1989 and 1992–1995, among the most disadvantaged: all cancers increased from 1.14 to 1.28 times higher than the least disadvantaged; lung cancer increased from 1.53 to 1.93 times higher; respiratory system diseases increased from 1.79 to 2.41 times higher; and accidents, poisonings and violence increased from 1.42 to 1.53 times higher (Heath et al., 2000).

- Between 2009 and 2011, the most disadvantaged died of diabetes, chronic obstructive pulmonary disease and lung cancer twice as much as the least disadvantaged (Australian Institute of Health and Welfare, 2014).

- As of 2011, the most-disadvantaged Australians die 1.3 times more frequently than the least disadvantaged. If all Australians had the same mortality rate as the least-disadvantaged population, 54,200 fewer people would have died between 2009 and 2011 (Australian Institute of Health and Welfare, 2014).

Social inequality and health inequality are linked and both are a product of the social organization of society. If the first is minimized and the second improved by policies targeted at reducing inequality, then the whole society will benefit. As the Black Report put it: 'Eliminating social inequalities in health offers the greatest opportunity for achieving overall improvements in the nation's health' (Townsend and Davidson, 1988: 200).

The Classical Marxist Approach

The Marxist tradition in the sociology of medicine specifically attempts to link diseases to structural economic and political developments. Marxists argue that disease and its treatment are the outcome of a capitalist economic system. The key text in the Marxist tradition is Friedrich Engels' *The Condition of the Working Class in England* (1974). Engels argues that disease is a direct outcome of capitalists' pursuit of profit at the expense of safety. By safety, he means not only industrial matters, but housing conditions and food quality more generally. Engels drew together a wide range of materials in 'social medicine', and essentially laid the basis of a sociology of health. He made three central points.

The first was that what people suffer from is not the product of their own individual make-up. This contrasts with the prevailing view in the nineteenth century and in the twentieth century of medicine and psychology, which focus solely on the individual. He develops his argument using examples. Accident proneness (which is still in vogue in industrial psychology) is the product of industrial organization and not a psychological characteristic of individuals. It is the product of management techniques where workers have to work at a forced pace, independently of the risks they put themselves at. His analysis of alcoholism locates it not in the psychodynamics of the individual, but in the miseries of industrial cities. Living in slums, malnourished, at risk of sudden death, and living an impoverished life turned people to drink. Hence the starting point of Engels' account of disease was social organization, and not an approach that focused on and blamed the individual.

Second, and continuing from this first point, Engels argued steadfastly for a social explanation of individual circumstances, rejecting explanations that pointed to divine providence as the source of an inevitable inequality. Explanations of disease, and of people getting what they deserve, are always close to the surface in Western thought. Witness the saying 'Cleanliness is next to Godliness'.

Third, Engels argued that sickness and disease are primarily the product of social conditions and not inevitable biological occurrences. Not only are orthopaedic disorders caused by working conditions, but also tuberculosis, typhoid and syphilis were the product of working conditions and living standards. For Engels the Industrial Revolution and the private ownership of property resulted in 'social murder' (Engels, 1974).

The Political and Economic Functions of Medicine

Medicine in advanced capitalist societies is oriented towards curing disease through the application of sophisticated drugs and the use of high-cost technology. Paradoxically, the major causes of mortality and morbidity in these societies, though alleviated by such treatment, are not generally amenable to cure by these regimens. At the same time, medicine places responsibility for these diseases with the individual, and to the extent that it is involved in preventative medicine, it is along the lines of admonishing individuals to modify their own lifestyle patterns (Calnan, 1984; Neubauer and Pratt, 1981). The leading causes of mortality and morbidity in the developed world today are ischaemic heart disease, various cancers, mental and nervous disorders and chronic respiratory diseases, which are not the result of endogenous bodily processes, but of social conditions. Further, these illnesses are not amenable to cure via the application of intensive care or the use of drugs (McKinlay and McKinlay, 1977, 1989; Miniño et al., 2004, 2010). Indeed, this is nothing new, as those within the medical establishment have also shown, since current health standards derived less from new discoveries and technologies than from environmental health control of housing, nutrition and water supplies, prior to the 1930s (Cochrane, 1972; Dubos, 1959; McKeown, 1965, 1979; Weitz, 2010: 14–47).

In this general characterization, Marxists explain health care and medicine in contemporary society as part of the capitalist mode of production. Waitzkin argues:

technologic forms of treatment (and the associated high costs) whose effectiveness is dubious at best makes sense only when analysed from the structural features of capitalism. That is, although [technologic treatment] appears irrational given our health care needs, they become quite rational when seen from the needs of the capitalist system, especially since they support the expansion of monopoly capital and private profitability of the health care sector. (Waitzkin, 1981: 342)

This perspective is shared by Renaud (1975), who argues that health needs are treated by medicine in such a way as to be compatible with the capitalist organization of the economy:

The dominant engineering approach of contemporary scientific medicine equates healing and consumption, i.e. in more general terms, health needs and the commodity form of their satisfaction, thus legitimating and facilitating capitalist economic growth despite its negative health consequences. (Renaud, 1975: 559)

From this perspective, the health-care industry has four interrelated economic functions in capitalist society: accumulation of capital; provision of investment opportunities; absorption of surplus labour; and the maintenance of the labour force (Rodberg and Stevenson, 1979; Waitzkin, 2000).

In addition, the organization of health care provides three important ideological functions. First, by providing health care – however inadequately – it legitimates the status quo, acting as an agent of social control by rendering what are basically social problems to an individualistic level. Second, in its equation of hospital care and the consumption of drugs as health care, it reproduces the capitalist mode of production. Third, it reproduces the capitalist class structure both in the organization of health workers and in the consumption patterns it generates (Navarro, 1976; Waitzkin, 2000).

In summary, to quote Renaud:

This view of health and illness is congruent with the larger capitalist environment because it commodifies health needs and legitimates this commodification. It transforms the potentially explosive social problems that are diseases and death into discrete isolable commodities that can be incorporated into the capitalist organisation of the economy in the same way as any other commodity on the economic market. In an incredible *tour de force*, it succeeds in providing cultur-ally valued solutions to problems largely created by economic growth and even makes these solutions to a certain extent profitable for capital accumulation and thus for more economic growth. With scientific medicine, health care has grown into an industry which helps maintain the legitimacy of the social order and which in part creates new sectors of production. (Renaud, 1975: 564)

The dominant class supports a conception of illness as an individual phenomenon and denies the salience of social structures in the production of ill health. This is paralleled in the field of health-care consumption, where the individualistic aetiology gives rise to technologically based curative therapies that are capital-intensive and hospital-based (Waitzkin, 1986). From a Marxist perspective, contemporary capitalist health-care organizations systematically neglect the environmental, occupational and social production of health and disease (Doyal and Pennell, 1979).

The Medical Profession in a Marxist Analysis

The medical profession is seen as central to the control of labour (Johnson, 1977), especially through its control of the sick certificate, while the theories of disease it develops and enforces – individualizing, and ignoring social factors – perform an ideological function in stabilizing the status quo.

Medical knowledge and technology do not have a separate existence from capitalism: rather they are the products of it (Navarro, 1983). Thus medicine cannot be saved from capitalism by freeing it of its class bias, since this is an integral part of medicine. The biologism (the belief that social relations can be understood as natural phenomena), the scientism (the belief that social relations are susceptible to the methods of the natural sciences), the mechanism of medical knowledge (the belief that the mind is separate from the body, and the body constructed as interdependent parts), and the positivism of its concepts of disease (that diseases have singular causes that attack independent parts of the body, and are cured by drugs and technology) are not capitalist overlays on medical knowledge, but constitute medical knowledge under the capitalist mode of production (Navarro, 1980). Thus Navarro does not operate with a dichotomous model of an uncontaminated medical knowledge overlaid by a capitalist ideology; rather medicine under capitalism is capitalist medicine: 'It is a social relationship in which class relations are the key' (Navarro, 1980: 523).

Waitzkin (1989, 2000) demonstrates the link between the class structures of capitalism and the micro-level structures of the clinical setting. He shows how the doctor–patient interactions reflect class structures. Doctors, he argues, on the one hand directly voice the explicit ideological messages that legitimate the current class structure of society. In their equation of health with economic productivity, they maintain the social relations of capitalism. At the level of the reproduction of labour power, doctors reinforce the position ascribed to women in capitalist society, as unpaid domestic labourers responsible for the nurturing of the next generation of workers. On the other hand, Waitzkin argues, doctors implicitly act as agents of social control, enforcing these ideologies, and acting as agents of medicalization. Providing a twist on C. Wright Mills (Mills, 1959), he argues that this is accomplished by rendering public issues into private troubles. As Waitzkin puts it 'In medical encounters, technical statements help direct patients' responses to objectified symptoms, signs and treatment. This reification shifts attention away from the totality of social relations and the social issues that are often root causes of personal troubles' (Waitzkin, 1989: 223).

In this analysis, the medical profession performs the ideological function of sustaining an image of the way society should be organized. The social context of illness is glossed over, and through medicalization, more and more social problems are rendered into technical, scientific ones. Through their control of sickness certificates, diagnostic categories, and access to mood-altering drugs, doctors in their daily practice enforce the ideologies of capitalism. By locating depression in the minds of women, they deny the reality of the exploitative position of the domestic labourer, and by prescribing tranquillizers do not question the status quo but actively support it. By treating industrial injuries as physico-anatomical events, and by repairing the worker, they place him or her in jeopardy of suffering:

> The exclusion of social context from critical attention is a fundamental feature of medical language, a feature closely connected to social control and ideology. Inattention to social issues, especially when these issues lie behind patients' personal troubles, can never be just a matter of personal inadequacy, or the inadequacy of professional training. Instead this lack is a basic part of what medicine is in our society. (Waitzkin, 1989: 222)

Modifications of Classical Marxism and Changes in Capitalism

In Welfare State capitalism (1950–1980), the state managed the economy, guaranteed minimum living standards and administered social citizenship (Marshall, 1963; Turner, 1986a). Central to Welfare State capitalism was the commitment to full employment by the state, citizenship mediated by universalistic welfare policies, the participation of labour in mass consumption, and (in Australia) a negotiated truce between capital and labour through arbitration. Professionalized medicine flourished in this environment, providing ideological support for the individualism of capitalism, legitimating state involvement in civil society and the economy, providing an investment sector for capital and, to some extent, satisfying human needs.

Each of these characteristics and functions of Welfare State capitalism has been wound back in post-1970s capitalist Welfare States. As one commentator has put it: 'Economic and social history since the mid-1970s has to be regarded as a period of conflict centred on the articulation of state and economy, which was constitutive of welfare state capitalism' (Berger, 1990: 75). The structural basis of Welfare State capitalism has been undermined with the decline in the industrial sector and the globalization of capital investment strategies. Concomitant with this has been a restructuring of the disciplining of labour. The break-up of organized industrial unions has meant that labour is not represented in a monolithic fashion by its unions (hence enterprise bargaining) and the reconstruction of the 'free' individual in neo-liberal ideology. Consequently, the maintenance and control of labour has declined as a concern of the state. State policy is now directed towards control over the costs and quantity of medical services, i.e. to intervene in the clinical process – thus challenging medicine's claim to a technical base. These changes at both an international and domestic level have resulted in a restructuring of the role played by medicine. Demands are now being made that, as part of the state sector, it succumb to fiscal control. In this process, capital unsettles medicine's ideological functions by commodifying its practices more and more overtly. Thus medicine has become caught between the state and the market, and is losing its independent and dominant position in the health sector.

Changes in Class Theory and the Sociology of Health

Given the complexity of both ownership patterns and the development of a managerial class in modern society, the classic account of class has been modified by researchers such as Erik Wright. Social class, in Erik Wright's schema, is measured in terms of the types of control people have at work (Wright, 2000; Wright et al., 1982). These are ownership of the workplace, control over budget decisions, control over other workers, and control over one's own work. Certainly, following the work of Marmot on Whitehall civil servants, it is clear that fine distinctions in the hierarchy of work have significant impacts on the experience of sickness and disease.

Another virtue of Wright's work is that it allows for a combination of stratificational analysis and class analysis. In a study of substance-use disorders, for example, it appears that social class and socio-economic status may operate independently. It seems that members of the working class, using Wright's schema, are vulnerable to substance abuse from the beginning of their working life. On the other hand, those becoming self-employed, that is, changing their socio-economic status, become more vulnerable to substance abuse – a condition which has been labelled secondary vulnerability to substance abuse (Wohlfarth and Vandenbrink, 1998).

While Wright has attempted to modify class analysis to keep it in use under changed conditions, others have largely rejected it. For many sociologists, class is now largely redundant under the impact of postmodern analyses that claim to focus on complexity, difference and identity. The main arguments are that class is no longer the source of identity, and that consumption provides the basis for identity. Postmodernist theorists are far more likely to point to social change such as globalization and the transformation of culture, without reference to class (Jameson, 1991). Thus, as Bradley puts it, 'seduction and repression become the twin axes of class domination' (Bradley, 1996: 69). Postmodern culture means the end of class society, as class is dissolved by individuation and as perceptions of risk replace class identity (Beck, 1992). Bauman (1992) argues that class is now based on consumption rather than exploitation in production, giving rise to new patterns of inequality, including a new poor group excluded from consumption. Class as both an empirical reality (that is, as a category within which people live and identify themselves with) and as a theoretical tool has been weakened by changes in contemporary capitalism. As Bob Holton has put it, the strong class model of class as community has gone, and the analytic purchase of class as the unitary explanation of inequality in capitalist societies has been modified (Holton, 1996).

Others such as Esping-Andersen (1993) have suggested a post-industrial class structure, which incorporates gender, ethnicity and age. Like Bauman, in addition to four occupation-based class groups, he argues that there is a large, new, surplus population group: an underclass. Their analysis at least then keeps a critical edge to it, highlighting points of contradiction and antagonism in the social structure. Notwithstanding these analyses, there is clear evidence of the impact of class structure in the areas of health, voting behaviour and education, and also clear evidence that there is not much intergenerational mobility. On these grounds, Higgs and Scambler (1998: 90–6) have sought to retain the usefulness of class for the sociology of health in five propositions:

1. Just because people are not aware of class does not mean that it has no impact.

2. 'Society' is both the outcome of and the process of social action. Thus 'it is not class relations but rather their effects that offer themselves for study' (p. 91).

3. The bottom and the top of the class structure are not in question, and the evidence for the existence of a capitalist class is incontrovertible.

4. An international global perspective on class is necessary, though much neglected in empirical research.

5. The flaw in both neo-Marxist and neo-Weberian analysis is 'a misguided attempt to "map" too many aspects of an increasingly complex and subtle pattern of social differentiation on the sole basis of occupational data' (p. 93).

Overall, then, the evidence for the class basis of inequality is strong. At the same time, sociologists have had to accommodate transformations in the social structure, both modifications of the traditional class basis of capitalist societies, and especially of gender and ethnicity as sometimes competing, sometimes complementary sources and explanations of the cause of inequality.

Transformations of the Medical Profession

Since the 1970s, the state has been attempting to transform the delivery of health through encouraging participation by the private sector, and to alter individuals' attitudes to the health-care system by seeking to make them more self-reliant and responsible. Private health insurers, but also corporate investors in the private health sphere (who used to be allies of the medical profession) now find the profession too slow to adapt to the requirements of profit maximization, and they are attempting to implement their own controls over medicine's technical and clinical activities. In Australia and America, insurance organizations provide lists of the tests they will and will not make payments for, thereby limiting the doctor's clinical freedom (White, 2000a).

In this context the ongoing commodification of health care, and in general practice, the development of entrepreneurial and corporate medicine, are particularly important. These changes are, in Australia, linked to globalization and the spread of foreign investor companies in the health-care sector (Collyer and White, 1997), which in turn are occurring in an overcrowded market of medical suppliers.

The development of entrepreneurial medicine and corporate investment in medicine, that is, the formation of the medical-industrial complex (Relman, 1980), are shaped by changes in the organization of labour and industry in Australia. These changes are usually encapsulated in the phrase 'post-Fordist' and in the transformation from mass production to 'flexible specialization'. In advanced capitalist societies, large-scale factories and production-line systems are in decline, and with them the need for a docile industrial working class. Rather, the need is for a more self-reliant and autonomous workforce who control their own time. There are significant implications for general practitioners in these transformations. First, there is no longer the requirement for the external supervision of the workforce by the medical profession. Further, the alliance between employers and the medical profession has been weakened. The profession no longer serves a clear-cut social control function (especially control over the sick certificate), and capital resists tax drains on its profit base that may be used for the delivery of health care to the population that it no longer requires. Capital comes to see investment in medicine that is structured around the control of the individual as wasteful. The quality of health care moves to reflect these changes in the labour market. What is now required are forms of medical intervention that reflect the autonomy of the workplace.

These changes can be summarized as the move to a focus on lifestyle forms of knowledge and practice. It is not coincidental that in the period from 1980 to 1990 the number of joggers and gyms has increased, as have programmes of alcohol moderation and dietary self-regulation. The Hospital Corporation of Australia spent AUD $3 million setting up a national network of occupational health centres aimed at reducing worker absenteeism and worker compensation costs and improving productivity and lifestyles (*Australian Financial Review*, 17 July 1986; Crawford, 2000; Gillick, 1984). Intertwined with these changes in capital's management practices are neo-liberal attempts to resurrect a nineteenth-century form of governance (Gordon, 1991). In this citizens are required to accept, and health policies emphasize, the internalization of medical norms of behaviour, and these prioritize the self-seeking, self-sustaining individual – the sovereign individual of liberal capitalism (Abercrombie et al., 1986).

Technological Change

Paralleling these political and economic changes are technological ones. Technological change has been most significantly discussed in the context of the deprofessionalization thesis. Haug (1973) argues that with the rationalization of medical knowledge (especially through new technologies such as computer-based diagnostic systems) and with the development of an increasingly knowledgeable public, the social distance between the practitioner and the patient narrows. However, technology has not taken over the general practitioner's role, nor does the cultural authority of medicine appear to have slipped. Even allowing for a large component of informal care in the provision of health care, around 85 per cent of the Australian population visit a general practitioner each year (State and Territory Health Ministers, 2007: 7). Second, new medical technologies have either been kept under the control of the medical profession, or the interpretation of the significance of findings using the new diagnostic technologies is still in the hands of the profession (Haug, 1988).

Nevertheless, administrative technologies are being developed which are having an impact on practitioner autonomy. These developments are two-edged. On the one side, they open new opportunities to general practitioners to be integrated into the community health systems, opening electronic links with other practitioners. On the other, they bring doctors' daily work practices and diagnostic and prescribing activities under surveillance (Lewis and Majoribanks, 2003).

For example, in May 2015, the government announced that all Australians will be automatically enrolled into a centralized 'eHealth' system. Replacing a previous online patient tracker that patients had to opt-in for, the eHealth system will automatically collate vital health information about each Australian. Although patients can manage their records by choosing to 'hide' certain parts of their medical history, all information is by default accessible to registered medical practitioners, who can review each citizen's medical history and add to it as they see fit (eHealth, 2015). Though the new eHealth system has yet to be trialled, it is poised to integrate general practice into the wider health system, but also increase surveillance of the general practitioner. In particular, referral radiology and referral pathology costs are likely to be open to scrutiny, as would practitioner-initiated repeat visits to the doctor. These could then be seen as 'over-servicing'. The only way to overcome such an allegation is the acceptance of treatment protocols.

Haug's deprofessionalization-of-medicine thesis alerts us to social changes at the level of the rationalization of knowledge, and perhaps the increasing challenge to expert knowledge. At the same time, the argument can be very neatly reversed. The codification of knowledge actually requires more expert knowledge. As Beck (1992) has argued, we need to trust experts to identify what it is that puts us at risk in the environment, before we can actually know that we are at risk. A modern example of this is the development of self-tracking health devices. With the proliferation of smartphones and internet-enabled devices, there has been a major influx of smartphone apps and standalone technologies that 'track' various health metrics – weight, diet, sleep, exercise, etc. Generally, these apps and devices claim that they can help the individual 'reclaim' their health from the medical profession. Although some studies have shown that using self-tracking technologies can lead to a greater sense of autonomy and can create more transparent relationships between humans and the technologies that shape their everyday life (Lupton, 2013), their use and dissemination still depends on an internalization of knowledge, metrics and standards pre-established by the dominant medical profession and discourse (Freund, 2004). Neither smartphone users nor app developers would be able to make sense of their self-tracking without first understanding what is important and meaningful to track.

Thus while we can potentially challenge expert knowledge, we simultaneously must take more and more of it on trust. Put succinctly by Giddens (1992), we may challenge expert systems but we still trust individual experts. By and large the consumerist challenge to medicine is not that it isn't any good, but that it does not deliver well enough or fast enough.

Commodification

There is another major social change at work in medicine: commodification. This refers to the process whereby parts of everyday life are converted into objects for sale on the market. In health, this process includes the increasing need to buy medical services to gain better health status. Increasing areas of health care have become commodified for exchange on the market, and fewer and fewer areas of non-market-based resources are available to individuals.

Central to commodification is the cash nexus. On the one hand, the Australian Medical Association (AMA) has always insisted that the patient 'pay' for the professional services of the GP. On the other, the 'open pocket' implications of a universally funded fee-for-service model have resulted in high patient turnover and facilitated a form of medical intervention that does not incorporate preventative medicine; for example, 41.7 per cent of GPs agree that 'the competitive environment in urban practice favours bad medical practice'. Pressure to see patients, and to compete with entrepreneurial clinics, leads to a 'see them quick' outcome in general practice. An even greater number, 68 per cent, thought that bulk billing (when the doctor directly bills the government rather than the patient) led to superficial care, over-servicing and 'entrepreneurial' (i.e. profit-maximizing) practice. However, at the same time, 39.1 per cent of the respondents rejected the statement that 'the system of payment is too tightly tied to fee for service for each individual and there should be the possibility of other mechanisms for payments of GPs' (Department of Health and Human Services et al., 1992). The GPs in this survey, then, held contradictory views on the problems of payment and possible solutions. Competition leads to bad care, but steps to minimize competition – based on changes to Medicare and bulk billing – are rejected.

Another effect of the commodification of health services is the development of entrepreneurial medicine, known as 'the 24-hour clinic'. These clinics are able to undertake expensive advertising and provide convenient 24-hour access, satisfying the demands of some consumers and threatening more conventional general practices. These 24-hour clinics have been criticized, both by the government and the medical profession, for their high patient turnover, for causing fragmentation in the quality and continuity of care, and for their 'profligate use of investigations, drugs, and specialist referrals and patient recall' (Doessel, 1990: 6). However, the fact that they bulk bill, without patient co-payment, means that they are financially attractive to patients, particularly those already in jeopardy because of poverty. Furthermore, patients tend to use the 24-hour clinics for uncomplicated, simple medical problems, and for services such as the issuing of repeat prescriptions. Bulk-billing clinics may thus be clearing the market of uncomplicated cases, since patients appear to keep their own GP for what they regard as significant medical problems. Thus GPs are having to deal with complex medical matters, and therefore may be more involved with intervention, prevention and following up chronic patients. So one source of GPs' concerns is that they get paid the same as those in the bulk-billing clinics, even though their services may be far more demanding. Equally, in order to compete, GPs have to push their turnover up, bulk bill, and may be 'confined by economic pressure to the consulting room ... rarely able to interact with community health professional colleagues, to participate in hospital practices or in the broader issues of health care and public health promotion' (Veale and Douglas, 1992: 14). Thus, the commodification of health care has benefits and drawbacks for both patient and GP, but ultimately puts effective health-care reform much further out of reach.

Corporate Medicine

Health insurance companies and corporate investors in health pose a serious challenge to the independence of GPs. For example, New South Wales' health funds have attempted to make doctors obtain prior approval for the prescription of certain drugs. The AMA rejected this development as being a shift towards an American-style 'managed care', where clinical decisions have to be made with one eye on the health insurer's specifications of what they will pay for, which leads to a 'sausage-factory' approach to treatment. The then-president of the AMA, Dr Keith Woollard, claimed that the attempt to introduce control over prescribing was 'an outrageous attempt at bureaucratic intrusion' in the doctor–patient relationship (Australian Medical Association, 1996).

The involvement of health insurers may be only part of the AMA's problem. As the government attempts to devolve more and more health-care costs onto the states, state governments are responding by contracting out their health-care services. One consequence is that US companies, at the invitation of state governments, are moving into the picture. For example, Kaiser Permanente, the largest US managed care organization, has become involved in South Australia's co-ordinated care programme. These attempts by local corporate and overseas capital to control medical expenditure represent significant challenges to medicine, and illustrate the redrawing of the boundaries of health-care provision. In this way, both globalization (the development of new markets) and commodification (the sale of services) feed into each other.

The Body, Social Structures and Bourdieu

Along with a focus on the forms of commodity and labour, any materialist account of health and illness must also account for the treatment and production of the body under capitalism. In medicine, the body is the unproblematic basis of our natural, biological existence, and the site of disease. In the social sciences, the argument is that our experience and knowledge of our bodies is a product of our specific historical, cultural, political and gendered existence. In this sense, the body is not a biologically objective entity but the canvas on which social relationships are painted. In classical sociology, Marx, Engels and Weber demonstrated both the shaping of the body as it was harnessed to the discipline of factory labour, and in this sense the malleability of its 'natural' form, which they took for granted. One of the earliest anthropological accounts of the body was produced by Marcel Mauss, who noted that every aspect of bodily deportment – from breathing, through to marching and swimming – was specific to the society which produced it and reflected hierarchies of inequality, especially based around education levels. Mary Douglas went on to argue that:

> the social body constrains the way the physical body is perceived. The physical experience of the body, always modified by the social categories through which it is known, sustains a particular view of society. There is a continual interchange between the two kinds of bodily experience so that each reinforces the categories of the other. (Douglas, 1973: 93)

Contemporary research goes further in rejecting the 'naturalness' of the body, providing alternative definitions and accounts of the body that highlight both the social shaping of our understandings of our body and our body as a lived reality. As Simone de Beauvoir, the French feminist philosopher, put it: 'It is not the body-object described by biologists that actually exists, but the body as lived in by the subject' (1953: 33). Feminist analyses of medical representations of the body – which will be discussed in detail in Chapter 8 – highlight the way in which medicalization produces women's bodies as sick and in need of constant care and surveillance. At the cultural level, women's bodies have been shown to be construed as inferior to men's, as less amenable to control, and as dangerous. Historians, particularly those influenced by Foucault, have also demonstrated how specific religious, political and economic contexts produce our knowledge of the body. It is against this background that we can see the contribution of the French sociologist Pierre Bourdieu. His work extends Marxist analyses by showing how class patterns of inequality are manifest in the body. For Bourdieu, the body forms physical capital alongside economic, social and cultural capital: 'The way people treat their bodies reveals the deepest dispositions of their habitus' (Bourdieu, 1984: 190). The well-shaped and -maintained body is used to show to others that we discipline and control ourselves and that we are worthy and, indeed, superior members of society. Bourdieu's concern is to locate this process within the production and reproduction of class differences. He argues that consumption patterns are determined by economic abilities to consume, and that in turn what we consume marks our class position.

The most obvious 'taste' in the context of embodied inequality is the literal taste of dietary consumption patterns (Bourdieu, 1984). For example, there is substantial statistical epidemiological evidence to show that individuals of affluent status in Western societies are likely to enjoy higher-quality diets, whereas individuals of lower socio-economic status preferentially consume energy-dense diets that are nutrient-poor (Darmon and Drewnowski, 2008). Using a Bourdieusian approach, Calnan and Cant (1990) showed that the habitus of food consumption was an underlying factor of such persistent differences, in a study that suggested that middle-class women emphasize a 'balanced diet' and 'everything in moderation', whereas working-class women emphasize the importance of a meal being 'substantial' and 'filling' though not necessarily nutrient-rich (Williams, 1995). In this way, a commonly assumed individually 'chosen' factor which determines the shape of the body (food intake) is in fact structurally determined.

The interplay of physical, social, cultural and economic capital is well illustrated in terms of childhood obesity. Among lower-class children, the tendency to obesity is filtered – or better, facilitated – by environments that produce a habitus of unhealthy eating and low physical activity, in areas well served by fast-food outlets but poorly serviced by recreational facilities and poor information flows about diet (Cohen et al., 2006). The immediate consequences include respiratory disorders, type two diabetes, depression and social exclusion (Storch et al., 2007). These children are at a 400 per cent increased risk of obesity in adulthood (Freedman et al., 2005) and will then be at risk of diabetes and increased risk of cancer (Ogden et al., 2010). Thus the working-class habitus and its resulting body will over the next 40 years create a circular effect of increasing disease in childhood, leading into adulthood, and produce the first generation in modern times to die before their parents of preventable diseases caused by social inequalities (Gerald et al., 1994).

For Bourdieu, 'habitus' also includes persistent class-specific ways of representing the body, a form of physical capital which enhances or limits access to scarce social resources and marks the individual's social location. Thus the middle and upper classes pursue exercise patterns that produce a lean, 'fit'-looking body, favouring jogging and swimming. The working class produces bodies in the gym, with physical bulk, muscularity and strength as their aims (Bauman et al., 1990). As Charlesworth (2000) has argued, following Bourdieu, for working-class male bodies, we have social conditions structured by necessity producing a lived tradition, a tradition that lives on through the desire to build a strong powerful body, a necessity that produces a pleasure in the strength, endurance and stoicism of the body, and which fosters an instrumental, quasi-mechanistic relation to the body. The body as the medium for producing effects in its own structure, its tissue, muscle and sinew, the body as tool of a labouring intent rather than the body as an end of pleasure-in-itself. (2000: 261)

In this way, class-based practices of dietary consumption and exercise serve to produce particular types of bodies. Such 'distinctions' (Bourdieu, 1984) have important health consequences associated with the production of particular body types. These produce the 'social gradient of disease' – that is, the concentration among the lower classes of conditions such as type two diabetes, hypertension and obesity (Saguy and Almeling, 2008). For example, obesity rates tend to be correlated with lower socio-economic status in developed countries (Senese et al., 2009; Zhang and Wang, 2004). For developing countries, the trend is the reverse, with the affluent being able to afford and make distinct their affluence through the consumption of precisely these energy-rich foods and sedentary lifestyle that marks low SES in the developed world (McLaren, 2007). Bodies and health are reproduced and distributed following the structures of inequality in society – economic, cultural and physical.

One of the clearest illustrations of the impact of inequality on the health of the body is the persistent differences in height between the upper class and those who are unskilled labourers. In Britain, while both groups have increased their height over the twentieth century as a result of better nutrition and living and working standards, the gap has persisted, with class I men averaging five foot nine inches and class V averaging five foot seven inches (using the British Registrar General's occupational scale) (Walker et al., 1988). Similarly, over the last 90 years, class differences in height, weight and body mass index have scarcely changed at all in Portugal (Cardosa and Caninas, 2010). The socio-economic habitus conferred on us in our height not only persists over generations but also is a marker for social mobility and increased social status. Swedish research has found that working-class school children who were taller experienced upward social mobility (as measured by educational attainment), while shorter upper-class children experienced downward social mobility (Cernerud, 1995).

Our habitus then acts as a settled way of interpreting and responding to the world – a set of world views, if you like – that focus and define reality, both economically and physically. Bourdieu argues that in contemporary society we show who we are in consuming 'taste', and that these symbolic forms of consumption mark out hierarchies of class-based inequality. Those dominant groups who have been most successful at developing their 'taste', and imposing their definition on other groups, are those with high 'cultural capital', those who know the range of tastes available across society. Since it takes time and money to learn the range of tastes available and remembering that this process is an economically unproductive one – for example, art or wine appreciation classes, or guided tours to Italy to view the paintings of the Renaissance, or hiring a personal trainer all cost money and produce no discernible product in themselves – it will be the economically dominant class's view of what is good taste that prevails. For Bourdieu, inequality is thus economic, cultural, physical and psychological, with poorer groups' concepts of good taste gauged as second best. Patterns of inequality then impact not only in the material bodily sense of poverty and sickness, but also in the emotional and psychological sense of exclusion from the upper reaches of taste which would demonstrate cultural signs of membership of the dominant group (Marmot, 2004; Wilkinson, 1999; and in terms of racial inequality, see Foreman, 2003).

Conclusion

In this chapter I have distinguished four ways of looking at health in terms of socio-economic factors. First, I highlighted the research that draws attention to the 'materialist' basis of people's health, that is, the correlation between social and economic environment – of housing, urban space, occupation and diet – and disease. These factors are materialist in the sense that, by and large, they operate independently of an individual's own actions. Second, I identified occupation (as measured by the use of the Registrar General's Classification of Occupations on death certificates) as providing a snapshot of the impact of inequality, especially inequality associated with income and occupation, on an individual's health. Third, I pointed to a socio-economic approach in which inequality along a range of variables – housing, education, income – can be shown to be linked to unequal experience of disease. Fourth, I outlined the Marxist account in which class is the central feature of capitalist society and the determining factor in the distribution of disease. In this explanation, class, as measured by the need to sell your labour power, is the determining cause of health inequality. This approach has had to take into account changes in the class formation and forms of production and consumption in contemporary society. On the one hand individuals no longer identify themselves as members of the working class as strongly. On the other hand, the increasing concentrations of capital and the decline in the industrial working class have meant significant changes in the role of the medical profession. Increasingly, individual medical practitioners and their practices are being taken over by large investment companies, and the change to lifestyle-based interventions, often run by large companies, means that clinical medicine may not be as dominant as it was.

Pierre Bourdieu developed an innovative theory of the relationship of the body to our class position in society. He saw health as socially patterned and reflected in the individual's body. Health is then a source of capital we can use to gain valued social goods – jobs, education and social status. Bourdieu's position thus complemented Marx's belief that social class as determined by the economy was central to modern societies, but he also argued that other forms of capital exist, which he labelled cultural, social and symbolic. Possessing these forms of capital allows us to position ourselves in society.

From the Marxist perspective, medicine plays both an economic and an ideological role in contemporary society, which can be summarized as follows. First, medicine is object-centred rather than person-centred, treating the human being as a thing. Second, disease is seen as a condition to be treated by chemical or electrical intervention to restore balance in the body, rather than the outcome of social relationships. Third, health is defined as fitness to carry out a social role – in particular, your ability to sell your labour. Fourth, medicine focuses on the individual and individualistic conceptions of lifestyles, thus deflecting attention from the social, political and economic environment. Fifth, these functionalist and individualistic perspectives lead to an emphasis on curing, with two results:

(a) technologically based curative medicine provides the basis for ongoing capital accumulation – that is, profitability; and

(b) in focusing on the individual, the role of environmental issues in causing ill health is obscured and the capitalist organization of production is protected (Doyal and Pennell, 1979).

Summary

- In this chapter I have argued that the material organization of society – and especially the exposure to physical hazard, whether in the workplace or the home – is responsible for a great deal of disease.

- An account of this relationship can be presented either descriptively in terms of occupation, or (more sociologically) in terms of socio-economic status or class analysis.

- In the Marxist analysis, medicine is shown to be part of the capitalist economy, in which technological developments and therapies are pursued for their profitability.

- Medical knowledge acts to make the damage done by the capitalist system look 'natural' and biological, and it depoliticizes the person's experience of disease, in a context where it is in fact politically and economically caused.

- Transformations in capitalism, particularly the rise of corporate investors in health care, are changing the role of the medical profession as it becomes more and more a part of wage labour.

Discussion Questions

1.   How does the material organization of society shape people's health?

2.   In a Marxist analysis what is the function of modern medicine?

3.   Capitalist societies produce capitalist health-care systems. Do you agree with this?

Further Reading

Marmot, M. (2004) *Status Syndrome: How Your Social Standing Directly Affects Your Health and Life Expectancy*. Oxford: Bloomsbury. Text based on research into the social gradient of illness.

Townsend, P. and Davidson, N. (eds) (1988) *Inequalities in Health: The Black Report and the Health Divide*. Harmondsworth: Penguin. The classic in the field of structural health inequality.

Wilkinson, R. (1996) *Unhealthy Societies: The Afflictions of Inequality*. London: Routledge. A very thorough summary of the impact of the material organization of society on health.

For ongoing empirical and theoretical developments in the Marxist sociology of health, consult the *International Journal of Health Services* under the editorship of one of America's leading Marxists, Vincente Navarro.

6

PARSONS, AMERICAN SOCIOLOGY OF MEDICINE AND THE SICK ROLE

○ Parsons argued that contemporary society should not be understood as capitalist. Rather it was modern, and while it had a capitalist economy, it had a non-capitalist social structure. Medicine was a key example in his argument.

○ He held that the professional role in modern society was a distinctive one, based on altruism and a service ethic of care. It thus acted as a brake on the egotism and competitiveness of market relationships.

○ Parsons also argued strongly against any understanding of sickness as purely biological. Cultural and social norms will determine what counts as disease and how it is treated. For him, to be sick is to enter the 'sick role', which is controlled by the medical profession. Their task is to prevent individuals from trying to opt out of their social roles, which, Parsons acknowledges, may be detrimental to their health.

○ While Parsons' analysis has been subject to extensive empirical criticism, this should not obscure the theoretical power of his analysis of medicine as an institution of social control and of the way in which social structures determine an individual's health and disease.

The major alternative to Marxist accounts of health and illness, and of the nature of modern society, has been that provided by Talcott Parsons (1902–1979), one of the most influential American sociologists of the twentieth century. Whereas Marx examined those aspects of society that were bringing about change and conflict, Parsons' focus was on those factors that bound society together. Parsons was strongly influenced by the development of sociology in America as an intellectual field. Under the impact of Edward Ross (1938), American sociology rejected both the individualism of utilitarianism and the collectivism of class conflict in its search for a paradigm that would facilitate its professional formation and secure it a place in the American university structure. Ross developed an analysis based on socialization and social control. Thus the focus was on group processes at the broadest societal level, and the processes which bound the group together and brought about social stability (McMahon, 1998).

In Parsons' work this is rendered into a question. What is it, he asked, about the way that our social relationships are organized that makes for solidarity and stability? In particular, in the face of the individualism, self-interest and egotism of modern society, what is it that holds social relations together? This problem had already been formulated by the French sociologist Émile Durkheim, and as developed by Parsons was clearly put: if the psychologists and economists are correct and we are only organisms that attempt to minimize pain and maximize pleasure, then there is no basis for social solidarity. At every turn, we will try to maximize our own interests and undermine other people's. This is particularly so, as Durkheim pointed out, in a capitalist society where pursuing self-interest and maximizing profit, on the market, is the basis of social life. When individuals meet in the market, profitability is what drives their interaction, and the goal is realizing self-interest. Parsons argued that social life would be impossible if it was based only on economic interests and solely dependent on the utilitarian pursuit of self-interest by individuals. Society, to cohere, needs social institutions that will stand against the profit motive and self-interest. He argued that the professions, and especially medicine, were key social institutions which were not motivated by self-interest nor driven solely by the profit motive. His sociology contrasts and explores the non-rational, altruistic and other-worldliness of the professions with rational, egotistical, this-worldly economics. In this Parsons departs radically from Marxist sociology. For Marx, the economy was the dominant factor in the development of capitalist society. Parsons is arguing that in modern society other groups form, which are not the product solely of the economy, and which perform the central social function of stabilizing the social system.

Parsons is in the tradition of sociology called structural functionalism. He conceptualized society as a social system of interrelated social structures, each of which plays a specific function in bringing about stability and integration of individuals and their social roles. Society is the outcome of various actors performing their social roles (for example, mother, teacher, doctor) in specific social institutions (the family, the classroom and the hospital). The institutions perform the specific functions necessary for the continuation of social life. The family socializes the next generation, the teacher prepares the next generation for work, and the doctor repairs and rehabilitates, allowing individuals to continue performing their social roles.

Prior to Parsons, health had been the focus of sociological research in the USA. The Lynds (Lynd and Lynd, 1931) examined it in their study of Middletown (actually

Muncie, Indiana), and Ogburn (1922) used it as an example of cultural lag – of people's resistance to 'new' science and technology – while Koos (1954) made it a major focus in his *Health of Regionville*. Wardwell (1952) focused on chiropractors as a microcosm of the marginal social role. In general, the concern of these studies was with the circumstances under which people resisted the move to scientific medicine. Put the other way round, medicine was used as a lens through which to view the shift from traditional to modern society. By contrast, Parsons' structural functionalism can easily be portrayed as a celebration of the America of the 1950s, and his eulogization of the medical profession is part of this. His argument may be seen as medico-centric and biased on behalf of the doctor in ensuring patient compliance. At the same time, though, Parsons' sociological explanation of the sick role raises important questions about professions and their power.

The medical explanation of disease is that it is a biological event, a fact of nature. Parsons shows that there is too much ambiguity in medical knowledge to decisively tell the 'facts' of disease, and that being sick is a social accomplishment. Further, while he may have a favourable view of the medical profession, he argues more generally that medical practice and health have to be seen in the context of the broader social structure, and especially in terms of the family and the occupational structure of the USA (Parsons, 1958).

Parsons and the Professions

Parsons' major theoretical argument was an attack on utilitarian doctrines of self-interest, economic models of action and any understanding of human action as behaviourist. To put it plainly, any understanding of human action had to include reference to normative standards about the ends we want from life and the exercise of choice about how to achieve those ends.

It is in this context that we must see Parsons' theory of the medical profession and his argument that professions are occupations which do not reflect economic self-interest.

—BOX 6.1—

CHARACTERISTICS OF THE MEDICAL PROFESSION

1. Doctors are universalistic in their practice, i.e. ideally they operate without reference to the patient's class, gender, ethnicity or religion.

2. Doctors are affectively neutral, in that they do not pass moral judgements on the individuals they are dealing with.

(Continued)

(Continued)

3. They are oriented towards the good of the collective.

4. They are functionally specific, i.e. they deal only with the problem at hand and do not enquire into other factors (e.g. doctors deal with the problems of your body without asking questions about your morals).

The profession delivers a highly specific service to all against a background of non-discriminatory approaches to individuals. In other words, the doctor–patient relationship is the exact opposite of the business relationship based on economic contract. Parsons argued that this non-economic, normative framework was essential for the therapeutic regime, at the level of doctor–patient. It allowed the patient to feel as if they were a person whose problems could be treated in a non-judgemental fashion, and thus allowed healing to take place. At a more general level, given the isolation of individuals in modern society, it was essential to bring about normative order at the level of the social structure, because it reintegrated people back into the social system.

Parsons' characterization of the profession has not fared well with the passage of time. Contemporary sociologists of the professions are more likely to emphasize the self-interested practices of social closure, of seeking to maintain their occupational autonomy, their pursuit of high incomes and the maintenance of their social status. Whereas Parsons emphasized the long period of training, the knowledge base and the commitment to service and ethics, contemporary sociologists point to the gate-keeping exercise of closing off training options for other health practitioners, the self-interest and the venal motivation of the profession.

Contemporary analysis of the doctor–patient relationship emphasizes the ways in which universalistic criteria are not applied. Women can be shown to be the recipients of tranquillizers; the poor who cannot afford treatment go neglected; and other cultures' views of the body, health and disease are ignored. It is a well-established finding that the length of a medical consultation depends on your class, gender and ethnicity (Johnson et al., 2004; Peck and Denney, 2012). One study of how cardiac specialists make choices about who to operate on is very significant. It showed that in addition to technical discussions, the specialists made assumptions about whether or not the patient was 'deserving' of surgery. It found that when these issues arose, the surgeons made similar assumptions to those that lay people do about lifestyle, smoking and other social factors. Medical discourse is a blend of the social and the technical, not just the purely technical (Hughes and Griffiths, 1996).

The concept of a unitary medical profession that was central to Parsons' analysis has been overtaken by fragmentation in the profession itself, with professional organizations usually favouring specialist practitioners, lowering the status of general practitioners. An increasingly educated public is disenchanted with modern medicine, the over-prescription of drugs and over-use of technology. This has given rise to a growing alternative medicine sector supported by consumer groups. The presumption of the skilled supply of information and technical skills by the doctor, and unskilled and grateful consumption by the patient, has become a thing of the past. At the same time, many medical practitioners have embraced these changes, with many of them practising as, or referring patients to, non-orthodox practitioners. A survey of general practitioners in Wellington, New Zealand (Leibrich et al., 1987) found that 94 per cent knew of complementary practitioners in their area (hypnotherapist, acupuncturists and chiropractors); 80 per cent referred patients to non-medical practitioners; 24 per cent had received training in complementary practices; and a further 54 per cent wanted such training. The study also found that many doctors practised complementary therapies without training – four out of ten, for example, practising hypnosis, and three of these practising chiropractics. A more recent study in the UK indicated that nearly 40 per cent of General Practitioner partnerships in England provided their National Health Service (NHS) patients access to some form of complementary therapy. In approximately 20 per cent of practices, complementary therapies, most commonly acupuncture or homeopathy, were delivered by general practitioners or other members of the primary health-care team (Thomas et al., 2001). Further problems in Parsons' characterization of the profession can be demonstrated in empirical studies showing practice and treatment variations among medical practitioners, especially in diagnosing and prescribing.

Diagnostic Variations

The social processes in medical work can be demonstrated in studies of medical practitioners' activities when the same condition has been diagnosed. That is to say, even when doctors diagnose the same condition, how they treat it will vary in terms of laboratory test orders, prescriptions, referrals and requests for follow-ups. For example, whether or not the doctor orders a laboratory test varies from 1 to 50 per cent (Davis and Lee, 1990). What causes such variations is the subject of much study. These decisions are not the product of science; they are related to social variables to do with the practitioner. One study found that the continuous presence of 'influential practitioners' – medical staff who were especially aware of the procedures for testing and accepting patients – decreased the number of blood chemistry tests by 70 per cent (Anderson et al., 1991). It has been suggested that there are at least four major variables which affect the way doctors treat patients: their background and training; the way their practice is organized; the characteristics of their patients; and diagnostic characteristics. Other studies have examined whether or not doctors treat the same condition in the same way, and have found marked differences. Davis and Lee (1990) found in their study of New Zealand doctors that there are clear differences in the management of patients. Older doctors, without postgraduate training, are less likely to order laboratory tests and more likely to write a prescription. This is also true of those in solo country practices. Patient characteristics will also affect the doctor's treatment. Older patients are less likely to receive a script or follow-up, while women are more likely to have a test, and to be followed up. A patient's weight too is a cause for stigmatization if they are obese, with health-care professionals demonstrating substantial prejudice. The overweight and obese are taken to be lazy, indifferent to their health, unintelligent and resistant to change. Medical professionals actually think that by shaming these individuals they will react positively to attempts at weight loss. In fact the opposite is the case – in stigmatizing them they receive poorer treatment and less access to health services. The stigmatization further contributes to health inequalities since obesity in the population follows the social gradient of disease and affects the poor and lower classes (Puhl and Heur, 2010).

For sociologists, what is at issue here is not the correctness of the treatments, but the fact that they vary, and that they vary according to the social characteristics of the patient and the doctor. In short, these studies seriously undermine Parsons' concept of the medical profession as disinterested practitioners of a scientific practice. They do, however, support his contention that being sick is a socially negotiated role.

Prescribing Activities

Similarly, it can be shown that prescribing is the outcome of social factors, rather than clinically objective criteria. This is illustrated by the fact that when the list of drugs that doctors may prescribe is limited, they change their prescribing habits without an effect on morbidity or mortality. This is especially the case with antibiotics, which, if controlled, can lead to a reduction of costs by up to 25 per cent (Smith, 1988). However, since most postgraduate drug education is carried out by drug companies, and these companies spend large amounts of money encouraging general practitioners to prescribe their products, it can be very difficult to change doctors' prescribing habits. Watkins et al. (2003) conducted a study of factors influencing UK general practitioners' prescribing practices. They found that general practitioners with the highest prescribing costs (i.e. those whose prescriptions contributed the most to overall government expenditure on pharmaceutical subsidies) saw drug company representatives more frequently than doctors with lower prescribing costs. High rates of prescribing were also associated with doctors feeling frustrated by short consultation times, or dissatisfied with consultations that involved provision of advice only. Under these circumstances it is difficult to introduce non-drug-based therapies, even in areas where it is known that non-clinical interventions (such as dietary change) will have an impact (Sinclair, 1989). It is important to point out that this prescribing behaviour is not the result of patient pressure to leave the surgery with a script. This is commonly claimed by doctors. But in a study of general practitioner consultations with patients experiencing a sore throat or upper respiratory infection, Butler et al. (1998) found that, while one-third of patients expected to receive a prescription for antibiotics, the rest (two-thirds) consulted their doctor mainly for reassurance, pain relief or advice on prevention, and were happy to not receive a prescription. Doctors in the same study, however, cited patients expecting to receive antibiotics as the main reason for their over-prescription.

Parsons: People Act Rather Than Behave

Parsons was also keen to develop a second major argument in his sociology: that human beings act, and make choices and decisions, rather than responding to the environment in a passive way. In this argument, Parsons makes one of the fundamental contributions to the sociology of health and illness. If the medical view of disease is correct, then disease is purely the biological response of the human organism to environmental factors over which we, as conscious individuals, can have little effect. Parsons, following the German social theorist Max Weber, argued that, on the contrary, humans make sense of their world, they interpret it, give it meaning, and make choices about their participation in it. In this sense, disease is not purely biological. Even calling something a disease is the outcome of social, political and cultural circumstances. Parsons' basic argument is that sickness is a social and not a purely biochemical condition. He develops this argument in two ways. The first is to discuss whether or not medicine is a science.

Parsons argued that the self-proclaimed status of medicine as a science is problematic on two grounds (even if in his analysis of the profession he took it at face value). In the light of historical studies and comparative anthropology, it appears to be irrelevant whether illness is presented to be cured by magic, science or religion: the cure may take place and the system be legitimated, or death occurs and nature, the devil or lack of knowledge are invoked and the legitimacy of the system put beyond question. The second problem of medicine's claims to be scientific is that within the model of science it adheres to, it is not scientific. Parsons pointed to examples of resistance to discoveries, of fads in medical practice and of elements of magic in medical treatment. A good recent example of a surgical fad in the UK is the 'epidemic' of surgery for glue ear, which peaked between 1984 and 1989 and which has since steadily declined with no apparent clinical basis other than the judgement of the surgeons (Black, 1995). It is this, the element of magic in modern medicine, which Parsons makes most of. His point is that people often get better because they expect to do so, rather than anything to do with the treatment. In making this point he was reflecting the concern that had developed in the 1950s with the placebo effect: that individuals who believed they were being treated with medicine respond as if they were – even when they were not. So while medicine's claims to legitimacy in society are based on technical knowledge, there are gaps in the knowledge which it practises. These voids range from the unknowability of some aspects of medical knowledge and consequently the impossibility of treatment, to uncertainty in the practice of treatment, that is, the difficulty in showing a causal relationship between a complaint, a treatment and a cure.

Given these problems in medicine's claims to scientificness, Parsons concluded that being sick is a social role and not primarily a biological or physiological condition. Let me give two more examples of the way in which the social and the medical interact. Let me give two examples of the way the social and the medical interact, the use of drugs in treatment procedures; and the experience of pain following surgical procedures.

Following the Western model of health, we would predict that drugs should have a straightforward effect on the biochemistry of the body – the administration of a drug should cure the condition it is targeted at. Further, it should work the same way independently of to whom it is administered. However, studies by sociologists have shown that this is not the case (Price, 1984). When a new drug is trialled it is done through what is known as a double-blind trial. This means that patients are separated into three groups. The experimental group is given the new drug. The control group is given a placebo that is a chemically inert substance such as sugar. A third group is given nothing. It is double-blind because the patients don't know who is getting what; and neither do the doctors who are administering the drugs. So no one is able to influence the treatment regime. In a study of ulcer drugs the findings are notable.

In a study of ulcer treatment drugs it was found that up to 90 per cent of those in the placebo group got better, in the same way as if they had been treated by the active drug (Moerman, 1981). This is the placebo effect, and it cannot be explained by Western medicine, which separates the mind from the body (Romanucci-Ross and Moerman, 1988). As far as Western medicine is concerned, drugs are biochemically active substances which should have an impact on the body in a straightforward way. However, for sociologists these findings show that the way people define the situation will be important for what happens. This argument was put by the sociologist W. I. Thomas (1923), who said 'What people believe to be real, will be real in its consequences'. In other words, if you think that you have received a drug your body will respond as if you had received the drug. This argument has been developed by sociologists into a broader formulation: the way in which you define the situation will affect your experience of the situation.

This finding was confirmed in a study of post-operative pain (Egbert et al., 1978). Two groups of surgical patients were treated very differently in a hospital. One group was talked to extensively about what they would experience, how the surgery would be conducted, and how they would feel after the event. The second group was treated as normal – little discussion was held with them and they were treated in a routine way. What was the effect of this? Those in the first group reported significantly less pain, requested significantly less post-operative pain relief, and were discharged from hospital much earlier than the second group. The way in which the situation was defined affected the outcome of the operation, even though it was exactly the same operation in both cases. Thus sociologists argue that even in cases which look like the real workings of nature – drugs and pain – social factors play a significant role.

Modern medicine has not been totally deaf to sociological studies. But even when the medical profession attempts to pay attention to the social factors of sickness, it is still generally resistant to sociological explanations. Kaptchuk et al.'s (2008) study, which looked at the placebo effect in sufferers of irritable bowel syndrome, found that not only did the placebo group report a steep decline in symptoms, but also it was most effective when paired with regular and 'friendly' interaction with a medical professional. Despite this admission of the effect of medical authority on wellness, the study still framed the placebo process as a 'sham' used to 'dupe' patients into feeling better – denying the authenticity of social interventions into health outside of psychological manipulation.

The second way Parsons set out to establish that sickness and disease are social phenomena was to ask what the role is of individual choice in sickness and disease. Since sociology deals with action, rather than behaviour, Parsons asked very radical questions: How much choice do we have in what we do? What happens to us? And how much of it is produced by the way society is organized? In the context of the sociology of health, are sickness and disease conditions imposed on us, or do they involve motivational factors on the part of the individual? Or is there interplay between choice, disease and the environment? Parsons' answer was that people can make choices about their illnesses – we can enter into disease, so to speak. It was on the basis of this argument that he conceptualized sickness: not as a biological condition, but as a social role.

The Sick Role

Parsons conceptualized the sick role against the background of two developments: one in American medicine, the other in his ongoing development of sociology. On the first count, the concept of psychosomatic illness was starting to be taken seriously by American medicine. The patient's outlook, personality and motivation were seen as essential parts of the patient's interaction with and experience of illness. This meant that the patient's responses to disease had to be taken into account in the treatment. On the second count, as Parsons developed his sociology – the voluntaristic theory of action – he advanced the argument that individuals have choices to make about their social relations and experiences. Given that being sick was primarily a social event, it followed that people could decide to be sick. This raised a significant problem for Parsons. He argued that it was possible that people could voluntarily decide to be sick, that is, to adopt the sick role in a deviant way to escape the requirements of their social life.

However, if this was the case then social life was potentially impossible. Given the strains of careers and marriages and the need always to be improving ourselves – as the American dream demanded – people may well opt to be sick and therefore escape the burdens of social life. This was deeply worrying for Parsons. People must be prevented from arbitrarily or, in a totally voluntaristic way, abdicating from society. Hence the sick role. The sick role is defined not by subjective feelings (of feeling lousy, or not coping, or of being tired all the time), but by the reactions of others and a pattern of action displayed by the claimant to the role. Put simply, between feeling sick and being sick lies entry into the sick role, and it is surrounded by guards that have to be overcome.

BOX 6.2

THE PATIENT'S RIGHTS AND DUTIES IN THE SICK ROLE

1. Legitimate withdrawal from social obligations – of work and family.

2. Exemption from responsibility for your condition – you cannot get well on your own but need help and support.

3. You must want to get well.

4. You must seek technically competent help.

A person can only legitimately enter the sick role if he or she desires to get well and seeks technically competent help. In exchange, the person will be exempted from other roles and will not be held responsible for his or her actions. The key step in this process is the approach to technically competent help, for only the doctor can ultimately sanction entry into the sick role.

People can only be sick if they are legitimately defined as patients, a state which can only come about through the intervention of the medical profession and, consequently, on biologically legitimated grounds. The irony of the sick role is that Parsons, dedicated to establishing the integrity of a sociological explanation of health and disease, develops a sophisticated analysis of the social function of medicine, but in the end hands the province of health and illness back to the medical practitioners. He is logically driven into this position by postulating the professions as the institutional bulwark against the self-seeking individualism of capitalism.

In a modern society the medical profession, according to his schema, incorporates achievement values and is universalistic, functionally specific and affectively neutral in its fulfilment of community interests rather than its own self-interest.

In Defence of the Sick Role

Not surprisingly, there is extensive criticism of Parsons' concept of the sick role. Parsons' model best fits those situations in which sickness is acute and the patient is the passive recipient of altruistically provided medical skills. His model has difficulties with chronic illness and physical disabilities such as diabetes, or normal but transient experiences such as pregnancy which may affect only part of the patient's social roles, and with conditions in which moral evaluation crosses over diagnoses, such as alcoholism or venereal disease. Nevertheless, research inspired by the concept of the sick role still continues.

For example, one use of sick role theory has been the postulation of the empowered sick individual who adopts a positive attitude towards his or her condition and its management. The ideas of 'patient empowerment' developed from qualitative analysis of patients' experiences have challenged the dependency aspects of Parsons' formulation, and particularly the idea of an authoritative doctor and a passive patient. But are these patients as autonomous and empowered as claimed? Does chronic illness allow them to escape the social control functions of the sick role, preventing the sick from forming a subcultural group which may come to enjoy its status? Crossley has studied the 'empowerment' responses of HIV-positive people, and argued that Parsons' model alerts us to structural features of illness that empowerment cannot overcome (Crossley, 1998). These relate to the fact that the chronically ill, as part of their stance, overemphasize their independence from technical and clinical help, especially in the case of AIDS. To construct themselves as empowered, chronically ill groups must construct an oppositional group to define themselves against, usually medical professionals. Second, Crossley points out that the move to empowerment, and the associated development of self-help groups, paradoxically leads to a 'disease-identity' dependency, in which the disease-state and the diseased-self become central.

Chronic disease has changed the temporal structure of the sick role such that it is no longer the acute process that Parsons had in mind. Long-term illness means that individuals cannot put their life on hold and enter the sick role. This has given rise to new forms of qualitative research in narrative analysis (as we saw in Chapter 4), which has been used to examine the experience of chronic illness. Some of these studies have shown that the concept of the sick role can also inform explanations of individuals' experiences of long-term chronic illness. A study into long-term brain injury found that there is a direct relationship between 'a survivor's somatic symptoms and their initial and continued acceptance of [the] sick role' (Barclay, 2012: 6). Similarly, research on cancer patients has demonstrated the impact of the sick role on chronically ill individuals.

─BOX 6.3─

THE SICK ROLE, CANCER AND LIMINALITY

Little et al. (1998) found that for those being treated for cancer of the colon:

- no matter how long since they had been diagnosed as having cancer, their ongoing identification was as a cancer patient;

- they had ongoing problems in communicating about the nature of the illness, its treatment and diagnosis to people close to them; and

- they had a heightened sense of the passage of time, and the limited amount left, and associated with this a feeling of powerlessness.

Paralleling the biological experience of cancer is a social process of disengagement and weakening of social links. Little calls this 'liminality', that is, a lesser experience of the normal stimuli of social life.

In the first stage of liminality, the key characteristic is of a loss of a sense of control, and of uncertainty. In the second stage, the person takes steps to construct a story of their illness, a narrative, which will make sense of their experience and allow them to communicate with others. Their attempt to give it meaning to others also gives it meaning for them. This liminal state of constructing and communicating meaning in the face of the inexplicable stays with these people for the rest of their lives. As Little and his colleagues have put it: 'The experience of liminality is firmly grounded in the changing and experiencing body that houses both the disease and the self' (Little et al., 1998: 1493).

Yet another interesting way of thinking about the usefulness of the sick role is in terms of examining the experience of doctors who become patients. Because of their 'insider' knowledge, and their equivalent status to the person treating them, these individuals problematize the consultation. Some seek to retain control of the consultation; others aim for the status of an ordinary patient; while others think that they are special patients with special needs, since their pathology is complicated by their knowledge of it. Studies of these consultations show that the power of the sick role overwhelms the attempts of the individual medical practitioner as the patient tries to retain control of his or her illness. The social role of the presiding doctor works just as it does with a lay patient and subordinates the sick doctor (McKevitt and Morgan, 1997).

So while many of the criticisms of the sick role are very well made, it retains a great deal of utility as a theoretical tool for exploring the experience of sickness. There is also an implicit political analysis of the causes of disease in American society in Parsons' work. His argument was that sickness may be the only response open to an individual in a situation of intolerable strain.

Sickness and American Values

What are the strains in the social system that drive people to be sick? For Parsons, there were two crucial aspects of American capitalism that would drive people to sickness: activism and individualism. Activism embodies the belief in the achievement motive and a belief in social success based on merit. In this context, the sick role provides the alternatives of withdrawal and retreatism as a response.

This instrumental activism has further implications for health and sickness in American culture. Activism leads to a corresponding emphasis on youth. Ageing and retirement, then, become very problematic as aspects of the individual's self-definition. Ageing therefore becomes a disease in itself. Gustafson found that the elderly spend a good deal of time in nursing homes trying to gain control over time, their self-image and their status as autonomous individuals, which was 'desperate and ineffectual' because those around them (nurses, doctors and family) saw ageing as a patient career which was 'an unbroken decline towards death' (Gustafson, 1972).

Thus sickness may well be a response to, or outcome of, intolerable gaps between societal ideals and personal abilities, or it may be forced on you because you do not meet wider cultural criteria. Parsons also pointed to one institution that he thought caused disease: the nuclear family. Parsons is often criticized as an apologist for the American way of life. But in this regard he was in advance of his time. He argued that it was quite impossible for any one institution to bear the strains that the family had to bear in contemporary society. The claustrophobic, emotionally intense, and rigidly role-segregated family was as much a threat to health as it was a solution to socializing the next generation. In particular, Parsons argued that the married woman was most at risk of role strain in this environment, tending towards the 'neurotic illness of compulsive domesticity' (Parsons, 1954: 194).

In summary, Parsons' theory of the sick role derives from his conviction that sociology deals with the actions of goal-setting individuals. Thus sociology is not a behavioural science, because actors are knowledgeable – they set goals and organize ways of achieving those ends in a meaningful way within the range of options offered by their culture. Sickness is, therefore, a meaningful activity: people can choose it, or they can have it forced upon them by the exigencies of their social existence; and it is never morally neutral.

The End of the Golden Age of Doctoring

As we saw in Chapter 5, medicine as a profession has been seriously challenged by technological developments, commodification and the rise of corporate medicine. These developments were fully analysed in McKinlay and Marceau's (2002) paper 'The End of the Golden Age of Doctoring'. In it they identify eight trends that were unsettling the profession at the end of the twentieth century: the changed nature of the state which no longer supported professionalism; the bureaucratization of medical practice; the competitive threat from other health-care workers; the impact of globalization; the information revolution; changing patterns of disease, in particular the rise of chronic degenerative conditions; the erosion of trust in the doctor–patient relationship; and the fragmentation of the peak medical bodies themselves.

It is interesting to note in this context that Parsons in 1964 predicted the decline of the medical profession as medical work became more specialized and differentiated. Within the general process of differentiation, he pointed to a number of social changes mediating the professional dominance of the medical practitioner in the health-care system. These included the process of bureaucratization in which administrators take over management of the provision of services, such as control of the hospital and its processes of administering patients, who are no longer under the direct control of the practitioner. In this the clinical decision making of which patient should go to which ward is a non-medical one. Parsons points out that 'this is indeed the abdication of one of the most cherished aspects of the sovereignty of the traditional medical practitioners, but one that could scarcely be avoided unless the advantages of large scale organisation are to be abandoned altogether' (Parsons, 1964: 347). The financial planning and administration of the hospital or clinic also becomes a matter of administrative control, far beyond the reach of the doctor. The fiduciary responsibility for training doctors has been removed from the direct control of the profession and taken over by universities, within which medicine finds itself only one school in the broader faculty of science which has control over its curriculum and teaching processes.

The rise of medical research laboratories – in which key researchers may not be medical practitioners but scientists – challenges the medical claim to autonomy based on the 'art of medicine', as its practices must more and more conform to the findings of the laboratory. So whereas medicine once 'shouldered' (Parsons, 1964: 355) the responsibility for health alone, now it must share it with a wide range of other practitioners – administratively, academically, financially and institutionally. Indeed, this uncertainty about who is responsible for their health was one of the key reasons US patients identified as to why their trust in doctors and the medical profession as a whole had diminished (Zheng, 2015). So it is ironic that Parsons, the theorist who did the most to construct medicine as a profession, for sociological reasons, predicted its demise.

Conclusion

For Parsons, studying medical phenomena was only of interest to the extent that they illuminated sociological problems. In particular, he was vitally concerned with the problem of order: how did society cohere? Following Durkheim, he rejected utilitarian theories and pointed to a shared system of values. He was equally challenged by the Weberian problem of meaning: if there is no purpose in the world for actors then social organization is likely to fall apart. Thus order and meaning are two sides of the same problem for Parsons. The experience of illness – its treatment on universalistic, non-ascriptive and non-emotional grounds – solves the problem of values, through the therapeutic encounter with the medical professional. Simultaneously, the experience of illness also allows actors to choose a response to social strains. It generates a meaningful response to an intolerable situation.

Summary

- At the core of Parsons' analysis are key sociological questions: How is social order possible? How does society cohere? How is meaning established in a complex, competitive and individualist society? And what is the relationship of the individual to social structures?

- Parsons is also concerned to argue that modern societies are not capitalist societies but have other, non-economic institutions which bring about stability and integrate individuals. Key among these is the medical profession.

- Parsons argues too that individuals can make choices in their social life, and that one of those choices may well be to opt out: to go sick. In fact, one reading of Parsons supports the view that contemporary society is increasingly pushing individuals in this direction.

- The sick role, guarded by the medical profession, exists to prevent individuals opting out. The paradox is that while Parsons' analysis supports the sociological perspective that disease is socially produced, and not a biological fact, he gives control over it to a group whose legitimacy is based on a claim to 'biological' knowledge.

Discussion Questions

1. According to Parsons, what is the social control function of the medical profession?

2. Being sick is more than just biological; it's a social role. Discuss.

3. What are the rights and duties of someone in the sick role?

Further Reading

Holton, R. and Turner, B. (1986) *Talcott Parsons on Economy and Society*. London: Routledge and Kegan Paul. The book provides a good overview of Parsonian sociology in general and of his sociology of health, in Chapter 2, 'Sickness and Social Structure: Parsons' Contribution to Medical Sociology'.

Parsons, T. (1978) *Action Theory and the Human Condition*. London: Free Press. This book includes chapters titled 'Health and Disease: A Sociological and Action Perspective' and 'The Sick Role and the Role of the Physicians Reconsidered'.

7

FOUCAULT AND THE SOCIOLOGY OF MEDICAL KNOWLEDGE

o Like Parsons, and against Marx, Foucault argues that there is more to modern societies than economics. In particular, following Max Weber, he points to the development of bureaucratic surveillance of the population as a dominant feature of society.

o The development of professional groups whose claim is both to understand human beings (knowledge), and to prescribe to them how to act (power), is a central part of his analysis of Western societies.

o Medicine, which Foucault analyses in a historical perspective, provides a case study of this process, in the way in which it constructs our understanding of the body and of disease.

o Foucault's concepts of anatomo-politics (the internalization of scientific concepts of health and normality which are administered by professional groups on the basis of their claim to scientific knowledge) and biopolitics (the linking of the human body to organized knowledge so as to achieve social control) provide a link between the individual and social structures.

There are considerable parallels between the work of Parsons and the French thinker Michel Foucault (1926–1984). Neither considers medicine to be mainly about healing. Both see it as an institution of social control. Both demystify medicine and its claims to scientificness. Both argue that sickness is constructed as deviant behaviour in modern society. For Parsons, this can be the motivated deviance to enter the sick role and avoid social obligations. For Foucault, it is the identification of the sick person as diseased by the 'helping professions' of modern society. Parsons' sick role can be subsumed, in Foucault's theory, as one of the ways in which we develop an internalized self-control, incorporating ideals of 'normal' behaviour.

Foucault: The Most General Picture

The focus on economics as the centre of modern societies, especially in Marx, is inadequate in light of the development of administrative power linked to the state. In a fundamental sense, modern societies are bureaucratic societies, and information needs to be generated, monitored, evaluated and used as the basis of planning. The development of administrative power takes place against the same background as the development of the modern social sciences – criminology, penology, psychology and sociology – and the modern medical sciences and psychiatry. The development of administrative power goes hand in hand with the development of disciplinary power to manage free labour. This disciplinary power contrasts with the exemplary power of violence characteristic of previous ages. Violence, as controlled by state authorities, becomes an underlying sanction – a hidden but available threat – while control is sustained primarily through the disciplinary power of surveillance. By surveillance, Foucault means two closely related phenomena:

1. The collection and organization of information that can be stored by agencies and used to monitor the activities of an administered population.

2. Direct supervision or control of subordinates by superiors in particular organizations – schools, factories, prisons, universities, hospitals and bureaucracies (Giddens, 1987).

The concepts which link these eclectic elements together are anatomo-politics (the politics of the body) and biopolitics (the politics of population). The power over life, of biopower, emerged with the development of the modern state and its need to guarantee the health of its population. On the one hand, there was an increasing concern with the manipulation of the body as a machine, with

> its disciplining, the optimisation of its capabilities, the extortion of its forces, the parallel increase in its usefulness and its docility, its integration into systems of efficient and economic controls, all this was ensured by the procedures of power that characterised the disciplines: an anatomo-politics of the human body. (Foucault, 1976: 139)

On the other hand was the concern with population. This was

> the species body, the body imbued with the mechanics of life and serving as the basis of the biological processes: propagation, births, and mortality, the level of health, life expectancy and longevity and with all the conditions that can cause these to vary. Their supervision was effected through an entire series of interventions and regulatory controls: a biopolitics of the population. (Foucault, 1976: 130)

Foucault's analysis of modern society moves around the three interrelated aspects of the body, power and knowledge. The body is both the target of and is constituted by the power relations focused on it, which render it obedient and docile. These power relations are not external forces but internalized 'self-control'. Power, for Foucault, is an all-embracing aspect of all social relationships in which it flows like an electrical field. It is not something that one group has and the others do not. Thus the medical power which shapes and forms the body is relational; those whose bodies are being shaped in turn react back on medicine.

Foucault's Sociology of Health

Foucault's work, in particular *The Birth of the Clinic* (1973), is a sustained attempt to analyse medical knowledge as the product of a specific historical period. His central argument is that modern medicine is a manifestation of an administered society in which the centralization of information about citizens is essential for social planning. Thus while Marxists focus on the economy, and Parsons on the social system, Foucault focuses on the development of the bureaucratic state in modern societies. Each theorist is identifying different aspects of modern society and this, in part, accounts for their different explanations of the causes and treatment of disease.

One theorist who similarly focuses on state formation, but who draws very different conclusions to Foucault, is Norbert Elias (1978, 1985; see also Goudsblom, 1986). Elias's argument, against Weber and Foucault, is that the developmental process in the West is a progressive, liberalizing and humanizing one. As the title of Elias's two volumes on the development of the West phrases it: we are involved in a civilizing process.

The overlap between the Foucauldian and the Eliasian analysis of health is considerable. Both emphasize the interaction between social structures and the development of personalities – they are both radically sociological in their assessment of how particular people come to be at particular times. They both argue that the history of medicine is not the history of the application of rational, scientific insights: rather, it is the record of cultural, political and economic changes in European society. Where they part company is in their assessment of the impact of these changes. Elias argues that the development of concerns with health and hygiene reflects a broader social movement, which reflects the increased 'delicacy of feeling' (1978: 115) between individuals. Health, and the maintenance of personal hygiene, are a reflection of this change. Further, health becomes the symbol of correct social relationships because, with the democratization of European society and the individualization of personality structures, it becomes a field of practice open to all. Our concern with our bodies and their presentation to others marks a long-term progressive development in European society, and not an administrative coup of a social system out of control.

For Foucault, however, following Weber, the development of scientific medicine, the internalization of norms of hygiene, and the development of a state administrative structure to enforce and coordinate public health are all aspects of Weber's Iron Cage (see Chapter 1). People are more and more cogs in the administered society.

The key to Foucault's analysis is the demographic transition of the late eighteenth and nineteenth centuries (Omran, 1971). In this period there were more live births, and death occurred later; this, combined with economic developments, resulted in the growth of large-scale cities and a crisis of urban control. Foucault argues that as the new cities developed and capitalism matured, new forms of knowledge about people developed.

> If the economic takeoff of the West began with the techniques that made possible the accumulation of capital, it might perhaps be said that the methods of administering the accumulation of men made possible a political takeoff in relation to the traditional, ritual, costly, violent forms of power, which soon fell into disuse and were superseded by a subtle, calculated technology of subjection. In fact the two processes – the accumulation of men and the accumulation of capital – cannot be separated. (Foucault, 1977a: 221)

Disciplines of Knowledge, Disciplines of Power: Power/Knowledge

This new knowledge was of people as objects to be counted and monitored, or, to use Foucault's word, surveyed. The new practices of sanitary science, penology, medicine and industrial hygiene, which all developed at this time, had as their object the interrelations of individuals and their lifestyles. New disciplines of knowledge developed whose aims were to predict and control the behaviour of individuals and to provide the state with information to control and monitor these individuals. Thus Foucault develops a play on words. The new academic 'disciplines' of psychology, psychiatry and medicine, and the social sciences, were also 'disciplines' in the sense of prescribing how people should act and behave, the lifestyles they should adopt, and in establishing norms of behaviour which they could enforce. It is for this reason that Foucault always writes of 'power/knowledge'. Knowledge is not disinterested – it is linked to forms of social control. Importantly, he is also suggesting that power is linked not only to economic relations, but also to the credentialled knowledge of the university. This leads to Foucault's central insight: the development of the modern social and medical sciences is the development of sophisticated power/knowledge of social control. Furthermore, he identifies the way in which these knowledges work through professional groups of helpers and healers, and are internalized by us as subjective realities. The new disciplines established the 'scientific' criteria by which we distinguish categories of people – the sane, the insane, the disabled, the deviant, the criminal and the sick (Foucault, 1967).

---BOX 7.1---

FOUCAULT'S SYNTHESIS OF CLASSICAL SOCIOLOGY

This can be analytically summarized as a description of modern society, in which we can see how Foucault has adapted Marx, Weber and Durkheim. His synthesis is one in which there is the application of scientific principles (rationalization) to an increasingly 'thing'-like body (alienation) in specialized institutions (bureaucratization) in the interests of restoring the individual to normal functioning. In presenting this analysis of modern society, Foucault seeks to link the individual to social structures through the internalization of the norms of society. Thus Foucault provides a twist to the Orwellian fantasy that we are controlled by external technologies of surveillance. Rather, he locates social control in our subjective realities. We have internalized scientific concepts of normality into our daily life.

Foucault's History of Medicine

Following Jewson (1976), we can schematically outline Foucault's history of medicine. The period from the Middle Ages to the eighteenth century was one of *bedside medicine*: doctors were dependent on the patronage of the patient and at their command. Disease was something that happened to the whole person and was conceptualized as a lack of balance in the human being, involving both physical and spiritual factors. The ethos of the period can be summarized in the doctor's question: 'What is the matter with you?' The question underpins a holistic orientation to the patient, and a relationship in which the doctor needed to retain the favour of the patient.

The Industrial Revolution of the nineteenth century and urbanization resulted in the growth of huge hospitals to house the sick, and marks the period of *hospital medicine*. The patient became dependent on the now-professional doctor, while disease became a problem of the pathology of a specific organ, distinct from the whole existence of the individual. The question directed by the doctor at the patient, 'Where does it hurt?', catches many of the characteristics of this period. The medical practitioner wants and elicits only specific information that stays narrowly physical. The patient has to reply or forfeit the right to treatment. From the mid-twentieth century on is the period of *laboratory medicine*, in which both patient and doctor are displaced by scientific tests. A cellular theory of disease is developed. Disease becomes a biochemical process, the domain of scientists and laboratory technicians, in which statistical tests of biological normality displace the patient as person entirely. Healing no longer depends on any charismatic ability of the practitioner, but is caught in the phrase 'Let's wait and see what the tests say'. Thus, in an argument closely following Max Weber, Foucault charts the disenchantment and increasing scientization of life. We learn more and more about the workings of the body as an artefact of the laboratory, and less and less about health and happiness.

The Body

The drive to construct the body as a research topic is the product of social change as well as factors intrinsic to sociological theory.

With changes in social life the body has become a focus of study in anthropology, history, philosophy and sociology. Demographic changes, especially the ageing structure of capitalist societies, and the declining death rate in third world countries, have literally made the number of bodies problematic. The body as a carrier of commodities and lifestyles, whether in the gym, on the jogging track, or in the accoutrements of the fashion label, has highlighted the role of the body as a symbolic marker of social status. Medical technology increasingly renders concepts of a 'natural' body almost impossible to hold, and has highlighted the social shaping of the body. Definitions of death are now clearly seen to be the outcome of professional interest groups, as ways of maintaining bodily function to maintain organ viability are developed. Indeed, the whole area of organ transplant has raised the problem of what constitutes the person and the body. In short, there has developed a widespread interest, from the popular press through to the most arcane of scholarly studies, in the social construction of the body.

Within sociological theory, these social changes have allowed the development of what might be called the 'hidden' agenda of classical sociology – the relationship between knowledge, nature and social structure. For better or for worse, classical sociology has been read as having an implicit correspondence theory of truth – that our knowledge reflects a pre-existing, objective nature – about the way in which both natural and social scientific knowledge are produced. The materialism of Marxism led to a biologism in its accounts of the body, of ethnicity and of gender. The positivism of Durkheim, and the concept of homo duplex (the pre-social, organic self transformed by forms of social solidarity) on the one hand, led to a focus on observable social facts. On the other hand, it led to an exclusion of the body which was construed as a biological imperative, which if taken into account would undermine the attempt to study social facts and would provide the thin edge of the wedge for biological reductionism to enter sociology. Weber, the most relativist of the classical sociologists, both ontologically and epistemologically, did not develop the implications of his work, particularly on discipline, in terms of the body.

The hidden keel of classical sociology, though, was the insight that the production of knowledge, in both the natural and the social sciences, was a social accomplishment. Marx and Engels both critically evaluated Darwinian biology as the product of liberalism and utilitarianism. Durkheim, explicitly in *The Elementary Forms of the Religious Life* (1915), argued that Kant's categories of understanding were grounded, not in the individual's mind, but in the social and moral structure of the society that produced them. Weber pointed out that the content of mathematics (and therefore of the natural sciences) was the product of culture just as was the conscience. In short, within classical sociology there was an ambivalence about the status of nature as an ontological given and about the autonomy of our knowledge of reality: 'nature' was a problematic concept.

It is this insight that has been recaptured by the Foucauldian approach, and which has allowed the hitherto seemingly natural body to become a focus of study. The status of the body, whether defined medically or in racial or gendered terms, has come to be seen as a social accomplishment and not the product of science or nature. The various natural aspects of our existence can be demonstrated to be socially based. On the one hand, our bodies are socially constructed within the context of class, gender and ethnicity, and therefore reflect the structures of legitimation and domination of these structures.

Historical and Metaphorical Representations of the Body

That we live in a world of metaphor and myth is nowhere more clearly illustrated than in our understanding of the body. As Helman has argued, myth and medicine converge on the body. The significance of the media attention to heart transplant patients can only be understood in a context that recognizes that transplanting the heart involves dealing with the most important mythical organ of selfhood. Watch Helman, a surgeon and anthropologist, play with the metaphors for us:

> For a while, after the operation, all those familiar idioms, such as 'to take heart', 'with all my heart', 'from the bottom of my heart', 'a heart to heart talk', had a peculiar new salience, a double meaning both medical and metaphorical. During the operation the recipient was literally 'heartless' for that brief − and now mythological − pause, as the surgeon lifted the old broken heart out of the body, and handed it to an assistant, before replacing it inside the empty chest with the healthier heart of another. In this exchange, both donor and recipient had 'lost their hearts' to one another, so that afterwards, with his heart now 'in the right place', a man who had once been 'sick of heart' could resume his everyday life, as 'hearty' as before. (Helman, 1985: 3)

Similarly, the very first skull-and-scalp transplant in 2015 used a more banal but equally mythical set of metaphors to make sense of the complex procedure. Though the surgeons explained that the transplant largely came down to a matter of 'plumbing', when everything was finally 'flowing' again, 'life' took on an anthropomorphic quality:

'It went from something that was cold and gray and lifeless to something that is pink and healthy and vibrant', Dr Klebuc said; 'You could see the life start to crawl back into the tissue' (Hawryluk, 2015). An event that was otherwise reported in a heavily biological language culminated for the surgeons – and their public – as a mystical experience of the body, its functions and its connection to selfhood.

Understandings of the body reflect their social and cultural period. In medieval times, the body was conceptualized theologically as the reflection of God's divine plan (Alford, 1979). Speech disorders, for example, were seen as manifestations of the effect of the soul on the body, rather than malfunctioning physical parts (O'Neill, 1980). With the development of the modern period and following Descartes, who drew an analogy between the body and the performance of clockwork, the dominant metaphor of the body became the machine.

─BOX 7.2─

THE CARTESIAN VIEW OF THE BODY

The Cartesian heritage has bequeathed three major components to our own socially structured understanding of the body.

- First, it is dualistic: the mind and the body are sharply distinguished, with the body being the subject of the natural sciences and the mind the subject of the human sciences. The two are also thought of as operating independently of each other.

- Second, it has left us with a reductionist image of the priority of the physical over the mental, in both the psychological and medical sciences. The material, physical base is the determinant factor in causal explanations.

- Third, it is positivistic. The argument is that since we are dealing with physical realities, the methods of the natural sciences are the legitimate ones for the study of human beings.

As a consequence, the body is no longer the microcosm of the universe, thought of as reflecting God's ordering of the cosmos, but as a machine reflecting the technical and production concerns of industrial capitalism (Rabinbach, 1990).

The image of the human body as purely natural and separate from social factors has been widely criticized by sociologists. The human body may be described as a physical reality, but it is simultaneously a metaphorical reality. As Foucault has argued, the task of genealogy 'is to expose a body totally imprinted by history and the process of history's destruction of the body' (Foucault, 1977b: 148). The dichotomy of the body as physical reality and the body as metaphor is broken in the analysis of the body as language – and both its physical reality and its metaphysical reality are linguistic accomplishments. The physical body does not exist without its metaphorical accomplishments. At the same time, however, metaphor does not exist in an idealist vacuum. The languages that we use to discuss the body are located in institutions and are bearers of power relationships. In this the body acts as the conduit of our understanding of social life. Thus it has been noted that concepts of the body act as political, social and ideological resources in society – the image of the body shapes our understanding of society, and our understanding of society shapes our understanding of the body.

The body, then, is the site of a complex series of interrelationships, comprising the frontier of society, the social self and the subjectively existing psychobiological individual. Understandings of it will also reflect the interests of dominant classes, as well as individuals' attempts to understand their social location (T. Turner, 1980: 122). This complex set of relationships can be illustrated in an analysis of the wide appeal of physiology books in the nineteenth century to urban audiences. As Cooter has argued, these books on the body provided an image of the body as 'regularity yet change, order yet progress' (Cooter, 1979: 79). Following an examination of the theories of Saint-Simon, Fourier and Comte and of developments in anatomy and physiology, he concludes:

> The physiological interest in differences in organisms (as contrasted with pre-18th century thought which emphasised sameness) which ultimately fed into organismic social theory, arose simultaneously with urban industrial society, not ahead of it or subsequent to it ... we must realise that the origins of the society and its dominant metaphor were in dialectical relationship, feeding off each other and becoming increasingly enmeshed. (Cooter, 1979: 81)

Indeed, it was exactly at this period that the words 'consensus' and 'consensual' came into common use to describe politics and society, but deriving directly from physiology. However, it goes further than just the exchange of words from the field of the natural sciences to the social sciences. In the nineteenth century, the human being became conceptualized as the human motor. As Rabinbach has put it:

> The protean forces of nature, the productive power of industrial machines, and the body in motion were all instances of the same dynamic laws, subject to measurement. The metaphor of the human motor translated revolutionary scientific discoveries about physical nature into a new vision of social modernity. (Rabinbach, 1990: 1)

Foucault's Body

It is these professional and institutional developments of the nineteenth century, Foucault argues, that show the 'body' as a transient social and cultural artefact, and not a part of nature. In the context of medical thought, Foucault argues that the crucial concepts of the body and disease must be seen as historical products. We believe, Foucault points out, 'that the body obeys the exclusive laws of physiology and that it escapes the influences of history, but this too is false. The body is moulded by a great many regimes' (Foucault, 1977b: 153; see Mauss, 1935 [1973] for an earlier analysis).

Foucault's point is that political and economic regimes actually produce the framework within which a human body can be understood. Further, he argues that the scientific understanding of disease and the body that modern society has produced is also historically and politically specific. As he puts it, 'the exact superposition of the "body" of the disease and the body of the sick person is no more than a historical temporary datum' (Foucault, 1973: 13).

Foucault gives special attention to the body because it is centrally located in the disciplines of criminology, medicine and sexology. As a consequence of its location in these fields of power/knowledge, we experience ourselves as subjects and as objects. Put another way, we have an image of our own body, and we are a body. This distinction has been captured in German by two distinct words: 'Leib' is our lived body, and 'Körper' is our physical body (Schilder, 1950). So the paradox is that the perception of our body is fundamental to our sense of self, but as an object, it is what connects us with others by its shared status as black, white, male, female, as the body of a child, a youth or an elderly person. Thus Foucault talks about a biopolitics focused on our bodies and their location in populations. It is on the basis of the establishment of the body by medicine that we are subject to specific mechanisms of social control.

The Anatomico-Metaphysical Register of the Body

Foucault identifies two periods in the conceptualization and control of the body, the transition between them involving a process in which legal and medical transformations are interlinked. These two periods are clearly dependent on Durkheim's distinction between mechanical and organic types of solidarity. Foucault argues that the medicine of the sixteenth and seventeenth centuries produced an anatomico-metaphysical register of the body. By and large, sickness, insanity and criminality were not distinguished. The sole aim of 'therapy' was to physically discipline the body through incarceration, bleeding and leeching, to force it back to 'normality'. Under a system of retributive justice, the focus was on the physical breaking of the body to enforce conformity and obedience, in a society characterized by centralized power.

Technico-Political Register of the Body

Modern medicine, however, produces a technico-political register of the body for submission and use. Rather than breaking the body, the aim is rehabilitation of the body/mind through the regulations of the factory, the prison, the hospital and the asylum. The body has been reconstructed: 'a materialist reduction of the soul and a general theory of dressage, at the centre of which reigns the notion of docility which joins the analysable body to the manipulable body' (Foucault, 1977a: 136). Under a system of restitutive justice the focus is on the moral reintegration of the individual by specialized institutions and workers – hospitals, prisons and asylums, doctors, criminologists, sociologists and psychiatrists. At the centre is the internalization of scientific concepts of 'health' and 'normality', which are administered by professional groups on the basis of their claim to scientific knowledge.

But precisely because the body is the site of social, political, economic and gender struggles to construct it, it is also the site of opposition to that structuring. On the one hand, our bodies are socially constructed within the context of class, gender and ethnicity, and therefore reflect the structures of legitimation and domination of these constructs. On the other hand, the awareness of this social location can open up alternative discourses of resistance, or reform to the structural shaping of our bodily selves, and the reshaping of our bodily selves within the contradictory fields this oppositional discourse provides.

Following the logic of the analysis of the body developed here, it is no accident that the body which Foucault understood may well have passed its historical moment. We can recapture the dynamics of the debate using an analytical model developed by Bryan Turner (Turner, 1992). Foundationalist, anti-constructionist approaches take the body as a given datum and examine the ways in which it impacts on society. In this approach, demographic studies of the relationship of the body to populations are prominent. Anti-foundationalist approaches – that is, social constructionist approaches – see the body as discourse, as the outcome of knowledge/power, and as reflecting in metaphor the material structures of society. The development of the latest imaging technologies in medicine provides a good example.

BOX 7.3

THE QUANTIFIED SELF

Since the 1970s, the technology to monitor our own bodies has steadily increased in sophistication. From simple pedometers to complex microcomputers worn on our bodies, we can monitor our exercise rates, weight loss or gain, blood pressure, sugar levels and cortisol levels. From a Foucauldian perspective, these developments are a new facet in the technologies of the self as, at an ever more finely focused level, we develop ourselves in terms of the prescriptions of the psy-professions to comply with

(Continued)

(Continued)

the normal. In addition, in the statistical representations of our wellbeing, we quantify our self-understanding in what appear to be scientifically objective data, which incorporates us further in the voluntary compliance with neo-liberalism that we manage our own health and wellbeing, while obscuring the structural constraints on individuals and groups to achieve health and wellbeing (Lupton, 2016).

As Williams has shown, the 'physical' body has all but disappeared in modern techno-medicine. We have plastic bodies, 3D-printed bodies, bionic/interchangeable bodies, genetically engineered designer babies, and the virtual bodies of the new surgical techniques in which surgeons operate at a distance via TV screens. These new forms of the body build on the older technological bodies of the ultrasound, the foetal monitor, the stethoscope and the blood count (Williams, 1997). The plasticity of the body is now a taken-for-granted part of medicine, and its users, in the techniques of plastic surgery. Our bodies can be remade on demand, and the expectation is that we will be remade in the process, becoming more socially or sexually desirable as partners. According to Williams, in 1997 there were 600,000 cosmetic surgery operations a year in the USA, with operations doubling in number between 1981 and 1987. As of 2012, that number has increased to 1.7 million operations per year, and is forecast to increase to 3.8 million by 2030 (Broer et al., 2014). We now have bionic/interchangeable bodies, which range from the 'fully' human – with no implants – to those with the titanium hip, the pacemaker and the cochlea ear, and from the fully original with no transplants to those with 'designer' additives of organs, produced by international capitalist firms (Hogle, 1995). In developing his review, Williams follows Frank, who argues that the Foucauldian gaze over the body of the patient has been dissolved with the creation of hyper-real bodies of technological–human blend, with no edges to distinguish the two (Frank, 1992). Bodies, and ourselves, become manifestations of the machines that create and document their 'life criteria'. Bodies are no longer a distinctive category in medical knowledge and practice. In the multiple screens of the VDU, the TV and the MRI, the monitors provide 'multiple images and codings in which the body is doubled and redoubled' (Williams, 1997: 1047).

Conclusion

Foucault's sociology of health has major implications for our understanding of society. In the first place, he rejects any idea that there is an evolutionary process of improvement in Western society. In providing this radical critique of liberal histories of the West, Foucault is at pains to point out that he is not passing judgement on whether or not this is a good system of control, only that it is a system of control.

His disagreement with liberal histories is concerned with their self-understanding of the present being a linear development out of a dark past into a rosy present. For Foucault, history is a series of radical discontinuities, which do not represent a progression towards the truth. Human knowledge depends on the society which gives rise to it, and as societies change so does knowledge, and truth.

All of social life involves power, and while the way power is manifest changes, from breaking the body to controlling the mind, this does not represent an improvement. If anything, it means that the workings of power have become more sophisticated and subtle. Associated with this argument is a reconstruction of how power should be conceptualized. In Marxism, power is wielded by the ruling class to enforce compliance on the part of the working class. In feminism, power is wielded by men to force women to comply with patriarchal images of their social roles. Foucault argues (as does Parsons) that power flows through all social relationships. It is not a tool wielded by one group over another. He develops this point in three ways. First, power does not need to be wielded by a group, since 'power' lies in being hidden: we have internalized the power structures of society to the extent that we are unaware of them. The second point is that if a group is targeted by another with more power, this, in fact, empowers the subjugated group. To be the target of the medical profession, or of the state, is to be empowered by being drawn into a power/knowledge field in which what is at stake is precisely the definition of the subjugated group. Thus to be labelled 'insane', or 'homosexual', or a 'drug addict' allows these groups to dispute their labels. Third, he rejects any idea that how we understand ourselves as individuals is 'natural'. The way that we understand ourselves, Foucault argues, is a product of professional discourses which provide us with a vocabulary to understand ourselves. We internalize these images and then take them for granted. These issues will concern us again in the next chapter as we examine feminist responses to Foucault.

Summary

- With Parsons, Foucault has produced one of the most powerful syntheses of classical social theory in the twentieth century, drawing together the themes of individualization, rationalization and bureaucratic administration.

- His historical analysis of medicine has relativized our understanding of the body as specific to society and not to nature.

- In his analysis of the development of the medical profession, he has demonstrated how modern society is dependent on individuals internalizing norms of correct behaviour, which are based on a claimed scientific foundation, and enforced by professional groups with state sanctions to back them up.

- His argument that power is diffuse in social relationships has challenged theories which emphasize its control by specific groups – either by capitalists or patriarchal men.

Discussion Questions

1. Modern medicine is a key part of our surveillance society. What does Foucault mean by this?

2. The social function of modern medicine according to Foucault is to make us monitor ourselves according to definitions of normality developed by the psy-professions. Can you think of the ways you comply with these definitions?

3. How does Foucault argue that the body is shaped by historical and social factors?

Further Reading

Armstrong, D. (1995) 'The Rise of Surveillance Medicine.' *Sociology of Health and Illness* 17: 393–404. Armstrong has worked extensively in the Foucauldian tradition and is very accessible.

Armstrong, D. (2002) *A New History of Identity: A Sociology of Medical Knowledge*. Basingstoke: Palgrave. A social and political history of medical texts using a Foucauldian framework.

Dreyfus, H. and Rabinow, P. (1982) *Michel Foucault: Beyond Structuralism and Hermeneutics*. Brighton: Harvester Press. This is still one of the best overviews of Foucault's work and is particularly good on biopower.

Turner, B. S. (1992) *Regulating Bodies*. London: Routledge. This brings together a series of essays on the body which use a Foucauldian approach.

8

HEALTH, GENDER AND FEMINISM

o In this chapter I argue that there are more women patients because of their social role, and because of the medicalization of their life cycle. It is not because they are biologically sicker than men.

o I represent the medicalization thesis, showing how it is particularly useful for understanding the patriarchal medical construction of women as inferior to men, and specifically of the use of medical technology to subordinate women.

o At the same time, there is wide diversity in feminist analyses of medical practices and knowledges, which are presented here, especially Marxist feminism and Foucauldian feminism.

o Foucauldian feminists have made important contributions to the social construction of the body, and to analysing screening programmes as forms of surveillance and medicalization of well women.

o The chapter concludes with an examination of the impact of gender roles on men's health.

In general, feminist health sociologists argue that medicine and patriarchy control women by enforcing passivity, dependence and submission as appropriate feminine traits. By focusing on the individual rather than their social location, doctors reproduce the situations that lead women to the surgery in the first place. Treating depression with drugs reinforces the traditional role of women which they are seeking to escape. In this the feminists also point to the role of multinational drug companies, who in their advertising 'reinforce patriarchal, sexist attitudes, medical authority [and] patient powerlessness' (Seaman, 1987: 35).

Aspects of women's lives surrounding their reproductive capacity have also been medicalized. Menstruation (Montgomery, 1974), premenstrual syndrome

(Figert, 1995; Laws, 1983; Offman and Kleinplatz, 2004), infertility (Becker and Nachtigall, 1992) and menopause (Bell, 1990; Kaufert, 1982) provide good examples. The early work of Young and Bacadayan (1965) attempted to develop a sociological analysis of menstrual taboos against biological and psychological theories. Analysing transcultural responses to menstruation, and therefore its cultural variability, they pointed to male solidarity as a form of social rigidity, and to the lack of communication between gendered groups as giving rise to menstrual taboos (Young and Bacadayan, 1965). The emphasis of these studies is on the symptomatology as the outcome of sociological factors of women's role in society. In this context, even the medically described physiological changes – osteoporosis and bone fractures in menopause, for example – must be seen to be in need of social appraisal rather than a straightforward case for clinical explanation (Townsend and Carbone, 1980). In the medical model, when dealing with menopause, doctors go to the extremes of either dismissing any symptoms as 'only to be expected', treating menopause as an illness requiring medication, or by offering psychological explanations. Each approach 'intentionally or unintentionally, amounts to a repression of the woman concerned' (Leeson and Gray, 1978: 103).

Women's illnesses are both a consequence of and a response to patriarchal society. In feminist analyses, medicine is shown to define women by their biology and their reproductive capacity: menses, pregnancy and menopause. Feminist sociologists also argued that medicine labels women's resistance to their social roles with a special set of diseases, for example hysteria, chlorosis, agoraphobia and anorexia nervosa. When defined as medical problems, which can only be resolved with medical solutions, women lose control of fundamental aspects of their experience – fertility, sexuality, menopause and ageing (Oakley, 1984). In a self-described 'radical feminist' study, Denny argued that in vitro fertilization, a seemingly female-centric technology, is actually just a new method for patriarchal medicine to force women to realize their social role through reproduction: 'Although IVF is promoted as a treatment for infertility, the emphasis on technology is about control of reproductive capacity. ... In radical feminist ideology women's desire for children is fueled by pro-natalist ideology and exploited by men eager to master nature' (1994: 70).

The history of modern medicine and its treatment of women is the history of the subordination of women. As Barker-Penfield (1979) pointed out, gynaecology was used to attack the first wave of feminism. Obstetricians and gynaecologists located the cause of women's 'problems' in the vagina and castrated women in their thousands. The explicit aim of the operation was to restore women to their normal social roles of housewife and mother. As gynaecology developed through the 1950s, a large number of complaints were seen as the product of the woman's rejection of femininity. Conditions which gynaecologists considered to be psychogenic, or caused by incomplete feminization, included: dysmenorrhoea, excessive pain in labour, menstrual irregularity, pelvic pain, infertility, a tendency to miscarry or deliver prematurely, excessive nausea in pregnancy, toxaemia of pregnancy and complications of labour (Ehrenreich and English, 1978; Holmes, 1980; Leeson and Gray, 1978).

In patriarchal medicine, women's bodies are defined in contrast to the good, healthy, male body, and found wanting. Hence women are, by definition, inferior, sicker and more at risk of biological disorder than men. In performing this analysis, patriarchal medicine moves from social category (of mother, of houseworker, of carer) to biological category (of menstruating, pregnant and menopausal) and combines by sleight of hand the two, obscuring the social basis of women's 'problems'. Women are sicker and more in need of treatments for what medicine claims to be biological problems. Women are medically constructed as inferior and sicker on account of their reproductive capacity.

Why are there More Women Patients?

Sociologists have traditionally distinguished between 'sex', which is biologically given in male and female, and 'gender', which is the learned social roles that go with being masculine or feminine. This distinction is currently under examination, since it is clear that the biological base is itself constructed by social groups and does not exist independently as some fact of nature. However, the distinction does allow us to focus on the ways in which being socialized as a woman will affect your experience of health and illness.

—BOX 8.1—

WHY ARE THERE MORE WOMEN PATIENTS? AN OVERVIEW

- The medicalizing of reproduction
- Screening programmes
- Caretaker roles
- Social role of mother and housewife
- The dangers of the 'cottage industry' of housework
- Marriage
- Feminization of poverty
- Socialization into presenting symptoms to doctors

The two consistent findings relating to the health of women are that they are diagnosed as suffering from more ill health and, paradoxically, that they live longer. In Australia, women's life expectancy is greater than men's, while non-Aboriginal women live longer than Aboriginal women (Australian Institute of Health and Welfare, 2006, 2014). However, between the ages of 15 and 44 women are *hospitalized* at a higher rate than men. This is largely because this is their period of reproduction; outside of these years they are hospitalized less than men (Department of Health and Ageing, 2005). Women go to the doctor more than men do – not just during their reproductive years, but throughout their entire life. In Australia, women visit the GP up to 20 per cent more often than men (Australian Bureau of Statistics, 2012a). In part this is due to antenatal care and family planning. Women are systematically targeted in *screening programmes* for cervical cancer and breast cancer, which urge them to have check-ups on a regular basis. The collection of statistical data in a positivistic way – in a way that predefines the reality to be known as the healthy functioning of women's reproductive organs – tells us little about women's health. Furthermore, it obscures the fact that what we do know about the health care that women receive is that it is often about reproduction and not illness.

Women are also over-represented in the health statistics as a consequence of their *caretaker* roles of children, for taking responsibility for other adults in the household, and for their extended family (Abel and Nelson, 1990; Berg and Woods, 2009). Women's role as the caretaker of infants and children, especially when they are sick or receiving preventative health services, contributes to the medicalization of women (Prout, 1988). Since the 1950s, the medical profession has been attributing disorders in children – asthma, colic, eczema – to psychological disorders in mothers (Contratto, 1984), and mothers seeking medical advice on behalf of their children are met with prejudice, hostility and derision (Lennane and Lennane, 1973). The mother is often given drugs – tranquillizers – to treat her for her child's problem (Phillips, 1983).

Medical assumptions about women can affect the doctor–child–mother relation-ship in other ways. The way that women respond to their disabled children, for example, raises tensions with medical practitioners. The medical professional focuses on the biomedical aspects of the disability and seeks to restrict the discussion to the language of medical science. Consequently, the family's perception of the condi-tion is seen as unrealistically hopeful, overly emotional and confused. However, an in-depth study of six mothers parenting disabled children found that, in contrast to the medical professionals' perspective, the mothers were quite aware of their posi-tion, which was an 'embrace of paradox'. This allowed them to control the swings between hopelessness and hope, between love for the child and a wish that the dis-ability could be eradicated, between long-term planning and short-term insecurity. Being aware of and coping with these paradoxes enabled the mothers to cope and maintain an orientation of hopefulness (Larson, 1998).

The salient point in these studies is that women are over-represented in the health system, not just because they are sick, but because childcare and birth have been medicalized, and because women are held responsible for the health of other adults in their domestic environment.

Women taking on the major burden of care is also linked to structural economic change. The contraction of the Welfare State, for example, has meant that the care of the disabled and the elderly are pushed back on women in the home as unpaid labour. Under neo-liberal health policies, health care is shifted from the public to the private sphere. Minimally, 15 per cent of working-age women in Britain are *caring* for the sick, the elderly or the disabled, often with enormous impacts on their own health and wellbeing (Carers UK, 2004; Opie, 1991, 1992). Women also have more contact with the health-care system either as caretakers of the aged and/or because they are over-represented among the elderly.

Early research suggested that while *marriage* was beneficial for men's mental health, it was a negative factor in women's mental health (Bernard, 1972). There is some evidence now though that marriage is healthy for women, and leads to fewer assaults and to fewer non-fatal accidents (Cheung, 1998). Family roles also appear to be good for women. As Arber has argued: 'Family roles are important for women; women without children and previously married women have particularly poor health status especially those not in paid employment and living in local authority housing' (Arber, 1991: 425). It is notable, though, that this account is cut through with the wider problem of poverty, a burden that is systematically distributed by gender and affecting divorced women most. The *feminization of poverty*, then, sets up a vicious cycle wherein women's health is put at greater risk; they have fewer resources to cope with it, and in turn get sicker (Chant, 2012; Gimenez, 1989). It is hard to draw any strong conclusions about the impact of caring roles and paid work on women's health. On balance, the most likely conclusion is that paid work protects women from the stresses of their nurturing role and enhances their self-image (Lennon and Rosenfield, 1992).

The over-representation of women in the health system is also a result of the *social roles* women are forced into, which are unhealthy in and of themselves and becoming more so. They have lower status, work for longer hours, have lower wages, do more unpaid work, have greater social and emotional commitments, and get fewer hours of sleep and leisure (Bird and Fremont, 1991). There is evidence too that the house is physically a dangerous *workplace*. Women homeworkers have been found to have high cancer rates, which may be attributable to the unregulated toxic materials in the 'cottage industry' of the home (Morton and Ungs, 1979). Exposure to pesticides in the home is now implicated in the cause of Parkinson's disease, with an American study finding a 70 per cent increase in the risk of getting Parkinson's among those who used household insecticides for the equivalent of a 70-day period. Even those in the lowest exposure group had a 40 per cent increase in the chance of getting Parkinson's (Stephenson, 2000). Doyal has reported that of the 6245 deaths in home accidents in 1971, 35.3 per cent happened to men, while 64.7 per cent happened to women (Doyal and Pennell, 1979: 74). In 2005, Australian women were twice as likely as men to be part of accidents in a home – both their own and someone else's (Australian Bureau of Statistics, 2006).

The final factor in providing an explanation for the apparent high numbers of sick women is that women and men are *socialized* to experience and report their bodily sensations differently. Women are more likely to consult doctors on how they feel, whereas men are more likely to avoid a consultation unless it is based on physical factors. It is for this reason that men are less likely to be diagnosed as suffering from stress or depression, and more likely to be diagnosed as having a physical ailment (Verbrugge, 1989).

These assumptions about the health and mental states of women flow through to prescribing habits. In a 1996 study, the prescription habits of doctors were monitored with a startling discovery:

> One physician we observed consistently recommended one particular migraine drug to male patients and another to females. When queried about this, he said that the medication he suggests to men is his true drug of choice for migraine. But because the drug can also cause weight gain, he does not recommend it to his female patients. (Forsythe, 1996: 567)

BOX 8.2

PATRIARCHAL MEDICINE – PRESCRIBING, TREATING AND DIAGNOSING WOMEN

- An Australian study found that, independently of presenting complaints, women are *prescribed* more antibiotics, hormones, and drugs affecting the central nervous, cardiovascular and urogenital systems. They also receive more drugs for allergies and immune system disorders, ear and nose problems, topical applications and skin preparations (Sayer and Britt, 1997).

- Clear differences in the *treatment* of men and women also come out in directions by the doctor to restrict activities. The likelihood of being prescribed activity restrictions is four times higher for female patients of male physicians than men with equivalent physical symptoms (Safran et al., 1997).

- In contested diseases – that is, ones in which there is no medical unanimity about the condition, such as chronic fatigue syndrome – women are more likely to be *diagnosed* as having a psychiatric disorder. In one study, 85 per cent of women presenting with what could be chronic fatigue syndrome were given a psychiatric diagnosis, while only 30 per cent of men were so diagnosed (Broom and Woodward, 1996).

Pharmaceutical advertising can also reinforce the gendered construction of particular illnesses or conditions. Take the distinction between migraines and cluster headaches, for example. Migraines are classified by the World Health Organization as 19th in the top 20 debilitating human conditions (World Health Organization, 2004). Cluster headache is rarer than migraine but has been said to have such extreme pain that it has been nicknamed 'suicide headache'. Though they are both, at their core, simply extreme versions of a headache, their epidemiology is vastly different. Migraines affect 19 per cent of females and only 6.1 per cent of males (Miller et al., 2007: 142), whereas cluster headaches affect men more than females at a rate of 5:1 (Lance, 1982: 207). Kempner studied patterns of advertising by pharmaceutical companies for migraine treatments. Her results indicated that by consistently marketing these products towards women, pharmaceutical companies help to create the impression that migraine is a 'women's disorder', in turn ensuring that women are more likely than men to seek help for, and be diagnosed with, migraines (Kempner, 2006).

Conversely, cluster headaches have been marketed, characterized and treated as hyper-masculine phenomena. John Graham, one of the pioneers of headache studies, constructed the profile of the cluster headache sufferer as 'ambitious [and] hard-working'; they are 'a harder-drinking and harder-smoking lot' than their fellows; they have 'athletic prowess' and are 'red-blooded'; overall, 'theirs is a male disease' (Graham, 1972: 181–2). Compare this to the profile of the migraine sufferer, who is 'neurotic', 'prone to excess amounts of stress' and 'generally unable to cope with daily life' (Diamond and Solomon, 1999: 48). The effect of these profiles means that whereas cluster headache sufferers are pitied for their debilitating condition, and told to help prevent and treat their episodes actively with intense physical activity (Manzoni and Torelli, 2005: 118), migraineurs are blamed for the burden they put on their loved ones and the health-care system (Broom, 1989: 122; Stovner et al., 2007: 193) and are told to respond passively, to take sedative medication, lie quietly in dark rooms, and isolate themselves until the episode has passed and they no longer present a difficulty to those around them.

Regardless of the actual biological differences between migraines and cluster headaches, the construction of their epidemiology has serious consequences for the wellbeing of both male and female headache sufferers. Men are not allowed to be ill unless their illness is appropriately 'masculine', and women are disempowered, individualized, and blamed for being sick at all.

Medicalization

The medicalization of women is an all-pervasive aspect of their lives in modern society. Even the words used to describe women in medical textbooks – which are supposedly scientific – are pejorative. Take, for example, 'infantile' uterus, 'failed' trial of labour, or placental 'insufficiency'. As Pfeffer points out, there are also 'irregular' menstrual cycles, hormonal 'imbalances', 'hostile' cervical mucus, 'irregular' shedding of the lining of the uterus, along with 'blighted' ovum and 'incompetent' cervixes (Pfeffer, 1985).

Medicalization can be demonstrated to work at the institutional level, where it is reflected in diagnosis and treatment. A web of powerful social assumptions underlie medical thinking about women. Women are less likely to receive treatment for physical conditions and are diagnosed as having 'psychosomatic problems'.

This deferral of treatment can mean that when women are finally treated they are older and sicker, and therefore less likely to benefit from treatment. Medicine reinforces the image of women as emotional, passive, despondent, feminine, seductive, manipulative, subjective and untrustworthy. These assumptions shape the doctor–patient interaction. A study of the interactions between male doctors and middle-aged female patients found that 'women were remorselessly confirmed in traditional family and domestic roles and more than one instance of a woman's refusal to do housework resulted eventually in hospitalisation and electro-convulsive therapy' (Barrett and Roberts, 1978). Further, the higher the status of the doctor the more sexist and unequal the doctor–patient relations became.

Are Women More Depressed than Men?

Women are diagnosed as 'mad' more than men. Men are not labelled mad, but 'bad'. Men are criminal, violent and imprisoned, while women are depressed, treated more with ECT and insulin shock therapy, as well as psycho-surgical techniques such as lobotomies. Those women most at risk of being diagnosed mad are the married, those with children and the unemployed (Ussher, 1991).

It is a well-established finding from the earliest sociological analyses of psychiatry (Brown and Harris, 1978) that women are diagnosed as depressed more than men, and the pattern has gone virtually unchanged over a 20-year period (Meltzer et al., 1995). Indeed, the statistics are quite staggering, with women having a 50 to 100 per cent higher incidence of depression than men. Research in the USA suggests that women are two-thirds more likely to be diagnosed as depressed than men (Bertakis et al., 2001; Kessler et al., 1994).

There is no evidence that there are any biological explanations for the differences in depression rates between men and women (Harris et al., 1991). It can be argued that gonadal steroids affect the central nervous system structure and functioning. But even if this is so, researchers exploring the issue have pointed out that the effect of the androgens 'may be context dependent, with the context determined by a person's past history, expectations, environment and biological substrate' (Rubinow and Schmidt, 1996: 984).

It has been argued that women do not have a higher rate of depression, but that women seek health interventions more often when they experience low levels of ill health. This gets taken up as depression, especially on self-scaled questionnaires and in averaging women's depression across a range of scales, and results in an over-representation of apparent depression (Bertakis et al., 2001; Newman, 1984).

In comparison with biological explanations, there is considerable support for the argument that the different depression rates can be explained by the different roles that women have. When men and women have been exposed to the same stressful (but not gender-specific) occurrences, they have the same rates of depression (Nazroo et al., 1997). When women are exposed to stress around children, housing and reproduction, they have higher rates of depression (Nazroo et al., 1998).

This appears to be supported by studies which show not that women are more depressed than men, but that they are most noticeably diagnosed as depressed when they are of childbearing age (Bebbington, 1996). It also appears to be the case that men and women respond differently to stress and that men internalize stress and anger, while women express it. There is some support for this argument, in that if you count alcohol abuse and drug dependency in men, then their rates of psychiatric disorder can equal that of women. Put another way, what women report as depression, men mask with drinking (Kessler et al., 1994; Meltzer et al., 1995). This is supported by British data, which show that while women are diagnosed more with major depressive disorder, agoraphobia and simple phobias, men are diagnosed more with alcohol abuse, substance abuse and antisocial personality disorders (Jenkins et al., 1998).

Against this background set of findings and general characterization of feminist accounts of medicine, we have to set the contributions of specific forms of feminism.

Different Forms of Feminism

Feminism is neither unitary nor internally coherent as a social theory. Rather it is made up of diverse and contradictory strands. A distinction can be made between the different theoretical bases of the various strands – liberal, radical, Marxist and Foucauldian – and this has implications for the analyses of medicine and explanations of health and disease in contemporary society. The general concepts of feminism have also been criticized by postmodernist feminists as being part of modernist social theory. The confidence of asserting that 'patriarchy' did or does something to women, that there is an all-pervasive male gaze, and that power is centralized in the patriarchal institutions of the state have all undergone significant challenges (Barrett, 1992). So too has the idea that womanhood, or the feminine, is a universal and intrinsic characteristic of women. Rather, the fluidity of concept and of the variability in the practices of what it is to be 'a woman' have been held up by poststructuralists and postmodernists, as well as activists from non-European, non-middle class and non-academic backgrounds (Anthias and Yuval-Davis, 1993).

Liberal Feminism

One of the basic tenets of liberalism is that the economic fate of every individual should be determined through their own efforts rather than by birth or heredity. This claim is manifest in various Equal Opportunities Commissions, which demand equal opportunities for women in the job market and the right to move to the upper reaches of it. There should be equal rights for women before the law, to jobs, pay, access to education and promotion. By contrast, but following the same logic, cultural feminists may sometimes be lined up with liberal feminists, emphasizing the caring and nurturing aspects of motherhood and that this should be emphasized to give women a legitimate place in society. Equality will come about by developing an essentially different role for women in society. Furthermore, by doing this, women will develop spiritual power and liberation by being in touch with their bodies (Rossi, 1977).

Liberal feminists focus on the clear inequalities in women's participation in medicine, and especially in the specialities. Where women do get into postgraduate medicine, it is often in the spheres of psychiatry and paediatrics – two areas associated with care and nurturing. The patriarchal nature of the medical profession can also be demonstrated in the gendered structure of the medical workforce. The overall numbers of women entering medical training have been increasing. However, women graduates do not tend to go on to postgraduate work, or to positions in teaching hospitals. They typically end up in part-time GP work, with smaller caseloads and lower fees than their male colleagues (Thomson, 1998). For liberal feminists, medical knowledge is not problematic. The problem is the lack of equality for women to participate in it.

Liberal feminism is open to the same critique as liberalism in general. It overlooks the structured relations of power that exist in society in terms of economic power, and in terms of patriarchal power. Neither more working-class doctors nor more feminist ones will transform the class or patriarchal structure of society. Equalizing participation rates of men and women in medicine without changes in the material structures of society will not transform medical practices.

Radical Feminism

Radical feminism asserts the fundamental biological differences between men and women. Woman's body is privileged over man's, and it is in women's interest to wrest control of their fertility and reproductive abilities from men (Rich, 1992). For radical feminists, the family is the basis of the hierarchical sexual division of labour, and must be overthrown. Women are in a class of their own and the sexual division of labour is the most basic form of oppression. Firestone identifies women's role in childbearing as the cause of their oppression. Only when technology relieves them of this role will freedom be possible (Firestone, 1974).

Radical feminism claimed to be quite new and distinct from liberal feminism and Marxist feminism. With its claim that women's oppression was the source of all oppression, it was especially concerned with control of fertility and reproduction by men, and the way that this was manifest in the ideologies and daily practices of marriage, compulsory heterosexuality and motherhood. At the same time, radical feminism obscured the ways in which patriarchy is produced in specific historical moments. Patriarchy is political and not biological. The differences between men and women are presented differently depending on other circumstances. Ann Oakley, for example, charts the social, political and economic contingencies that shaped medical ideas about pregnancy. In war time, when there was no need to keep women out of the workforce, there was no discussion of their 'feminine' weaknesses (Oakley, 1984).

Marxist Feminism

The original formulation (Zaretsky, 1976) of Marxist feminism draws on Engels' argument in *The Origins of the Family, Private Property and the State* (Engels, 1948 [1884]). The initial division of labour is the family and it is based on both the existence of private property and biology. Within the family, which was a form of slavery dependent on the 'free' labour of the wife, Engels argued that the husband was the bourgeois and the wife the proletariat. The origin of this relationship was the fact that women bear children and therefore have a greater degree of certainty than men who the fathers of their offspring are. In a capitalist society, the owners of capital need to ensure that they are passing their property on to their legitimate heirs, hence the rigid control of their wives' fertility.

For more recent Marxist feminism, the interface between patriarchy and capitalism shapes women's health, as well as the ways in which the caring and nurturing roles of women are constructed as natural (Benoit and Heitlinger, 1998). Much of the literature on women's caring roles in society assumes that this is a natural function of women. Caring and femininity are presented as part and parcel of the biologically given nature of women. Feminist sociologists, anthropologists and historians are more alert to the variations that occur across societies and time in how women behave, and in what roles they perform. Caring is a highly variable activity that may under some circumstances not be the woman's role at all. In our society, Marxist feminists argue that women's caring role is a direct outcome of the interrelations of capitalism and patriarchy. Woman's role as a carer ensures in the first place that she is constructed as an unnoticed labourer in the private domain of the home, providing unpaid labour which reproduces both her husband and children. This is done at no cost to capital, which benefits by exploiting the husband as worker in the present, and the children in the future. The emotional, physical and social organization of the household and childrearing (that is, caring) is defined in capitalist society as not labour and not work.

Furthermore, this undervaluing of women's caring is reflected in the occupational structure of capitalist patriarchal societies. Women are over-represented in nursing, teaching, social work and, increasingly, general practice. They are marginalized from the rewards of the full-time, technology-driven, 'hard' specialist professions, and their caring work is seen simultaneously as part of – but not legitimate – work activities. Thus the Marxist feminists have a very different account of the way in which the medical and healing labour force is organized than liberal and radical feminists. While gender shapes the overall pattern of health care, specific features of the economy and state in different countries are also important (see Benoit and Heitlinger, 1998).

Patriarchal Science and Medicine

While organized feminist movements have identified sources of women's oppression in the political and private arenas, others have been developing arguments about the very structure of medical knowledge as sexist and patriarchal. Feminist sociologists of knowledge have raised key issues about the status of medical knowledge (Grosz, 1988; Smith, 1995). If science is disinterested, objective and 'factual' knowledge, then how does it participate in the subordination of women? Many feminists accept that there are social processes surrounding science, for example at the level of funding, or of the number of women in positions of power, but not in its subject matter. However, fact making in medicine is never straightforward or guided simply by science. Knowledge is always partial and perspectival, and always reflects the interests of those who generate it. As Evelyn Fox-Keller has put it, 'in characterising scientific and objective thought as masculine, the very activity by which the knower can acquire knowledge is genderised' (Fox-Keller, 1985: 79).

Grosz has identified three ways in which medical knowledge reflects masculinist interests (Grosz, 1988). First, it is sexist in the sense of discriminating against women by distinguishing them from the more positively valued image of men. This may be very clear, as in studies asserting that women have smaller brains. More commonly, it is through ignoring women entirely. An analysis of the articles published in the *Journal of the American Medical Association* between 1990 and 1992 found that women are under-represented in clinical trials. Among studies of non-gender-specific diseases, women were under-represented – excluded from, or were less than one-third of the subjects – in nearly three times as many studies as were men (Bird, 1994). Many major tests of new drugs or treatments do not include women in their sample population, even if the drugs are for use on women. It was only in 1986 that the National Institutes of Health in the USA, noting that there were few scientific data on women's health, issued a policy to encourage the inclusion of women in clinical scientific trials (Public Health Services, 1985). Notwithstanding this, the Institutes were unable to enforce the recommendation, and some very famous medical trials were initiated without women subjects at all.

BOX 8.3

FAMOUS CLINICAL TRIALS WITH NO WOMEN SUBJECTS

- The Physician's Health Study of 1988, which is supposed to demonstrate the effect of aspirin on reducing the risk of cardiovascular disease, is based on a clinical study of 22,071 men – with no women participants.

- The Multiple Risk Factor Intervention Trial, which studied coronary heart disease risk factors, used a sample of 15,000 men.

- The Baltimore Longitudinal Study on Aging, carried out between 1958 and 1978, contained no women and issued a report in 1984 on 'normal human aging' which made no reference to women (Auerbach and Figert, 1995).

The medical assumption is that what works for men will work for women, but there is no evidence to support this position, and in fact, as Bird (1994) suggests, in adopting such a strategy women's lives are being put at risk.

Second, Grosz argues that medicine is patriarchal in its claims about knowledge. Men are rational, logical, clear and unemotional; women are the opposite. Male knowledge is objective, truthful and independent, while women's knowledge is intuitive, emotional and unreliable. Third, medical knowledge is phallocentric: women are represented in general terms that refer only to male characteristics.

Feminism and the Critique of Technology

The feminist critique of medical knowledge has been extended to a critique of medical technology. Technical innovations are always socially located in their practices and outcomes. The technical is not the application of rational, scientific knowledge to self-evident practical problems. Technical innovation is a political process that is always linked to power relations. Feminists argue that Western science and technology embody stereotypical male values of domination, control, power and objectivity. In terms of women, they result in medically invasive solutions to the socially constructed images of women as problematic. This feminist critique of technology demonstrates the way in which technology both is produced out of social relations and shapes social relationships. Nowhere is this clearer than in the area of reproductive technology. The concern is that the new technologies will be used to construct women as 'mother machines' (Corea, 1985) and as 'living laboratories' (Rowland, 1992). The conversion of women into 'scientific' spare parts is shown in medical language 'of disembodied parts of women – "the ovaries", "ripe eggs", and recovering these parts even as they materially scrutinise, alter or remove these parts of women's bodies' (Steinberg, 1990: 86).

The claim that technological innovations represent improvements in the area of childbirth has been challenged. The start of the modern period of technical intervention into childbirth was in the seventeenth century, with attempts to measure the birth canal (Wertz, 1980). This link between a mechanistic view of the body and childbirth culminates in the current construction of childbirth, in which women are 'fragmented into body parts by the practices of scientific medicine' (Martin, 1987: 21). Even allowing for some weakening of this paradigm in the transition away from the body as machine, there has been a more subtle form of social control through the ideology of natural childbirth, which has increased medical control into the post-birth period (Arney, 1982). The technology of artificial insemination and reproduction has also been analysed as a specifically laboratory approach to the problem of women's infertility. Instead of putting money into screening for the well-known causes of infertility such as chlamydia, it is put into high-technology, capital-intensive, laboratory-based research. The public portrayal of this is one in which the marvels of science are linked to the magic of motherhood (Bunkle, 1984).

─BOX 8.4─

UNJUSTIFIED TECHNICAL INTERVENTIONS
IN PREGNANCY

There is continued technical intervention in pregnancy on no established medical grounds and this runs against the findings of major World Health Organization research and guidelines for best practice. Obstetricians continue to use a range of technical practices for which there are no clear scientific grounds. A study of 98 hospitals and 3160 low-risk births found extensive evidence of unwarranted interventions in the delivery (Williams et al., 1998):

- routine ultrasound scanning, routine foetal electronic monitoring during birth, induction, the prone position during labour (when the evidence is that the upright position is better), operative vaginal birth, artificial rupture of the membranes, Caesarean section and episiotomy;

- high rates of intervention for low-risk groups, and of substantial geographical variation in procedures: 72 per cent of the women had more vaginal examination than was expected; 53 per cent had artificial ruptures of the membrane; 38 per cent of the labours were augmented (again with substantial regional variation); 28 per cent had spinal blocks; over 25 per cent had instrumental delivery; and 46 per cent had an episiotomy (again with substantial regional variation).

At the same time that these medical 'breakthroughs' have been introduced, there has been no decrease in cerebral palsy rates in the past 30 years; low birth-weight rates have not gone down; and maternal mortality rates have not decreased in the past 10 years (Wagner, 1998: 30). What motivates the obstetricians are a range of non-medical factors. First, different countries have different standards of practice. For example, in Britain and its former colonies, forceps delivery is the norm, while in Europe it is vacuum extraction. Convenience of delivery time plays a large part in medical decision making, with the majority of inductions occurring on weekdays – as do emergency Caesarean sections. Fear of being sued also leads to a highly interventionist management of birth. In private fee-for-service hospitals the profitability of multiple interventions drives over-provision, as do the commercial investments of medical entrepreneurs in equipment such as electronic foetal monitors. Neither the interests of the patient, nor justified medical grounds, account for the behaviour of the obstetricians.

FOUCAULT AND FEMINISM AND THE BODY

It is within feminist thought that the most detailed examination of the social and gendered structuring of the body has occurred. It is through the practices of our bodies that we experience our sense of male- and femaleness (Gray and Saggers, 1994; Grosz, 1988; Grosz and De Lepervanche, 1988). The link to Foucault is in his analysis of power and of the body. As he put it:

> When I think of the mechanics of power, I think of its capillary form of existence, of the extent to which power seeps into the very grain of the individuals, reaches right into their bodies, permeates their gestures, their posture, what they say, how they learn to live and work with other people. (cited in Martin, 1989: 6)

For example, this has been explored in an examination of the learned throwing styles of boys and girls:

> There is a specific positive style of feminine body comportment and move-ment, which is learned as the girl comes to understand that she is a girl ... The more the girl assumes her status as feminine, the more she takes her-self to be fragile and immobile, and the more she actively enacts her own body inhibition. (Young, 1990: 153)

Women's movements and bodily presentations are restricted by cultural mores of modesty; and the routines of women's daily lives are made up of make-up and beauty practices which constitute her body in the ideal of femininity. Out of these practices, the woman's body is produced, 'a practised and subjected body' (Bartsky, 1988: 71) of inferior status to men's.

Both feminists and Foucault have pointed to the centrality of the body in social relationships (Butler, 1993). The body is the focus of professional monitoring by doctors, the site at which we internalize social norms of correct appearance and dressage. Many commentators have welcomed a symbiotic blending of both femi-nism and Foucault (Crowley and Himmelweit, 1992; Flax, 1987; Hennessy, 1993). This is because Foucault's view of power as an ever-present yet diffuse aspect of social relationships allows feminists to provide an account of how it is that women incorporate, as well as resist, patriarchal images of their body. Following Foucault's argument, that to be targeted by those wielding power is itself to be empowered, also provides feminism with a sense of women as active agents (Bordo, 1985: 93).

The adoption by women bodybuilders of the male aesthetics of body shapes demonstrates (to the women in an empowering sense and to the men in a threaten-ing sense) that the body can be moulded independently of biological understandings of its limits (Mansfield and McGinn, 1993). The utility of taking on aspects of the

(Continued)

(Continued)

male discourse is further illustrated by Waterhouse in a study of the adoption of male dress by lesbians in the nineteenth century (Waterhouse, 1993). While potentially entrapping the women inside the masculinist discourse of viewing potential sexual partners as objects, cross-dressing simultaneously provided the only avenue for lesbian women to see each other. Alternatively, the dominant discourse of female subjugation to male desire can be held at bay, as Edwards shows in her study of prostitutes, not by taking on aspects of the dominant male discourse (body shape or dress) but by withholding access to parts of the body associated with acts of intimacy – most notably kissing the mouth (Edwards, 1993).

The Foucauldian-feminist position allows us to explore the paradoxes of medicalization.

> In a society that relies heavily on the authority of the scientific explanations of reality, it seems only 'natural' that women would want a scientific-medical explanation for their feelings and the experiences of their bodies. Pointing out and documenting just how the 'natural' is really 'social' or 'cultural' is the particular contribution of the sociological perspective. (Auerbach and Figert, 1995: 124)

Take, for example, the disputes among feminists about the existence of premenstrual syndrome (Laws, 1983) and menopausal syndrome (Kaufert, 1982; Townsend and Carbone, 1980). To accept the condition as a 'real' one gives women an explanation of their feelings, and provides a valid vocabulary of motive for these women (Mills, 1940). On the other hand, it represents a medicalization of women and a subsequent loss of control over their bodies and lives. This debate has to be seen, as debates over all diseases can be, as the outcome of political and social struggle, worked out at the level of the individual body (Figert, 1995). The paradox of women's participation in their own medicalization has been well captured by Riessman: 'There are times when the interests of women from the middle and upper classes are served by the therapeutic professions, whose political and economic interests are in turn served by transforming these women's complaints into illnesses' (Riessman, 1983: 14). The end of the process, though, is always the same: problems whose sources lie in gendered social relationships and roles are medicalized, technical solutions are proffered, and the underlying causes hidden from view.

Women are not always passive recipients of patriarchal medicalization (Riessman, 1983). In the first place, women are not unequivocally positive about medical technology and make well-established critical appraisals of it (Birke, 1980). Equally, they are not passively dominated by it. American research has found that some women experience 'technocratic control' over their bodies in childbirth as empowering and not as part of a patriarchal technology (Davis-Floyd, 1994), while other women find the new reproductive technologies empowering and liberating. While it is true that the new technologies call into existence new subjectivities, this allows for new forms of power/knowledge, in which control over the process is at least open to women (Denny, 1996). Women also appraise the usefulness of drugs, neither expecting nor passively accepting antidepressant drugs. It appears too that doctors are not unconscious prescribers of tranquillizers either, offering women a variety of alternatives, and often seeing the prescription as a point of last resort (Gabe and Thorgood, 1986). Thus the macro-level assessment of the medicalization of women is open to at least some modification at the level of daily life. What could be concluded is that there is a continuum, ranging from total control by the practitioner at the institutional surgical level through to a negotiated order at the level of the doctor's surgery, where women enter into dialogue to construct their own experience of their relationship with both patriarchal doctors and their place in the social structure.

However, the differences between the two theories – between feminists and Foucault – is also large and, some argue, irreconcilable. Foucault himself makes no mention of gendered bodies, but operates with a 'masculinized' model of the body and its disciplinary regimes (McNay, 1994). Additionally, where Foucault sees dispersed power fields, feminists see organized patriarchal power. The feminist criticism of Foucault is that his concept of power is nebulous. He has been accused of phallocentrism, and of being blind to women's plight (McNay, 1991; Phelan, 1990). His argument is, by and large, that power is not centralized, that in modern societies it flows and empowers as much as it subjugates. In this he differs quite markedly from feminist accounts of power as something wielded by men over women. Cooper (1994), for example, discusses women's fear of darkened streets as something that flows through social relations – both men and women feel it – but it disciplines women to keep off them.

Bringing Out the Foucauldian-Feminist Position: Screening

Liberal feminists have welcomed screening programmes for women as redressing the imbalance of services. Further, they have argued that such programmes are empowering for women since they direct them to services and make them aware of their bodies. Thus mammography and cervical cancer screening have been widely supported. But is this an advance for women? Foucauldian feminists argue that such screening programmes of otherwise well women are, in fact, aspects of the medicalization of women. Women, who are already marginalized, are being targeted yet again by the 'helping professions' with yet more aspects of their life being monitored and surveyed.

Screening programmes for women – particularly for breast cancer and cervical cancer – provide good examples of medical actions that can be explained in Foucauldian-feminist terms. Mass screening enshrines the examination of the individual woman's body linked to population-based disease statistics. In what appears to be a humanistic step forward, taking into account women's desire to know about and control their bodies, mass public health campaigns have been initiated. The claim is that early stages of cancer will be caught, that more women will live longer, and that overall women will benefit from the procedure.

However, the target in screening is the 'abnormal' few, the pursuit of whom justifies the observation of the 'normal' majority. The 'invisible' diseases justify the monitoring of the whole target population in the rise of what Armstrong has called 'surveillance medicine' (Armstrong, 1995). Health promotion campaigns target the healthy population using fear campaigns and emphasizing the risks that people are putting themselves at by not having check-ups (Lupton, 1995). Furthermore, they target young women who are least likely to get breast cancer. As Kuni puts it: 'A darker side of the lay press campaigns is the use of fear and guilt to achieve compliance. Statistics are often misused, and the judgment of women who question the value of mammography is criticised' (Kuni, 1993: 186). Breast cancer, and its associated mass mammography, raise many of the issues concerned with medicalization of women's bodies, patriarchy and surveillance. The very focus on breast cancer is a particularly powerful expression of the ambiguous position of women in society, being at once a site of masculinized feminine sexuality, as well as the source of nourishment in motherhood (Batt, 1994).

Breast cancer is a life-threatening, common disease with no clear lifestyle-factor explanations. It thus reflects many of the problems that organized medicine has had to face in its 'war against cancer'. Put simply, there has been a failure to identify the causes of cancer and this has left medicine with a public relations problem. Mass screening for breast cancer can be seen as the actions of a professional group to control a potential crisis of confidence in their ability to deliver what they promise (Mitchell, 1987).

Mass screening does not prevent breast cancer, but is intended to detect it before it becomes symptomatic. The claim is that through early treatment the death rate will be reduced. Early randomized trials of women in screening programmes, compared with those who were not, found that deaths were reduced in the screened group, but overall the evidence is mixed (Dilhuydy and Barreau, 1997; MacDonald, 2005).

- In a major review of the epidemiological literature, Hurley and Kaldor (1992) concluded that the best demonstrated use of mass mammography was for women over the age of 50.

- Other researchers are even less persuaded that mass screening achieves much at the survival level, estimating one death fewer in every 15,000 women screened (Skrabanek, 1988).

- Randomized trials of the mortality benefits of mammography compared to direct physical examination suggest that physical examination is as successful as mammography (Kuni, 1993).

- There is little evidence that there has been any improvement in the treatment of breast cancer, so early detection does not mean enhanced survival (Kearsley, 1986).

The assumptions of the screening programme about cancer are also seriously questioned. As Kuni has pointed out, there is virtually no evidence that early detection improves mortality, because cancer of the breast is not restricted to the breast but spreads systemically to distant sites very early. 'In humans, some 90 per cent of nodal metastases occur before the primary tumour reaches a diameter of six millimetres, close to the limit of detectability' (Kuni, 1993: 186).

The problem of the false positive is also a significant one, with estimates of over-diagnoses ranging from an accepted minimum of 10 per cent to an upper level of 30 per cent (Brewer et al., 2007; Kleit and Ruiz, 2003). A false positive has serious costs, including high anxiety, unnecessary tissue biopsies, and scarring at the biopsy site. The false negative problem is also significant. That is, the woman has breast cancer but is told that she doesn't. Clinically, of course, the false negative is far more problematic than the false positive. On the advice of the medical practitioner, the false-negative woman leaves the medical system reassured that she has nothing to worry about. Overall, for all the above reasons, the costs of mass screening appear to outweigh any benefits. As Miller has demonstrated, there are no benefits in the age range 40–49, and the degree of benefit for women over 50 has been overestimated (Miller, 1993).

Screening programmes, then, have to be seen as having minimal medical justification. Indeed, there is a good deal of evidence that the screening may be harmful. Women, though, are induced to be dependent on technological fixes such as mammograms. A British study found that women preferred a technological check-up to breast self-examination. The women said that they preferred the former because it was performed by experts (Calnan, 1986). Rather than conclude that women participate in the construction of their own docile bodies, these women's position has to be seen in the overall context of the interrelationship between medicine and technology. Because breast cancer and cervical cancer are 'invisible diseases', the only way to detect them is through technical checks. The technical then becomes the solution, even though it does not do anything about the problem. In a society that takes the technological as the solution to social problems, it is very easy to slip into the argument that the presence of high technology means that the solution is at hand, for both the doctor and the patient (Bates and Lapsley, 1987).

At the same time, the discourse of empowerment leads women into a double bind: they are frail and potentially always sick, yet they are autonomous and active agents. However, their activism actually leads them further into subjugation. If anything, screening programmes have subverted feminism, incorporating some of its central points – autonomy, self-responsibility and control of the body – into a medicalized patriarchal gaze. This has been brought out by a study of cervical screening, which argued that it was 'a site for state, professional and male surveillance and control, through preventive services which many may feel obligated to participate in' (McKie, 1995: 442). Similarly, a study of the rhetoric of breast-cancer awareness campaigns in the US found that these initiatives effectively amounted to 'pinkwashing': 'talk about women that does not necessarily empower women' (Pezzullo, 2003: 365).

Feminist approaches to breast cancer emphasize that women must step out of the victim role that medicine constructs for them, and which is embedded in screening programmes. Rather, a politics of breast cancer must be constructed, developing an analysis of the environmental causes of breast cancer, as well as of the ways in which the current health system shapes individuals' understanding of and access to treatment (Brown et al., 2006; Wilkinson and Kitzinger, 1994). The experiential aspects of breast cancer, with care and support groups, must be developed to complement the current focus on high-tech interventions.

Men, Gender and Health

Men's health, as determined by their gender, has posed a recent challenge to feminist sociology. The recognition that both men's and women's health are shaped by gender is a recent development, especially for men's bodies (Sabo and Gordon, 1995). In Australia, a National Men's Health Conference was held in 1995, one consequence of which was the preparation by the Commonwealth Government Parliamentary Research Service of the background paper 'Testosterone Poisoning or Terminal Neglect? The Men's Health Issue' (Fletcher, 1996). The title pithily captures some of the major debates in feminism and gender studies around men's health.

The dominance of feminist analyses has meant that the concern has been on the impact of gender roles on women and their bodies. It seems now that, for theoretical reasons as well as the practical reason to do with men's diseases, this focus needs to be sharpened to examine the effect of gender on men and women. A feminist sociology of health which rigidly distinguishes between men's and women's health will always fall back onto the dichotomies of biomedicine.

The oppositions of feminist theory – especially radical feminism – between men and women operate on an already existing cultural and political map of the differences between the genders, which no matter what the intent of the theorists, simply reproduces the already existing social reality. Theoretically, the assumption that women's health is determined by gender, and that men's is not, leaves intact the biomedical assumption that men are healthy and well unless physically, demonstrably sick. It also means that women, on the other hand, are sick and diseased unless demonstrably well, which, given the medicalization of their reproductive cycles, is unlikely to be the case. Furthermore, Hearn (2012) points out that, because gendered analyses have tended to be 'explicitly about women ... and only implicitly about men', and that general body analyses 'are often implicitly about male, masculine and men's bodies (and not about women)', then men's bodies 'remain unnamed, decisively *unmarked*, in a similar but different way to "white bodies" in Western societies' (2012: 307, italics in original). Though this can lead to various forms of cultural domination, Hearn argues, it can also 'reify the body and neglect what men do, the practices that make and re-make men', thereby erasing their experience of health (2012: 308).

To ignore men's health, then, is to leave the dichotomy between men and women intact at a theoretical level and inhibit any political movement towards equity and egalitarianism between them. In this sense, the Marxist–feminist position, which seeks solidarity across groupings of men and women, and Foucauldian feminism, with its oppositional stance to professionals and their bureaucratic categories – including those of 'male' and 'female' – are far more productive theoretical orientations. A feminist theory that distinguishes between men and women also collapses the sex/gender distinction which has been central to feminism. While the argument has been made that women's gender is constructed on a false set of social assumptions disguised as science, and that therefore women are not biologically determined, the same argument has not been made as strongly for men (Courtenay, 2000). This is particularly intriguing given the fact that at least a part of the 'biologically' male population claims that their social, ascribed masculine gender is at odds with their own sense of their feminine gender (Lewins, 1995).

Empirically, a quick scan of population health data categorized by gender shows that men's health is equally socially determined by their gender role.

BOX 8.5

MEN'S HEALTH AND GENDER

- Australian females born in 2012 can expect to live an average of 84.3 years while a male can expect to live 79.9 years. Calculations of potential years of life lost (PYLL) from a disease or injury – an indicator of the number of years lost to premature death from injury or illness – show that in 2004 males had 75 per cent more PYLL than females. Two of the largest contributors to this gap were ischaemic heart disease and suicide (Australian Institute of Health and Welfare, 2006, 2014).

- In 2004–2005, the Australian Bureau of Statistics National Health Survey reported that more young males than females aged 15–17 years were in either excellent or very good health (85 per cent of males compared with 80 per cent of females). Despite this, in 2003, PYLL measures for young men were almost three times that for young females (ABS, 2004).

- Injury and suicide account for a large proportion of deaths among young men. In 2011, the male suicide rate was 2.5 times higher than that of females. Among people aged 15–24, men were more than twice as likely to die from injury or poisoning as women (Australian Institute of Health and Welfare, 2014).

(Continued)

(Continued)

- Males suffer from a substantially higher rate of cardiovascular disease, diabetes, chronic respiratory diseases and cancers (Australian Bureau of Statistics, 2012b). Men use primary health services less, delay seeking help when they are sick, and participate in more life-threatening drink-driving and violent behaviours (Fletcher, 1996).

- Older men have a death rate 61 per cent higher than the age-standardized rate for women. They have higher death rates from all causes, with lung cancer rates 387 per cent higher; suicide rates 286 per cent higher; bronchitis, emphysema and asthma 196 per cent higher; and stomach cancer 139 per cent higher (Fletcher, 1996).

Men's gender also has a significant impact on how they understand and experience sickness and disease. In a study of prostate ill health, Cameron and Bernardes (1998) used questionnaires and in-depth interviews with a large sample of men in Britain. They found that men tend not to discuss their physical symptoms, with 6 per cent of their respondents not even telling their spouse of their painful and intrusive condition. Men conceptualize the workings of their body in a machine-like fashion, focusing on technicalities such as amount drunk in relation to urine output. One respondent had kept records for five years of all liquid intake and output. Men also have a highly individualistic view of their health. While they are interested in information and in hearing of other sufferers' stories, they did not want support groups, and efforts by the National Prostate Health Association to bring groups together have failed. Men delay seeking medical advice for even the most overt physical symptoms, including one respondent who only came to medical attention following an emergency admission to hospital for urine retention. They also found that men make 'bad' patients in the sense of refusing to present for check-ups and examinations. Interestingly enough, some of the respondents claimed that they could only have their digital rectal examination if it was done by a man, since only 'men understand what you are going through'. This study reflects the social structuring of masculine identity in contemporary society. It can also be read as men actively trying to negotiate their gender identity in the face of chronic illness which challenges key attributes of their masculinity – their ability to stay in control, act rationally, and not complain and 'be a man'. Thus men's reactions to prostate ill health may well be to protect their sense of gender identity from threats.

Contemporary arguments in gender studies are that there is not just one masculinity, as suggested by both medical science and some feminists. Rather, there is a diversity in strategies for being male, for family structures which are not built on male dominance, and a plea for the recognition of the ways in which biographical ruptures and changes can occur in the gender identity and formation of men (Coltrane, 1994;

Connell, 1987; Courtenay, 2000; Morgan, 1992). Patriarchal ideologies of masculinity can be as dangerous and hazardous for men as they are for women. This is especially the case for 'hegemonic masculinity' (Connell, 1995), the dominant discourse of what it is to be male – the white Anglo-Saxon Protestant form of rational, domineering, aggressive and exploitative male. While it significantly benefits dominant male groups, it also results in the incredibly high death rates of young men as they seek to make the transition out of adolescence and into adulthood, adopting hazardous lifestyles resulting in violent death, drug abuse and suicide. It is this form of masculinity that is the one which is as dangerous to some men as it is to women.

Of course, the well-grounded fear of feminist theorists is that a turn to gender and a focus on masculinity will mean that 'men emerge both as the dominant gender and the real victims of masculinity' (Ramazanoglu, 1989: 346). Their argument is that even allowing that some men reject the tenets and practices of hegemonic masculinity, all men benefit by its existence.

BOX 8.6

GENDERED DISORDERS OF BODY IMAGE

Body dysmorphic disorder (BDD) is a condition in which an individual becomes obsessed with an aspect of their body as unsightly, under- or over-developed, or in some other way not normal. This perception is perceived as real but by medical standards is false, or if real, over-exaggerated. What is of interest to health sociologists is that both the experience of the condition and its diagnoses reflect common understandings of what the female and male body should look like. Thus BDD manifests itself as anorexia nervosa in women convinced that they are overweight, fat or unsightly, while in men it manifests as muscle dysmorphia where body mass and muscle development are perceived as too small. So not only is the body shaped in medical and professional literatures as complying with social assumptions about what is normal; but also we as individuals, when monitoring our body, practise what Foucault called technologies of the self to conform to societal and patriarchal understandings of what a 'good' body is (Bartsch, 2007).

Conclusion

In this chapter I have shown how the concept of patriarchy can be used to demonstrate the impact of the socially ascribed roles of femininity on women's health. I have argued that rather than being sicker than men or more unhealthy, it is the medicalization of women's bodies in a patriarchal and capitalist society that results in them being labelled sick more widely. Doctors act as agents of social control, enforcing compliance with socially determined roles and diagnosing, as sick, women who do not comply with these social roles. At the same time, any simple forms of feminist claims that patriarchy determines women's roles have had to be modified in the light of the fact that women also resist their medicalization. They are not unconscious dupes of the system, and any adequate theory of the way in which patriarchy determines their health has to take account of their ability to resist and transform their social roles. The role of Foucault has been particularly important in this regard. At the same time, however, feminist Foucauldians have shown how the empowerment of women, through self-help movements and health self-monitoring behaviour – such as breast examination – actually has increased the net of medicalization, as women voluntarily comply with the norms and the dictates of a medicalized set of social relationships. This has raised a range of theoretical issues for feminist health sociology.

Modernist feminists – radical, liberal and Marxist – challenged the social construction of the woman's body. The argument was that a distinction had to be made between sex and gender. Sex was given as the biological substratum of female and male, while gender was the learned social characteristics appropriate to masculinity and femininity, of being a man or a woman. In this model, the feminist sociology of health set out to show that what appeared to be given biologically as determinate was, in fact, a product of male social control of women, hidden inside claims to biological scientificness. Postmodernist theory challenges the binary oppositions that modernist feminism was built on: sex and gender, male and female, men and women. The 'factuality' of the body cannot be taken as prior to the ascription of gender characteristics. Rather, the biological understanding of the body is itself a socially accomplished project. Our bodies are simultaneously constructed by the discourse of normality, and enacted by us in that discourse, even when that enactment is oppositional (Gatens, 1992). One implication of this has been to draw attention to workings of gender on men's identity, with researchers highlighting the impact of masculinity on men's health.

Summary

- How we conceptualize the workings of society has important outcomes for what we discover about health and disease. For Marxists, the class dynamics of capitalism produce disease; for Parsons, disease may be produced by social strain, which the medical profession acts to moderate; for Foucault, an administrative state sets up professional models of deviance to facilitate social control of the population; for feminist theorists, contemporary society is patriarchal, and men use medical knowledge and practices to ensure that women comply with their social roles of mother and housewife.

- Feminists argue that there are more women patients because medicine has medicalized their life cycle, and targeted them for health-screening programmes at every stage of it. They are not sicker, but more medicalized.

- Neither are women more depressed than men, but patriarchal medicine is more likely to diagnose them as having psychiatric disorders than it does men.

- Medical technology can be shown to be unnecessarily yet constantly applied to women's bodies – whether at the level of mood-altering drugs or at the surgical level of intervening in pregnancy.

- Men's bodies, health and disease are also shaped by the requirements of patriarchal society – that they behave 'like men' – participating in hazardous activities, dying in accidents and killing themselves.

Discussion Questions

1. Patriarchal medicine controls women by medicalizing all stages of their life. Discuss.

2. What is it about women's social roles that results in more of them being diagnosed as mad?

3. Do our gender roles make us sick?

Further Reading

Butler, J. (1993) *Bodies That Matter: On the Discursive Limits of Sex.* New York: Routledge. The best of the Foucauldian feminists trying to resolve the paradoxes of 'doing gender' at the individual level, in the context of patriarchal structures.

Clarke, A. and Olesen, V. (eds) (1999) *Revisioning Women, Health and Healing: Feminist, Cultural and Technoscience Perspectives.* New York: Routledge. A collection of essays on feminist readings of health, with a special emphasis on modern medical technologies.

Kasper, A. and Ferguson, S. (eds) (2000) *Breast Cancer: Society Shapes an Epidemic.* New York: St Martin's Press. A collection of essays on the social construction of breast cancer, including chapters on breast cancer activism.

Pringle, R. (1999) *Sex, Medicine and Gender: Power and Authority in the Medical Profession.* Cambridge: Cambridge University Press. A good overall introduction to feminism and health.

9

RACE, ETHNICITY AND HEALTH

o   In this chapter, I use Max Weber's concept of status group to explore the role of ethnicity in explaining differences in disease rates. Ethnicity can be a category that a group chooses, as a way of empowering themselves, or it can be ascribed to them as a way of controlling them.

o   Empirical evidence on Australian Aborigines and African Americans is used to demonstrate that ethnicity works independently of class to produce and distribute disease.

o   The chapter continues the critique of biological categories to explain what the products of social life are. It presents the argument that 'race' is not a biological category, and that genetic explanations of disease are of limited use in explaining diseases that are mediated by social conditions.

In Marxism, class is an objective feature of capitalist society which shapes individuals' lives whether they are aware of it or not. Against this type of economic Marxism, Max Weber argued that people formed ideas about themselves and others, independently of class processes. He called these ideas 'status groups'. His key point is that status groups are not based on purely economic interests, which, Weber argues, are never sufficient to form a community. Weber defines a 'status situation' as 'every typical component of the life fate of men that is determined by a specific, positive or negative, social estimation of honour' (Gerth and Mills, 1948: 187). Status groups are also based on similar lifestyles. They are not dependent on economic standing, and there can be both negative and positive privileges attached to them, particularly in relation to access to the labour market. It is with the negative privileges that minority ethnic groups experience in terms of socio-economic status that we are concerned.

As Weber (Gerth and Mills, 1948: 190) points out, there is interplay between the claimed 'racial' bases to different ethnic groups, which provides a justification for the subordinate status of minority ethnic groups, even though the claimed 'racial' difference has no basis. What gives the claim to ethnic identity its sociological interest is that for some groups it is closely identified with their own understanding of their racial uniqueness – for example, New Zealand Maori or Australian Aborigines. I suggest in this chapter that these 'primordialists' are captured by the logic of medical knowledge, and it translates their political and social claim to 'ethnicity' into an elision of 'race', such that ethnicity just becomes another positivistic descriptor of a group. In short, the claim to ethnic status by a group based on uniqueness makes it vulnerable to cooption by dominant status groups. There is thus a dynamic interplay between categories of race and ethnicity, and between the primordialists and those who argue that ethnicity can be a chosen marker of status – the instrumentalists – for whom ethnicity is a resource rather than a defining characteristic.

The chapter also outlines the rise of the 'new genetics'. The claim is that our health is fundamentally fixed by our biological structure, in this case by our genetic structure. It shows that there is no evidence for this claim. Genetics may predispose us to disease, but it is social circumstances which provide the environment for it to develop. Rather, the function of genetic knowledge is to move disease yet one more step from the social environment, and to biologize social relations.

Race

Organized medicine is both shaped by and shapes racism. In the US, medically legitimated knowledge has been used to subjugate blacks and to justify their unequal social status. For example, it was used to justify the claim that African Americans could work uncovered in hot sun since they had thicker skin. Medical 'knowledge' was used to argue that environments known to be dangerous to health – such as malarial swamps – were not dangerous to African Americans (Alatas, 2010). There is also a long history of using African Americans for experimentation, sometimes horribly when patriarchy and racism intersect, as in the use of black women as guinea pigs for vesico-vaginal repair (Gamble, 1993). In terms of African American perceptions of the added dangers to their health posed by white medicine, these racist practices culminated in the Tuskegee syphilis experiments. Between 1932 and 1972, the US Department of Public Health conducted a natural history experiment. The argument was that with the successful treatment of syphilis, knowledge of its development to its end stage – tertiary syphilis – had been lost. The solution was to identify individuals with latent syphilis and then to withhold treatment from them. The 'experimental subjects' were 400 poor black sharecroppers with latent syphilis, who were deliberately allocated to a non-treatment regime to allow the disease to take its natural course. The men were given weekly medical examinations involving blood tests and spinal fluid taps, and were told that these were positive treatments which they needed to keep them healthy. In exchange for 'participating', the men were offered a hot meal and promised that they would not receive a pauper's funeral.

A medical experiment such as this could only be planned and carried out against the background of deeply racist assumptions about the value of black lives. It also reflected racially informed perceptions of black sexuality. The study was carried out with the background assumptions that black men had bigger penises than white men, that this was linked to greater libidos and that they therefore were less moral in their sexual behaviour, and thus, if not explicitly deserving of contracting syphilis, at least implicitly so (Haller, 1971). The estimate of preventable, horrible deaths ranges from 28 to 100 men. The study was well-known throughout American medical circles and had been reviewed by state ethics committees and passed. It was not discontinued due to any pressure from the medical profession, but as a consequence of a journalistic exposé (Jones, 1981, 1992).

The sorting of the population into races based on a claimed biological basis has been a prominent feature of twentieth-century medicine and some of the social sciences, such as biologically reductionist forms of anthropology, psychology and socio-biology. However, it has been well demonstrated that there is no basis for the division of the human species into races. Biologists themselves reject the category of race, pointing out that there are more genetic differences within a group than across human groups. There is an 85 per cent greater variance within population groups than across those that we label 'races' (Lewontin, 1973). In short, race is a socially ascribed characteristic, not a biological one. Even when a disease seems to be restricted to a racial group – for example sickle cell anaemia in black minority ethnic groups – the disease is responsible for only the smallest percentages of the group's morbidity and even less for its mortality. In 1977, the age-adjusted death rate in the USA among black groups was 37 per cent higher than among white groups. The proportion contributed by sickle cell anaemia was 0.3 per cent (Cooper and David, 1986). In the US case of African Americans, the wider picture of the social patterning of disease is overwhelming. In 2013, infant mortality rates for black Americans were twice as high as for white Americans. In 2013, age-adjusted death rates for the black population exceeded those for the white population by 47 per cent for stroke, 20 per cent for heart disease, 46 per cent for cancer, and an alarming 823 per cent for HIV (Centers for Disease Control and Prevention, 2013).

The commonality of our genetic make-up overwhelms any claimed differences. Race is not a biological category, but rather it is a social category and precisely illustrates the hold that the appeal of science has in our culture. The construction of race as a scientific term turns it into a 'factual', objective account and explanation of the contemporary state of social affairs. It is then used to displace other sociological explanations. For example, the impact of gender rather than 'race' appears to be a significant risk factor in the case of high blood pressure (Krieger, 1990), as does social class rather than skin colour (Dressler, 1991). However, if these conditions are presented as a consequence of biological inevitability, of 'race', then the social processes around them can be dismissed.

Ethnicity

One of the ways in which erstwhile 'racial' groups have been able to fight for political recognition is through their 'ethnic' identity. Thus the argument is that race, grounded in a claimed biological reality, is in fact an ideological tool of oppression, while 'ethnicity', grounded in a political process of self-claiming and political mobilization, is empowering. It has also become possible for members of ethnic groups to establish special cases of vulnerability for themselves in terms of disease, to appeal for resources and then health-care services. By and large, this is a good process where it is clear that the group does suffer from specific detriment, such as when an ethnic group is concentrated almost entirely in one industry with consequent impact on its health. It is also true that this appeal to ethnicity challenges biological models of disease by drawing attention to the cultural and social aspects both of the causes of disease and of ways of dealing with disease.

Ethnicity refers to the self-ascribed cultural and linguistic characteristics of a group claiming a common origin. In terms of the history of sociology and social movements, it represents the opposite to the category 'race'. There are two broad perspectives on ethnicity in sociology, captured in the shorthand phrases of 'primordialists' and 'instrumentalists' (Smaje, 1996). For primordialists, ethnicity is a powerful shaper of people's identity, organizing their whole orientation to the world, and being the key to their identity. The instrumentalists argue that, on the contrary, ethnicity is a political resource, which can be mobilized to advance social, political and economic interests of specific groups.

Hence there is a dichotomy set up between those explanations of ethnicity as a subjectively experienced reality and more structuralist accounts emphasizing the interrelations of socio-economic and racist factors in the construction of ethnicity. A sociologically useful concept of ethnicity must capture the dualism of individual identity and structured patterning of access to resources based on ethnicity.

Such an approach can be developed from the work of Max Weber. Weber argued that social groups seek to monopolize access to scarce resources through a process of social closure, in which they exclude competitor groups from areas of economic activity. Weber can be used to show the origins of ethnic identity in the maintenance of economic resources and the construction of identity to exclude outsiders:

> When the number of competitors increases in relation to the profit span, the participants become interested in curbing competition. Usually one group of competitors takes some externally identifiable characteristic of another group of (actual or potential) competitors – race, language, religion, local or social origin, descent, residence etc. – as a pretext for attempting their exclusion. Such group action may provoke a corresponding reaction on the part of those against whom it is directed. (Weber, 1968: 342)

'Ethnicity' develops in historically specific situations as a form of dominance of one group over another. It is a structural feature of society which differentially distributes access to economic goods, the labour market and social status. That is, independently of any personal attributes, membership of an ethnic group will structure your life experience. At the same time, ethnicity can be a chosen marker of identity by which groups distinguish themselves. Thus ethnicity is both enabling (conferring identity) and limiting (restricting choice and access to social goods). Put another way, ethnicity can be understood to have both a cultural and a material basis (Comaroff, 1987).

Aboriginality, 'Race' and Disease

What are your life chances if you are born Aboriginal in contemporary Australia? Life expectancy at birth is around 20 years shorter for Aboriginal peoples. When they get sick, Aboriginals die at a greater rate than non-Aboriginals, even of easily treated diseases. For example, Indigenous children born between 2010 and 2012 can expect to live 10 years shorter than non-Indigenous children born in the same span. Furthermore, from 2007 to 2011, Indigenous people died at five times the rate of non-Indigenous people; Indigenous Australians die from diabetes at a rate nine times that of the total population; mortality rates for all causes of death are higher for Indigenous than non-Indigenous Australians; and Indigenous Australians are much more likely to suffer from a chronic illness (Australian Bureau of Statistics, 2007; Australian Institute of Health and Welfare, 2014; Department of Health and Ageing, 2005). Indigenous people were 1.2 times more likely than non-Indigenous people to have cardiovascular disease, 3.3 times more likely to have diabetes, and 3.7 times more likely to have kidney disease (Australian Bureau of Statistics, 2013). Poverty and ethnicity combine in aboriginality to produce chronic disease and early death.

BOX 9.1

THE LIFE CHANCES OF AUSTRALIAN ABORIGINES

- Aboriginal and Torres Strait Islander people in Australia today have, on average, similar life expectancies to that of the total Australian population 100 years ago. The significant improvements in health and life expectancy that marked the twentieth century have not yet reached Aboriginal Australia (Australian Bureau of Statistics, 2002).

- While the infant mortality rate among Indigenous Australians has improved since the 1970s, in 2012 the death rate for Indigenous infants was still around twice the rate of the total population (Australian Institute of Health and Welfare, 2014: 302).

- Aboriginal children are 14 times more likely to be admitted to hospital than non-Indigenous children and more likely to die in hospital than non-Aboriginal children. This is largely due to respiratory and gastrointestinal infections (Carville et al., 2007).

- Life expectancy is considerably shorter for Aboriginal people than for non-Aboriginal persons. In 2010–2012, life expectancy for Aboriginal men was 10 years lower for males and females (Australian Institute of Health and Welfare, 2014: 301).

Despite these incredible inequalities in morbidity and mortality, Indigenous Australians access mainstream health services, such as private-practice general practitioners and the Pharmaceutical Benefits Scheme, 80 per cent less than the overall Australian population. What this leads to is a drastically high rate of hospitalization; for example, between 2010 and 2012, Indigenous Australians were hospitalized for preventable conditions 1.6 times more often than non-Indigenous people (Australian Institute of Health and Welfare, 2014: 325). Despite this, and even allowing for the provision of medical services through Aboriginal Medical Services and access to hospitals, overall spending on Aboriginal health is only 18 per cent higher than that spent on the non-Indigenous population. A significant proportion of this spending is accounted for by the high cost of delivery of services to remote locations where 26 per cent of Indigenous Australians live. The problem of a lack of resources is compounded by the problem of getting doctors to work in Aboriginal areas, such that there is a perennial problem in the delivery of health resources.

Socio-economic factors clearly aggravate the subordinate ethnic position Aborigines are in. At least part of the reason for Aboriginal health status is linked to their position in the working class. While it is very difficult to distinguish the impact of ethnicity from other social variables such as social class and gender, ethnicity does operate independently as a predictor of poor health. It is clear that when economic factors are held constant, there is a significant proportion of death and disease that is not explained – up to one-third (Bacquet et al., 1991). Ethnicity operates, following Weber's analysis of status groups, independently of class position as a predictor of poor health.

It is not only that Aboriginal people are members of the working class, but also that this interacts with their low ethnic status and they have a harsher experience of the working-class life: they are exposed to more environmental hazards, more pollutants and higher risks of occupational injury (Robinson, 1987). For example, the economic costs of being in the working class are higher for African Americans. It is well established that black groups, with the same educational qualifications as white groups, are paid less in the labour market and occupy lower-status positions (Farley, 1984; Grodsky and Pager, 2001). Thus there are big differences between black group and white group members of the working class. Class position interacts with ethnic status to produce ill health, for example, being strongly linked to higher blood pressure levels (Dressler, 1991).

The differences in sickness and death rates between blacks and whites are not biological, not natural, and not genetic. Aboriginal mortality is caused by lack of treatment of their conditions. This is the case, for example, in heart disease, diabetes and tuberculosis: diseases which have a mortality rate of up to five times the non-Aboriginal rate. There are significant differences in the treatment of ethnic groups in racially stratified societies. A study of the management of appendicitis in African-American children revealed that, compared to Caucasian children in the United States, African-American children have a much lower rate of hospitalization, higher rates of perforation of the appendix, lower rates of the less-invasive laparoscopic surgery, and a greater delay in surgical management of the condition (Kokoska et al., 2007). In Australia, Indigenous children are not treated in hospital, or not treated at all, for conditions that are routinely treated in non-Aboriginal populations – ear infections for example (Gray and Saggers, 1994). Furthermore, even when correctly diagnosed, non-white people often do not receive the treatment they need, or by the time they do, it is too late to help them. The treatment of coronary artery disease is a well-established surgical procedure, with recognized benefits for the patient. It is a procedure determined as nearly as possible on objective clinical grounds. Yet in New Zealand in 1983, when 822 coronary bypass operations were performed, only 10 were carried out on members of the minority Indigenous population, the Maori, despite the rate of heart disease being high among Maori people (Pomare, 1988). A more recent study produced similar results, showing that Pacific Islander and Maori people were less likely to receive coronary artery revascularization surgery despite higher rates of death from coronary artery disease among these population groups (Tukuitonga and Bindman, 2002).

Disparities in treatment between Indigenous and non-Indigenous people may also be a result of clinical services not being appropriately set up, in terms of their location and cultural sensitivity, to serve Indigenous people. In Australia, Indigenous women are 10 times more likely to die from cervical cancer than non-Indigenous women, and cervical cancer is the number one cause of cancer deaths among Indigenous women. This is despite cancer of the cervix now being considered one of the most easily preventable forms of cancer. The most likely cause of this is the low participation of Indigenous women in cervical screening (pap smear) programmes (Coory et al., 2002).

Racist Bias in Drug Trials

Medicine in ethnically stratified societies is also unscientific on its own terms, systematically excluding African Americans in the United States from the clinical trials of drugs. Hence if the alleged 'genetic' differences that medicine assumes exist between racial groups really do exist, then orthodox medicine systematically ignores them, with the result that drugs are being prescribed for a part of the population that they have not been trialled on. American blacks appeared less often than was statistically necessary in fully 50 clinical trials of new drugs reported in the leading journal *Clinical Pharmacology and Therapeutics* between 1984 and 1986 (Svensson, 1989). If some diseases do disproportionately affect different ethnic groups, then there is even more reason that they be included in trials.

Sociological explanations do not look for personality deficiencies in other ethnic groups, nor will they propose genetic or biological reasons for why this or that group has the health problems it has, though racist medicine in a capitalist society does. The Rockefeller Foundation, for example, funded extensive research into the 'germ of laziness', which was said to infect African Americans (Ettling, 1981). Instead, socio-logical explanations focus on the poorer access to education, appropriate dietary knowledge and unsafe work conditions which systematically put subordinated eth-nic groups at risk of chronic illness and early death. Rather than biology or genetics, the evidence for discrimination faced by minority ethnic groups with potential impacts on health significance over lifetimes is very well established.

Against an overall background of political discrimination – in the US case, at the level of civil rights and participation in the political processes (Mann, 1993) – ethnic groups face severe economic discrimination, at the basic level of access to loans, and to the basic underpinnings of participation in economic life, such as health care and health insurance, adequate schooling and access to the justice system (Myers, 1993). This flows over to the explicit outcomes of lower wages, participation in the informal sector of the economy with its increased exposure to health hazards at work, as well as the more hidden problems of under-representation in training programmes, promotional movies and extended schooling (Darity et al., 1995). In a vicious causal circle, the outcome is then segregated residential areas, with increased exposure to the hazards of industrial ghettos and slums, poisoning, environmental hazards, accidents, and the corollaries of addictive and violent behaviour. To add injury to insult, political and economic inequalities are added to by a general disparagement and denigration of cultural values and health belief systems, and a stereotypical representation of ethnic groups as responsible for their own problems (Krieger et al., 1993).

Problems with the Appropriation of Ethnicity in Medical Explanations

There are some very strong objections to the ways in which epidemiologists and medical researchers have adopted the categories of 'race' and ethnicity (Sheldon and Parker, 1992). In medical research, the primordialist approach to ethnicity has been adopted, with no sensitivity to the alternative instrumentalist claim of the origins of ethnic identity in political and social movements. Rather than being part of the reform of a racist society, ethnicity is confused with race, such that the concept of ethnicity is often restricted to 'black' people. Medical research that does this just transposes ethnicity with race, and in no way challenges a racialist understanding of social life. Even more, the appeal to ethnicity by these researchers reflects a racialized society (Miles, 1982). Yet again, a seemingly scientific category, this time the politically correct one of 'ethnicity', is brought into existence to provide a seemingly timeless and inevitable explanation of the inequalities in the exposure to sickness and diseases of different groups. It is then used to cover over racism as a factor in the explanation of disease, lending itself to a blame-the-victim approach. For example, much of the research on ethnic variations in disease has the effect of emphasizing the differences between groups. It also focuses on exceptional diseases rather than the common ones which the rest of the population share and are mediated by the ethnic group's relationship with poverty and inequality. Similarly, it is often argued that the language 'difficulties' of ethnic groups make it difficult to get across the right health messages. Yet it is well established that communication between medical practitioners and their patients is a general problem of the health-care system, and not a specific linguistic problem of specific groups (Waitzkin, 1991). Racism, rather than ethnic culture, needs to be explored as the cause of different rates of sickness and disease among groups.

In summary, the sociological worry about the use of 'ethnicity' as an explanatory variable is that cultural and linguistic factors are not adequately distinguished from socio-economic factors, and indeed that they can be used precisely to deflect attention from socio-economic explanations of the differences in disease rates. It can be seen, then, that the sociological concerns with ethnicity are similar to those concerns with lifestyle explanations of the cause of disease. They are at the wrong level of analysis, masking the structural aspects of exploitation and inequality, and they almost inevitably lead to policy formulations that blame the victims – either for their own behaviour, or for their culture's impact on the individual. Indeed, the use of ethnicity is even more worrying for a sociologist of the structuralist kind, because it has the immediate appeal of using a sociological category with hidden conservative implications.

The Genetic Explanation

Genetic explanations are often offered for, and used to justify, the hierarchical inequalities of modern societies. Genetic explanations of disease are based on the assumption that social life needs to be explained in terms of the characteristics and behaviours of individuals. These behaviours in turn are properties of the individual's brain. The behaviour can be quantified and individuals can then be ranked in terms of how much or how little of the characteristic they have. A normal range is constructed, with abnormal individuals identified and seen as in need of medical care. The behaviour is then seen as a property of the brain, with a specific location in the brain, and the product of specific biochemical reactions. Some biochemical changes may be caused by the environment; others are fixed immutably in the brain. Thus an equation of hereditability can be drawn up. Dealing with the abnormal conditions involves tracking down the 'genes' responsible for them and then, through eugenics, trying to eliminate them (Adams, 1990; ten Have, 2001).

Genetic explanations of disease can be characterized as reductionist and determinist. That is, they reduce the complexities of social life to a lowest common denominator. They are reductionist in that they explain complex wholes (the social shaping of death and disease) by the working of the parts (individuals, who in turn are explained by the workings of their parts). The complex processes of human society are reduced first to individuals, then to their genes. From this it is concluded that an understanding of the workings of the smallest part – the gene – will provide an explanation of the workings of the whole. At the same time, they suggest that many sicknesses and diseases are the inevitable outcome of biology. The seemingly 'scientific' characteristic of these assumptions performs a political function of diverting attention away from the social causes of disease and death.

Genetic explanations are a form of biological determinism: what human beings do is a consequence of biochemical properties that make them up, and these biochemical properties in turn are made up of the genes that constitute them. These elements, it is argued, determine human actions.

So human society is reducible to genes, and genes cause human society to take the shape that it does, rather than social factors. This gives an inevitability to the social organization and disorganization of life. Genes, having a basis in scientific knowledge and therefore appearing as 'value-free' facts, supplant other social explanations and deny them any validity. Their scientific basis is used to close down debates about economic, social or political causes of individuals' health and disease.

The Appeal of the Genetic Explanation

Debate about the role of genetics in determining human attributes, and therefore of certain human characteristics being unchangeable, has been part of the background noise in twentieth-century scholarship on ethnicity, health and life expectations. Arthur Jensen (1969) and Hans Eysenck (1971), two psychologists, proposed highly deterministic accounts of the genetic determination of the Intelligence Quotient (IQ). They argued that the distribution of IQ – and on IQ tests black and working-class children do poorly – reflected real differences among different genetic and class groups in society, and that remedial policy interventions in the schooling system would have no impact on these students. 'Head start' programmes to redress the social disadvantage of being black and being working class, and increased funding for working-class schools, would have no impact and would raise false expectations for these children and their parents. So not only can nothing be done, but to attempt any change is wrong as well (Kamin, 1974).

A more recent contribution to this debate is the work of Hernstein and Murray (1994), in their book *The Bell Curve: Intelligence and Class Structure in American Life*. They claim that IQ tests are not biased against ethnic minorities and that intelligence differences thus measured are objective, scientific and heritable. Thus, if blacks measure low this is because they are less intelligent, and, furthermore, since intelligence is heritable, there isn't much that can be done to improve their position. Race and racial differences are grounded in – that is, unchangeably located in – biology.

The resurgence of the genetics debate has to be seen in the context of the latest developments in medicine that allow for the testing, identification and intervention in the genetic make-up of humans (Marteau and Richards, 1996). The development of these increasingly well-funded technologies and procedures has brought serious concerns about the likelihood of increasing oppression based on gender and race (Draper, 1991). Biological determinists extend their claims about the inheritance of cognitive ability to things as disparate, and presumably unrelated, as brain and penis size, rate of sexual maturation and of length of menstruation (Rushton, 1989), as well as providing support for the racist popular ideas that different groups have different characteristics because of their colour.

Genetic explanations of disease are very appealing in modern societies since they tend to deflect attention from social explanations of disease; people become diseased and die because of their genes and not the way society is organized. Genetic explanations minimize the responsibility of governments to undertake interventions to protect individuals from the consequences of social organization. Genetic explanations also tend to justify inequality as natural and inevitable. Academics have called this the 'geneticizing of society' (Wertz, 1992) or simply 'geneticization' (ten Have, 2001), in which a fatalism about health, disease and life chances is fostered. The focus on genes breaks any link between the individual's health and illness and the society they live in. This is often linked with a naïve optimism about the breakthroughs in treatment that genetics might lead to. Williams, for example, enthuses that following the mapping of all the genes of the body, the determinants of disease will be discovered and 'physicians will simply inject corrective gene carriers into the blood stream of the patient in much the same way as drugs are administered now' (Williams, 1997: 1044). Other professional biologists have cautioned against any optimism that 'knowing' the genetic determinant of a human characteristic will enable us to plan for individuals with these characteristics. For a start, many of the things that are highly valued in society are social characteristics that are unlikely to have genetic markers (Gould, 1981; Lewontin et al., 1984). Take, for example, celibacy in male and female religious practitioners which, by definition, cannot be genetically determined. Yet all the major religious cultures produce celibate practitioners, which can only ever make sense in religious and social terms, and never in genetic terms.

Genetic explanations are often linked to eugenics programmes. Eugenics is based on the claim that the characteristics of different social groups are based in their shared genes and that by systematically controlling the reproduction of the group, the genetic characteristic can be eliminated. It most commonly is the claim that entire subordinate groups in the population have a different genetic structure to the elite. It was given its most powerful statement during the Second World War, in Hitler's attempt to eradicate 'Jewish' genes, as well as 'homosexual' genes, 'gypsy' genes and 'retarded' genes, from the human race. Chorover argues that genocide is not a peculiarly Nazi aberration, but had many predecessors, including the forcible sterilization of Eastern European immigrants to the USA in the 1920s (Chorover, 1979).

Prior to this, and influencing the experience of life of the entire British nation, eugenic thinking was the backdrop to the development of psychological testing in Western societies. The founders of psychology, Karl Pearson, Francis Galton and, later, Cyril Burt (the developer of the IQ test), were motivated by a concern to eradicate heritable disorders which they thought were concentrated in the working class. Such claims are still made. In the *Medical Journal of Australia*, Reid and his colleagues claimed that the higher incidence in uterine cancer among working-class patients was due to a factor carried in the sperm of their working-class male partners (Reid et al., 1979). It was also claimed that working-class sperm had a simpler, more repetitive structure to its DNA than did middle-class sperm. This accounted for working-class people only being able to think simple and repetitive thoughts, Reid claimed, unlike the complex thoughts of the middle classes (Reid et al., 1979, quoted in Rose et al., 1984: 231). It is little surprise that against the historical background of the social uses of genetics, the new genetics raises fears that minority groups will be highlighted for medicalization and oppression (Bradby, 1996).

BOX 9.2

SOCIAL DARWINISM, EUGENICS AND THE IQ CONTROVERSY

Social Darwinism is the application of Charles Darwin's theory of evolution and the survival of the fittest to human populations with the aim of justifying the existing social order by claiming that it is natural, inevitable and unchangeable. Its fullest expression as a social movement is in eugenics, from the Greek, meaning 'well-born'. The claim is that the characteristics of different social groups are based in their shared genes and that by systematically controlling the reproduction of the group the genetic characteristic can be eliminated, if negatively valued, or enhanced, if positively evaluated. In its most common form it is the claim that entire subordinate groups in the population have a different genetic structure from the elite. It was most fully realized during the Second World War in Hitler's attempt to eradicate 'Jewish' genes, as well as 'homosexual' genes, 'gypsy' genes and 'retarded' genes so as to protect the 'Aryan' genes of the Germans. In the USA, it was used in the 1920s and 1930s to justify the forcible sterilization of tens of thousands of Eastern European immigrants on Ellis Island (Chorover, 1979). So eugenics is not a peculiarly Nazi aberration: it formed the basis of British psychology at the end of the nineteenth century and educational practices in the twentieth century. Social Darwinism provided the backdrop to the foundation of British psychology in the

(Continued)

(Continued)

work of Francis Galton (1822–1911) and Karl Pearson (1857–1936), and in the twentieth century, Cyril Burt (1883–1971). Their argument was that the position of individuals in society reflected their innate abilities, and that those at the bottom should be prevented from reproducing. Cyril Burt argued that intelligence was virtually entirely hereditable and that environmental influences played little or no part in its development. His work was used to fix in place the British class structure through the administration of the 11-plus exam, which sorted the population irredeemably into their class position. The fact that much of his research has been found to be fraudulent has had little impact on the belief in 'IQs' (Hudson, 1976). In America, in the context of a backlash against the civil rights movement of the 1960s and finding affinities with behaviourism, Arthur Jensen (1923–) and Hans Eysenck (1916–1997) proposed deterministic accounts of the genetic contribution to intelligence as measured on tests of the intelligence quotient. They argued that the distribution of IQ as measured by IQ tests – on which African Americans and working-class people do poorly – reflected real differences among racial and class groups in society and that remedial intervention in schooling would have no impact on these individuals. Indeed, they argued that the introduction of 'head start' programmes in schools would falsely raise the expectations of blacks and working-class students, thereby fostering resentment. The debate was continued in the work of R. Hernstein and C. Murray (1994) in their book *The Bell Curve: Intelligence and Class Structure in American Life*. They claim that IQ tests are not biased against ethnic minorities and that measured intelligence differences are objective, scientific and heritable. The racial and class structure of American society is therefore grounded in biology – natural and unchangeable. The political appeal of such 'scientific' evidence is very apparent.

The Sociological Critique of Genetics

The number of diseases with an irrefutable genetic base is limited. Even where they have been established, they do not lead to any straightforward conclusion either about how the individual should act, or social policies to minimize the disease. Take, for example, Huntington's disease, for which genetic markers are known, allowing individuals to be tested for their risk of developing it (Richards, 1993). Huntington's disease is a degenerative neurological disease which causes dementia and loss of motor control, and starts in middle age. Yet fewer than 10 per cent of those at known risk come forward for testing. The reasons for this are sociological. 'Scientific' evidence may exist, but since it doesn't tell people what to do, they can reject it. As there is no effective treatment for the disease, there is, in a sense, little point in knowing about it. Equally, because onset is in middle age, parents are reluctant to have foetal testing, partly because they reject the option of abortion that a positive result may put them under pressure to consider, and they decide in favour of a normal life until the onset of the disease. Lastly, individuals do not come forward for testing because to be found as a positive risk affects their health insurability for other health matters unconnected to their vulnerability to Huntington's disease. In short, the existence of biomedical knowledge is put through the prism of social life.

Associated with this decision-making process is the theoretical point that genetic knowledge does not eliminate uncertainties in medical and social life (Davison et al., 1994). A genetic explanation is a statement that the individual will probably get a disease. However, even the most certain medical probability can be overtaken by other events, like accidents. Inherent uncertainty applies to all of us, all the time, no matter what our chances of having a heritable disease are. Furthermore, not all of those with a specific genetic marker will go on to develop the associated disease. Most genetic disorders rely on interaction with the environment to bring about the disease. Thus the timing and severity of illness will be the product of environmental factors and genetics combined. It is also the case that common chronic illnesses involve more than one gene site. Coronary heart disease, hypertension and manic depressive illness appear to be of this type. The interaction of gene site and environmental variables leads to such complexity in predicting the likelihood of disease that the claim that genes have programmed some people to get diseases becomes unsustainable.

Do genetic differences between social classes explain the differences in the distribution of disease and morbidity? There is no evidence to support this argument and a considerable amount to show that genetic factors play only a small part in the health and disease of social classes. In a study of the length of life of identical twins reared independently (who, if the geneticists are right, should suffer from the same diseases and the same causes of death), Hayakawa (1992) found that rather than their shared genetic make-up, environmental factors played a greater role in determining their lifespan. It was also found that twins died of very different diseases rather than from a shared genetic predisposition to disease. Twin studies have consistently supported the argument that it is the broader social, political and economic environment, rather than what we are born with, that shapes our diseases and death.

It is far more coherent to talk of a genetic vulnerability to environmental risks which predispose individuals to disease. The risks are socially, politically and economically 'shaped', not genetically 'produced'. Diseases which are thought to have a strong genetic component disappear when environmental risks which allow them to develop disappear. For example, take the change in the pattern of disease in the population in the twentieth century. The working class now die of what used to be the killers of the ruling class: stroke, heart attack and cancer (Wilkinson, 1996: 66). Patterns of disease become transformed with changed social conditions.

As Willis (1996) argues, the focus on genetics diverts attention from the social and economic environment and tends towards an individualistic explanation of disease. At the same time, developments such as the Human Genome Project, the attempt to map all genes, have to be understood primarily as profitable sources for investment, rather than as humanistically motivated attempts to eradicate diseases.

Conclusion

In this chapter I have shown that racism – in the sense of organized discriminatory medical practices against groups based on skin colour and alleged biological differences – has pervaded Western medicine. Medical accounts of different-coloured skin groups have been used to justify and explain their patterns of sickness, disease and death as biological, natural and inevitable. In racialized societies (that is, ones with status hierarchies built on colour), there is interaction with class structures such that the subordinate group suffers far worse health than the bottom of the dominant working class. Thus in addition to class and gender, sociological accounts of the inequalities of disease and death must take into account the dynamics of racism. I also explored the non-economic basis of exploitation, in particular through Weber's idea that social groups can form 'status' groups, which may be positively or negatively privileged.

Against the concept of 'race', sociologists and members of minority groups have proposed the category of ethnicity. In its 'instrumental' form, this refers to the way in which members of subordinate groups can make a claim to health resources on the basis of their groups' needs and rights. When used this way, ethnicity functions as an enabling resource. Ethnicity has also been defined as a fundamental – that is, unchangeable – feature of a group, in what is known as the primordialist position. Sociologically, this has allowed medicine to use the term 'ethnicity' in a way which simply reproduces the category of race.

Two of the most common explanations of the cause and patterning of disease – that they are grounded in a 'racial' biology, or in genetics – are, in fact, unsupportable. Rather, the construction of medical explanations using race and genetics performs the function of obscuring what are in fact social and political processes. Genetics plays a particularly important role in our society at this level, operating as a thinly veiled justification for a wide variety of health differences: as individual, biological and unchangeable. This chapter showed, against this, that patterns of disease are social products and not biological processes.

Summary

- Exploring differences in disease rates across ethnic groups illustrates the utility of Max Weber's argument that social groups form independently of economic factors. Thus, against the Marxist position, ethnicity functions independently of class as a predictor of poor health and disease.

- The claim that there are 'racial' differences in the human species has been used to justify the unequal treatment of subordinate groups, which has produced sickness and disease among them. The claimed racial differences are then used to explain these inequalities as natural.

- Erstwhile 'racial' groups can retain their cultural uniqueness by mobilizing a claim to 'ethnic' identity, though they run the risk that their 'ethnicity' will then be used as an explanation for their poor health, diseases and death.

- Racial and genetic explanations of patterns of disease in society represent the biologically most reductionist explanations of disease, effectively ruling out any sociological explanations. The power of scientific explanations in our society is marked by the fact there is only limited utility in explaining disease genetically, and no evidence for the hereditability of IQs.

- Fundamentally racial and genetic explanations act to obscure the social basis of inequality in disease.

Discussion Questions

1. Is medicine racist in its practices and assumptions about different ethnic groups?

2. How does your ethnicity shape your health?

3. Ethnic groups are organized into a status hierarchy, and the lower down you are, the sicker you are and the sooner you will die. Discuss.

Further Reading

Krieger, N., Rowley, D., Herman, A., Avery, B. and Phillips, M. (1993) 'Racism, Sexism, and Social Class: Implications for Studies of Health, Disease and Well Being.' *American Journal of Preventive Medicine* 9 (suppl.): 82–122. A very thorough review of the issues, as indicated by its title.

Rottenburg, R., Schramm, K. and Skinner, D. (eds) (2012) *Identity Politics and the New Genetics: Re/Creating Categories of Difference and Belonging*. Oxford: Berghahn Books. An excellent overview of the debates in the new genetics.

10

CONCLUSION

In this book I have endeavoured to demonstrate the impact of class, professional power, gender and ethnicity, in both shaping what is considered disease, as well as providing an account of how class, patriarchy and racism produce and distribute diseases. In this conclusion, rather than summarize what has gone before, I want to draw out the implications of these sociological arguments, synthesized into practical statements about the relationship between social structures and disease, both at the level of the population and as experienced by individuals. To do this, I draw on, and add to, the work of the World Health Organization (WHO). In 1998, the WHO commissioned a team of experts to bring together all the best research on the social factors most important in determining the health of a population (Wilkinson and Marmot, 1998). Framing the report was the overwhelming evidence for the limited impact of organized medicine on health, and the need for structural solutions to the cause and patterning of disease.

At the most general level, the WHO identified social exclusion, the lack of social support, and exposure to stress as key causes of diseases and early mortality. These characteristics of individuals' social lives in turn are reflections of and shape their participation in the labour market. Thus issues of socio-economic status, social integration and health are all deeply intertwined. They can only be separated out analytically, and, for any given individual will form an interconnected mosaic that will determine how healthy they are in life and when they die.

The WHO team also argued that patterns of health and illness are laid down in childhood, and that the impact of an underprivileged childhood on a person's health is not likely to be overcome in adulthood. If we start off in poor health, we continue in poor health. Later medical interventions will not make up for the impact of poverty (and consequent poor nutrition, housing and clothing), a lack of health care and information for pregnant women, and lack of access to nursing care and advice following the birth of an infant. Lifetime patterns of health and disease are set down in the first years of life, and will not improve even if the individual experiences social mobility. In fact, the single best intervention that any government can make to improve the health of its population is the provision of universal, free care for mothers-to-be and newborn infants (Shi, 1994).

The experiences of poverty, homelessness and unemployment – that is, social exclusion from the basic minimums regarded as the norm in our society – have a major impact on health. Those already at high levels of risk to their health (the migrant, the Indigenous population and the refugee) are at high risk of social exclusion and at extreme jeopardy of continuing poor health and early death. It is a tragedy of modern societies that social exclusion is concentrated on those with stigmatized medical conditions such as AIDS, mental illness and physical disability, resulting in an impoverished social life and early death for many individuals.

Being a part of a social network, having social support in which one's self-esteem and one's interpersonal relationships are valued, is now known to be a significant factor in preventing early death and vulnerability to disease. Good social support results in a whole range of beneficial health outcomes, from carrying a successful pregnancy, through to recovery from heart attack. Lack of social support is intertwined with social exclusion, both of which are shaped by inequalities of income. The consequence is a sicker, shorter life.

There now appears to be extensive evidence that stress, in the sociological rather than psychological sense – of uncertainty about employment, lack of autonomy at work and lack of a sense of autonomy over life events generally – has a major impact on the autonomic and immune systems. The experience of stress is socially induced and not a characteristic of an individual's psychic make-up. Put simply, the social conditions experienced by individuals at the bottom of the labour market, and who experience greatest uncertainty about their future, are in a permanent state of 'fight or flight' response mode. This biological state makes them vulnerable to infection and disease (Peterson, 1999). Indeed, the focus on stress by sociological researchers constitutes the formation of a new way of explaining the physical outcomes of social organization on individuals and their bodies (Pearlin et al., 2005; Wilkinson, 1996: 193).

These sociological vulnerabilities – of social exclusion, lack of social support and stress – can in turn lead to the adoption of poor lifestyle habits - of poor diet and addictive patterns of behaviour. Rates of addiction, for example, are highly correlated with other aspects of inequality. The poor, the disadvantaged, the unemployed and the homeless, as well as those in low-status jobs, are most at risk of addictive behaviours. While addiction may be seen as an individual's response to social situations, from a sociological perspective, it is the social circumstances that bring about the individual's behaviour.

Like addictive behaviours, our diets are lifestyle choices which are determined by what is available to us. Consuming high-fat, sugar-rich and low-fibre foods is determined by our income and educational level. White bread and refined white sugar (poor dietary 'choices') are cheaper than wholemeal bread and raw sugar (good dietary 'choices'). The poor are put at double jeopardy – what they can afford, and what is marketed for their consumption, is most deleterious to their health. Again, it is important to keep in mind that this is not an individual lifestyle choice, but the consequence of a structurally determined and limited access to a good diet.

Social exclusion, lack of social support and the experience of stress are key determinants of disease, early death and the likelihood of individuals adopting unhealthy lifestyles. In Australia, poverty and ethnicity combine in aboriginality to produce chronic disease and early death. These social factors can operate at the socio-psychological level, as individuals respond, within the limited range of options open to them, to the experience of life in an unequal society. The structures of socio-economic inequality, gender and Indigenous social status leave much less scope for individual variation.

Socio-economic inequality, the combination of low status and poor income – in and of itself, causes sickness and disease. As already mentioned, Townsend and colleagues (Townsend and Davidson, 1988) found in an examination of the 78 leading causes of death that 65 are more common in manual compared with non-manual male workers. In other words, the further down the social hierarchy you are, the sicker you will become, and the sooner you will die. The interweaving of poverty, lack of education, and poor social integration results in diminished health at every stage of the life cycle. It is now clear that inequality of income - the difference between the richest and the poorest - is the single biggest factor in the development of poor health.

The 1998 WHO report does not address the impact of gender directly – which is unusual given the socially determined differences between men's and women's illnesses and death rates, as we saw in Chapter 8 – but a 2009 report, 'Women and Health: Today's Evidence, Tomorrow's Agenda' (World Health Organization, 2009), addresses all of the major structural obstacles that face the gendered health divide. Above all, the difference that generates ill health is the fact that women go to the doctor more, use more prescription drugs, and are hospitalized more than men throughout each stage of their life. On the face of it, this would lead one to conclude that they are sicker than men. However, from a sociological perspective this is not the case. Rather than being sicker, women in Western societies are medicalized. Normal aspects of their life cycle - menstruation, pregnancy and menopause - are turned into medical problems requiring medical supervision and intervention. Feminist sociologists argue that medicine, in a patriarchal society, ensures that women conform to the social role ascribed to them: mother, domestic worker and wife.

In our society, disease is thought to be an individual occurrence based purely in our biological make-up. Continuing inequalities in the pattern of chronic disease - despite medical developments over the nineteenth and twentieth centuries - are generally thought to be the product of either genetics or lifestyle. However, even if there is a genetic explanation (for a very limited number of diseases), this does not actually advance our health in any significant way. It may explain diseases, but it does not take into account our social location or the environmental factors which trigger the disease. Equally, there is little evidence for the role of lifestyle factors, conceptualized as independent from the individual's social position, as a cause of disease. Put simply, our bodies are located in social structures which, by and large, determine our morbidity and mortality.

A sociological perspective on the causes of disease locates individuals' behaviour in institutional and structural contexts - that is, in terms of the structures of class, gender and ethnicity that shape their experience of life. No longer is it enough to claim that individuals need to modify their behaviour, or that increasing expenditure on health-care technology will prevent disease. Rather, it is necessary to take into account societal influences, not as bothersome extras (getting in the road of real medicine), but as the major causative influence of disease.

Unequal societies result in unequal sickness and disease experiences, with those at the bottom getting sicker and dying sooner from what are known to be preventable and modifiable social circumstances. The more equitable the distribution of wealth, the healthier the population. As White has put it 'egalitarianism is not just idealist politics, it is good health' (White, 1991b: 47).

Discussion Questions

1. How does the World Health Organization explain sickness and disease as social factors?

2. Without social support we are more likely both to get sick and to die sooner that those with support structures. Discuss.

3. Fundamentally, the cause of sickness and disease is inequality. Do you think this is correct?

BIBLIOGRAPHY

Abel, E. and Nelson, M. (1990) *Circles of Care*. Albany: State University of New York Press.

Abercrombie, N., Hill, S. and Turner, B. (1986) *Sovereign Individuals of Capitalism*. London: Allen and Unwin.

Acker, C. (1993) 'Stigma or Legitimation? A Historical Examination of the Social Potentials of Addiction Disease Models.' *Journal of Psychoactive Drugs* 25: 13–23.

Adams, M. (ed.) (1990) *The Wellborn Science: Eugenics in Germany, France, Brazil, and Russia*. New York: Oxford University Press.

Ahern, M., Hendryx, M. S. and Siddathan, K. (1996) 'The Importance of the Sense of Community on People's Perceptions of their Health Care Experience.' *Medical Care* 34: 911–23.

Alatas, S. (2010) *The Myth of the Lazy Native*. London: Routledge.

Alford, A. (1979) 'Medicine in the Middle Ages: The Theory of a Profession.' *Centennial Review* 23: 377–96.

Althusser, L. (1971) *Lenin and Philosophy and Other Essays*. London: New Left Review.

Altschuler, A., Somkin, C. and Adler, N. (2004) 'Local Services and Amenities, Neighborhood Social Capital, and Health.' *Social Science and Medicine* 59: 1219–29.

American Psychiatric Association Committee on Nomenclature and Statistics (1980) *Diagnostic and Statistical Manual of Mental Disorders (DSM-III)* 3rd edn. Washington, DC: American Psychiatric Association.

Anderson, J., Jay, S., Zimmerer, J., Farid, R. and Anderson, M. (1991) 'Influencing Test Ordering in Primary Care Using Influential Physicians.' *Health Sociology* 9 (1): 170–82.

Angermeyer, M. and Klusman, D. (1987) 'From Social Class to Social Stress: New Developments in Psychiatric Epidemiology.' In *From Social Class to Social Stress: New Developments in Psychiatric Epidemiology*, edited by M. Angermeyer. New York: Springer-Verlag.

Anthias, F. and Yuval-Davis, N. (1993) 'Contextualising Feminism: Gender, Ethnic and Class Divisions.' *Feminist Review* 15: 62–75.

Arber, S. (1991) 'Class, Paid Employment and Family Roles: Making Sense of Structural Disadvantage, Gender and Health Status.' *Social Science and Medicine* 32: 425–36.

Arksey, H. (1994) 'Expert and Lay Participation in the Construction of Medical Knowledge.' *Sociology of Health and Illness* 16 (4): 448–68.

Armstrong, D. (1983) *The Political Anatomy of the Body*. Edinburgh: Edinburgh University Press.

Armstrong, D. (1995) 'The Rise of Surveillance Medicine.' *Sociology of Health and Illness* 17: 393–404.

Arney, R. (1982) *Power and the Profession of Obstetrics*. Chicago: Chicago University Press.

Arney, R. and Bergen, B. (1984) *Medicine and the Management of Living: Taming the Last Great Beast*. Chicago: University of Chicago Press.

Aronowitz, R. (1998) *Making Sense of Illness: Science, Society and Disease.* Cambridge: Cambridge University Press.

Auerbach, J. and Figert, A. (1995) 'Women's Health Research: Public Policy and Sociology.' *Journal of Health and Social Behaviour* 28: 115–31.

Australian Bureau of Statistics (2002) *Australian Social Trends 2002.* Canberra: ABS.

Australian Bureau of Statistics (2004) *National Health Survey: Summary of Results, Australia 2004–5* (cat. no. 4364.0). Canberra.

Australian Bureau of Statistics (2006) *Injury in Australia: A Snapshot, 2004–05.* 4825.0.55.001. Canberra: ABS. http://www.abs.gov.au/ausstats/abs@.nsf/mf/4825.0.55.001/ (accessed 2 July 2015).

Australian Bureau of Statistics (2007) *Australian Social Trends 2007.* Canberra: ABS.

Australian Bureau of Statistics (2012a) *Health Service Usage and Experience of Care.* 1301.0. Canberra: ABS. http://www.abs.gov.au/ausstats/abs@.nsf/Lookup/by%20Subject/1301.0~2012~Main%20Features~Health%20service%20usage%20and%20experiences%20of%20care~234 (accessed 2 July 2015).

Australian Bureau of Statistics (2012b) *Australian Health Survey: First Results, 2011–12.* 4364.0.55.001. Canberra: ABS. http://www.abs.gov.au/ausstats/abs@.nsf/lookup/4364.0.55.001main+features12011-12 (accessed 3 July 2015).

Australian Bureau of Statistics (2013) *Australian Aboriginal and Torres Strait Islander Health Survey: First Results, Australia, 2012–13.* 4727.0.55.001. Canberra: ABS. http://www.abs.gov.au/ausstats/abs@.nsf/Lookup/84BBCF1F0DA6424ECA257C2F001456B3?opendocument (accessed 3 November 2015).

Australian Financial Review (1986) '$3m Occupational Health Centre Plan.' 17 July.

Australian Institute of Health and Welfare (2006) *Australia's Health 2006: The Tenth Biennial Health Report of the Australian Institute of Health and Welfare.* Cat. no. AUS 73. Canberra: AIHW.

Australian Institute of Health and Welfare (2007) *Young Australians: Their Health and Wellbeing.* Cat. no. PHE 87. Canberra: AIHW.

Australian Institute of Health and Welfare (2014) *Australia's Health 2014.* Australia's Health series no. 14. Cat. no. AUS 178. Canberra: AIHW.

Australian Medical Association (1996) 'Doctors to Become Health Fund Lackeys?' Press release, 14 July.

Australian Medical Association (2005) 'Submission to the House of Representatives Standing Committee on Health and Ageing Inquiry into Health Funding.' Canberra: Australian Medical Association.

Australian Safety and Compensation Council (2006) *Estimating the Number of Work-Related Traumatic Injury Fatalities in Australia 2003–04.* Canberra: Commonwealth of Australia.

Bacquet, C., Horm, J., Gibbs, T. and Greenwell, P. (1991) 'Socioeconomic Factors and Cancer Incidence Among Blacks and Whites.' *Journal of National Cancer Institute* 83: 551–7.

Baggot, R. (1990) *Alcohol, Politics and Social Politics.* London: Avebury Gower.

Baragwanath, C. and Howe, J. (2000) *Corporate Welfare: Public Accountability for Industry.* Canberra: The Australia Institute.

Barbalet, J. M. (1998) *Emotions, Social Theory and Social Structure: A Macrosociological Approach.* Cambridge: Cambridge University Press.

Barclay, D. (2012) 'Impact of "Sick" and "Recovery" Roles on Brain Injury Rehabilitation Outcomes.' *Rehabilitation Research and Practice*, DOI: 10.1155/2012/725078.

Barker-Penfield, J. (1979) 'Sexual Surgery in the Late Nineteenth Century.' In *Seizing Our Bodies*, edited by C. Dreifus. New York: Vintage.

Barrett, M. (1992) 'Words and Things: Materialism and Method in Contemporary Feminist Analysis.' In *Destabilising Theory*, edited by M. Barrett and A. Phillips. Cambridge: Polity Press.

Barrett, M. and Roberts, H. (1978) 'Doctors and their Patients: The Social Control of Women in General Practice.' In *Women, Sexuality and Social Control*, edited by C. Smart and B. Smart. London: Routledge and Kegan Paul.

Bartley, M., Blane, D. and Smith, G. (1998) 'Introduction: Beyond the Black Report.' *Sociology of Health and Illness* 20: 563–77.

Bartsch, D. (2007) 'Prevalence of Body Dysmorphic Disorder Symptoms and Associated Clinical Features Among Australian University Students.' *Clinical Psychologist* 11: 16–23.

Bartsky, S. (1988) 'Foucault, Femininity and the Modernisation of Patriarchal Power.' In *Feminism and Foucault: Reflections on Resistance*, edited by I. Diamond and L. Quinby. Boston: Northeastern University Press.

Bates, E. and Lapsley, H. (1987) *The Health Machine: The Impact of Medical Technology*. Sydney: Penguin.

Batt, S. (1994) *Patient No More: The Politics of Breast Cancer*. London: Scarlett Press.

Bauman, A., Owen, N. and Rushworth, R. (1990) 'Recent Trends and Socio-Demographic Determinants of Exercise Participation in Australia.' *Community Health Studies* 14: 19–26.

Bauman, Z. (1992) *Intimations of Postmodernity*. London: Routledge.

Bauman, Z. (1998) *Work, Consumerism and the New Poor*. Buckingham: Open University Press.

Beaglehole, R. and Bonita, R. (1997) *Public Health at the Crossroads: Achievements and Prospects*. Cambridge: Cambridge University Press.

Bebbington, P. (1996) 'The Origins of Sex Differences in Depressive Disorder: Bridging the Gap.' *International Review of Psychiatry* 8: 295–332.

Beck, U. (1992) *Risk Society: Towards a New Modernity*. London: Sage.

Becker, G. and Nachtigall, R. (1992) 'Eager for Medicalization: The Social Production of Infertility as a Disease.' *Sociology of Health and Illness* 14 (4): 456–71.

Becker, H. (1961) *Boys in White: Student Culture in the Medical School*. Chicago: Chicago University Press.

Behar, J. (1983) 'The Nonorthodox Cancer Therapy Movement: Emergent Organisation in Healthcare Crisis.' *Journal of Sociology and Social Welfare* 10: 440–50.

Bell, S. (1990) 'Sociological Perspectives on the Medicalization of Menopause.' In *Multidisciplinary Perspectives on Menopause*, edited by M. Flink, F. Kronenberg and W. Utian. New York: New York Academy of Sciences.

Benach, J. and Muntaner, C. (2007) 'Precarious Employment and Health: Developing a Research Agenda.' *Journal of Epidemiology and Community Health* 61: 276–7.

Benoit, C. and Heitlinger, A. (1998) 'Women's Health Care Work in Comparative Perspective – Canada, Sweden and Czechoslovakia/Czech Republic as Case Examples.' *Social Science and Medicine* 47: 1101–11.

Berg, J. and Woods, N. (2009) 'Global Women's Health: A Spotlight on Caregiving.' *Nursing Clinics of North America* 44 (3): 375–84.

Berger, J. (1990) 'Market and State in Advanced Capitalist Society.' In *Economy and Society*, edited by A. Martinelli and N. Smelser. London: Sage.

Berger, T. and Luckmann, T. (1967) *The Social Construction of Reality*. London: Penguin.

Bernard, J. (1972) *The Future of Marriage*. New Haven, CT: Yale University Press.

Bertakis, K., Helms, L., Callahan, E., Azari, R., Leigh, P. and Robbins, J. (2001) 'Patient Gender Differences in the Diagnosis of Depression in Primary Care.' *Journal of Women's Health and Gender-Based Medicine* 10 (7): 689–98.

Bijker, W., Hughes, T. and Pinch, T. (1987) *The Social Construction of Technological Systems: New Directions in the Sociology and History of Technology*. Cambridge, MA: MIT Press.

Bird, C. (1994) 'Women's Representation as Subjects in Clinical Studies: A Pilot Study of Research Published in JAMA in 1990 and 1992.' In *Women and Health Research: Ethical and Legal Issues of Including Women in Clinical Studies*, edited by A. Mastroianni, R. Faden and D. Federman. Washington, DC: National Academy Press.

Bird, C. and Fremont, A. (1991) 'Gender, Time Use, and Health.' *Journal of Health and Social Behaviour* 32: 114–29.

Birke, L. (ed.) (1980) *Alice Through the Microscope*. London: Virago.

Black, N. (1995) 'Surgery for Glue Ear – The English Epidemic Wanes.' *Journal of Epidemiology and Community Health* 49: 234–7.

Black, N., Langham, S. and Petticrew, M. (1995) 'Coronary Revascularisation – Why Do Rates Vary in the UK?' *Journal of Epidemiology and Community Health* 49: 408–12.

Blane, D., Davey Smith, G. and Bartley, M. (1993) 'Social Selection: What Does it Contribute to Social Class Differences in Health?' *Sociology of Health and Illness* 15: 1–15.

Blane, D., Hart, C. L., Davey Smith, G., Gillis, C. R., Hole, D. J. and Hawthorne, V. M. (1996) 'Association of Cardiovascular Disease Risk Factors with Socioeconomic Position During Childhood and During Adulthood.' *British Medical Journal* 313: 1434–8.

Blane, D., Bartley, M. and Davey Smith, G. (1997) 'Disease Aetiology and Materialist Explanations of Socioeconomic Mortality Differentials.' *European Journal of Public Health* 7: 385–91.

Bloor, D. (1976) *Knowledge and Social Imagery*. London: Routledge and Kegan Paul.

Bloor, D. (1981) 'The Strengths of the Strong Programme.' *Philosophy of the Social Sciences* 11: 199–213.

Bloor, M. (1976) 'Bishop Berkeley and the Adenotonsillectomy Enigma: An Exploration of Variation in the Social Construction of Medical Disposals.' *Sociology* 10: 43–61.

Blumhagen, D. (1980) 'The Meaning of Hypertension: A Folk Illness with a Medical Name.' *Culture, Medicine and Psychiatry* 4: 197–227.

Bobak, M., Pikhart, H., Hertzman, C., Rose, R. and Marmot, M. (1998) 'Socio-economic Factors, Perceived Control and Self-Reported Health in Russia – A Cross-Sectional Survey.' *Social Science and Medicine* 47: 269–79.

Bollet, A. (1981) 'The Rise and Fall of Diseases.' *Journal of Medicine* 70: 12–16.

Bordo, S. (1985) 'Anorexia Nervosa: Psychopathology as the Crystallisation of Culture.' *The Philosophical Forum* 17: 73–103.

Bourdieu, P. (1984) *Distinction: A Social Critique of the Judgment of Taste*. Cambridge, MA: Harvard University Press.

Bourdieu, P. (1990) *The Logic of Practice*. Cambridge: Polity Press.

Bradby, H. (1996) 'Genetics and Racism.' In *The Troubled Helix: Social and Psychological Aspects of the New Human Genetics*, edited by T. Marteau and M. Richards. Cambridge: Cambridge University Press.

Bradley, H. (1996) *Fractured Identities: Changing Patterns of Inequality*. Cambridge: Polity Press.

Brewer, N., Salz, T. and Lille, S. (2007) 'Systematic Review: The Long-term Effects of False Positive Mammograms.' *Annals of Internal Medicine* 146 (7): 502–10.

Broer, P., Levine, S. and Juran, S. (2014) 'Plastic Surgery: Quo Vadis? Current Trends and Future Projections of Aesthetic Plastic Surgical Procedures in the United States.' *Plastic and Reconstructive Surgery* 133 (3): 293–302.

Broom, D. (1986) 'Occupational Health of Houseworkers.' *Australian Feminist Studies* 2: 15–33.

Broom, D. (1989) 'Masculine Medicine, Feminine Illness: Gender and Health.' In *Sociology of Health and Illness: Australian Readings*, edited by G. Lupton and J. Najman. Melbourne: Macmillan.

Broom, D. and Woodward, R. (1996) 'Medicalisation Reconsidered: Toward a Collaborative Model of Health Care.' *Sociology of Health and Illness* 18 (3): 357–78.

Brown, G. W. (1989) *Life Events and Illness*. New York: Guilford Press.

Brown, G. W. and Harris, T. (1978) *Social Origins of Depression: A Study of Psychiatric Disorder in Women*. New York: Free Press.

Brown, M. and Shavers, V. (2002) 'Racial and Ethnic Disparities in the Receipt of Cancer Treatment.' *Journal of the National Cancer Institute* 94 (5): 334–57.

Brown, P., Zavestoski, S., Linder, M., McCormick , S. and Mayer, B. (2003) 'Chemicals and Casualties: The Search for Causes of Gulf War Illnesses.' In *Synthetic Planet: Chemical Politics and the Hazards of Modern Life*, edited by M. Casper. New York: Routledge.

Brown, P., McCormick, S., Mayer, B., Zavestoski, S., Morello-Frosch, R. and Senier, L. (2006) 'A Lab of Our Own – Environmental Causation of Breast Cancer and Challenges to the Dominant Epidemiological Paradigm.' *Science, Technology and Human Values* 31 (5): 499–536.

Bunker, J. (1970) 'Surgical Manpower: A Comparison of Operations and Surgeons in the U.S. and England and Wales.' *New England Journal of Medicine* 282: 135–44.

Bunkle, P. (1984) 'Manufacturing Motherhood.' *Broadsheet* 118: 23.

Bunkle, P. (1988) *Second Opinion*. Auckland: Oxford University Press.

Bury, M. (1982) 'Chronic Illness as Biographical Disruption.' *Sociology of Health and Illness* 4: 167–82.

Butler, C., Rounick, S., Pill, R., Maggs-Rapport, F. and Stott, N. (1998) 'Understanding the Culture of Prescribing: Quantitative Study of General Practitioners' and Patients' Perceptions of Antibiotics for Sore Throats.' *British Medical Journal* 317: 637–83.

Butler, J. (1993) *Bodies That Matter: On the Discursive Limits of Sex*. New York: Routledge.

Callon, M., Law, J. and Rip, A. (1986) *Mapping the Dynamics of Science and Technology: Sociology of Science in the Real World*. London: Macmillan.

Calnan, M. (1984) 'The Politics of Health: The Case of Smoking Control.' *Journal of Social Policy* 13: 279–96.

Calnan, M. (1986) 'Women and Medicalisation: An Empirical Examination of the Extent of Women's Dependence on Medical Technology in the Early Detection of Breast Cancer.' *Social Science and Medicine* 18: 561–9.

Calnan, M. and Cant, S. (1990) 'The Social Organisation of Food Consumption: A Comparison of Middle Class and Working Class Households.' *International Journal of Sociology and Food Policy* 10 (2): 53–79.

Cameron, E. and Bernardes, J. (1998) 'Gender and Disadvantage in Health – Men's Health for a Change.' *Sociology of Health and Illness* 20: 673–93.

Cameron, S., Walker, C. and Beers, M. (1995) 'E. Coli Outbreak in South Australia Associated with the Consumption of Metwurst.' *Communicable Diseases Intelligence* 19: 70–1.

Canguilhem, G. (1988) *Ideology and Rationality in the History of the Life Sciences.* Cambridge, MA: MIT Press.

Capek, S. (2000) 'Reframing Endometriosis: From "Career Woman's Disease" to Environment/ Body Connections.' In *Illness and the Environment: A Reader in Contested Medicine*, edited by S. Kroll-Smith, P. Brown and V. J. Gunter. New York: New York University Press.

Cardoso, H. and Caninas, M. (2010) 'Secular Trends in Social Class Differences in Height, Weight and BMI of Boys from Two Schools in Lisbon, Portugal (1910–2000).' *Economics and Human Biology* 8 (1): 111–20.

Carers UK (2004) *In Poor Health: The Impact of Caring on Health.* London: Carers UK.

Carlson, P. (1998) 'Self-perceived Health in East and West Europe – Another European Health Divide.' *Social Science and Medicine* 46: 1355–66.

Carpiano, R. (2007) 'Neighborhood Social Capital and Adult Health: An Empirical Test of a Bourdieu-based Model.' *Health and Place* 13 (3): 639–55.

Cartwright, S. A. (1851) 'Report on the Diseases and Physical Peculiarities of the Negro Race.' *New Orleans Medical and Surgical Journal* May: 691–715.

Cartwright, S. R. (1988) *The Report of the Cervical Cancer Enquiry.* Auckland: New Zealand Government Printer.

Carville, K., Lehmann, D., Hall, G., Moore, H., Richmond, P., de Klerk, N. and Burgner, D. (2007) 'Infection is the Major Component of the Disease Burden in Aboriginal and Non-Aboriginal Australian Children: A Population-Based Study.' *Pediatric Infectious Disease Journal* 26 (3): 210–16.

Cassell, J. (1976) 'The Contribution of the Social Environment to Host Resistance.' *American Journal of Epidemiology* 104: 107–23.

Centers for Disease Control and Prevention (2005) 'Mental Health in the United States: Prevalence of Diagnosis and Medication Treatment for Attention-Deficit/Hyperactivity Disorder – United States, 2003.' *Morbidity and Mortality Weekly Report* 54 (34): 842–47.

Centers for Disease Control and Prevention (2013) 'CDC Health Disparities and Inequalities Report – United States, 2013.' *Morbidity and Mortality Weekly Report* 62 (Suppl. 3).

Cernerud, L. (1995) 'Height and Social Mobility: A Study of the Height of 10 Year Olds in Relation to Socio-Economic Background and Type of Formal Schooling.' *Scandinavian Journal of Public Health* 23 (1): 28–31.

Chandola, T., Brunner, E. and Marmot, M. (2006) 'Chronic Stress at Work and the Metabolic Syndrome: Prospective Study.' *British Medical Journal* 332: 521–5.

Chant, S. (2012) 'Feminization of Poverty.' *The Wiley-Blackwell Encyclopedia of Globalization*. http://onlinelibrary.wiley.com/doi/10.1002/9780470670590.wbeog202/abstract (accessed 2 July 2015).

Charlesworth, S. (2000) *A Phenomenology of Working-Class Experience*. Cambridge: Cambridge University Press.

Charlton, D. and Murphy, M. (eds) (1997) *Adult Health: Historical Aspects 1850–1980*. London: HMSO.

Chatty, R., Stepner, M., Abraham, B., et al. (2016) 'The Association Between Income and Life Expectancy in the United States, 2001-2014.' *Journal of the American Medical Association* 315 (16): 1750–66.

Cheung, Y. B. (1998) 'Accidents, Assaults and Marital Status.' *Social Science and Medicine* 47: 1325–9.

Chorover, S. (1979) *From Genesis to Genocide*. Cambridge, MA: MIT Press.

Clarke, J. and James, S. (2003) 'The Radicalized Self: The Impact on the Self of the Contested Nature of the Diagnosis of Chronic Fatigue Syndrome.' *Social Science and Medicine* 57 (8): 1387–95

Cochrane, A. (1972) *Effectiveness and Efficiency*. London: Nuffield Provincial Hospitals Trust.

Cohen, R. and Schnelle, T. (eds) (1986) *Cognition and Fact: Materials on Ludwik Fleck*. Dordrecht: D. Riedel.

Cohen, S. and Williamson, G. (1991) 'Stress and Infectious Disease in Humans.' *Psychological Bulletin* 109: 5–24.

Cohen, S., Doyle, W. and Baum, A. (2006) 'Socioeconomic Status is Associated with Stress Hormones.' *Psychosomatic Medicine* 68 (3): 414–20.

Collyer, F. and White, K. (1997) 'Enter the Market: Competition, Regulation and Hospital Funding in Australia.' *Australian and New Zealand Journal of Sociology* 33: 344–63.

Coltrane, S. (1994) 'Theorising Masculinities in Contemporary Social Science.' In *Theorising Masculinities*, edited by H. Brod and M. Kaufman. London: Sage.

Comaroff, J. (1987) 'Of Totemism and Ethnicity: Consciousness, Practice and the Signs of Inequality.' *Ethnos* 52: 301–23.

Conger, R., Elder, G., Simons, R. and Ge, X. (1993) 'Husband and Wife Differences in Response to Undesirable Life Events.' *Journal of Health and Social Behaviour* 34: 71–88.

Connell, R. W. (1987) *Gender and Power: Society, the Person and Sexual Politics*. Cambridge: Polity Press.

Connell, R. W. (1995) *Masculinities*. St Leonards, NSW: Allen and Unwin.

Conrad, P. (1992) 'Medicalisation and Social Control.' *Annual Review of Sociology* 18: 209–32.

Conrad, P. (2007) *The Medicalization of Society: On the Transformation of Human Conditions into Treatable Disorders*. Baltimore: Johns Hopkins University Press.

Conrad, P. and Potter, D. (2000) 'From Hyperactive Children to ADHD Adults: Observations on the Expansion of Medical Categories.' *Social Problems* 47 (4): 559–82.

Conrad, P. and Schneider, J. (1980) *Deviance and Medicalisation: From Badness to Sickness*. St Louis: Mosby.

Contratto, S. (1984) 'Mothers.' In *The Shadow of the Past*, edited by M. Lewin. New York: Columbia University Press.

Cooper, D. (1967) *Psychiatry and Anti-Psychiatry*. London: Tavistock.

Cooper, D. (1994) 'Productive, Relational and Everywhere? Conceptualising Power and Resistance within Foucauldian Feminism.' *Sociology* 28 (2): 435–54.

Cooper, R. and David, R. (1986) 'The Biological Concept of Race and its Application to Epidemiology.' *Journal of Health Politics, Policy and Law* 11: 97–116.

Coory, M. and Walsh, W. (2005) 'Rates of Percutaneous Coronary Interventions and Bypass Surgery after Acute Myocardial Infarction in Indigenous Patients.' *Medical Journal of Australia* 182 (10): 507–12.

Coory, M., Fagan, P., Muller, J. and Dunn, N. (2002) 'Participation in Cervical Cancer Screening by Women in Rural and Remote Aboriginal and Torres Strait Islander Communities in Queensland.' *Medical Journal of Australia* 177 (10): 544–7.

Cooter, R. (1979) 'The Power of the Body: The Early Nineteenth Century.' In *Natural Order: Historical Studies of Scientific Culture*, edited by B. Barnes and S. Shapin. London: Sage.

Corea, G. (1985) *The Mother Machine*. New York: Harper & Row.

Courtenay, W. (2000) 'Constructions of Masculinity and their Influence on Men's Well-Being: A Theory of Gender and Health.' *Social Science and Medicine* 50: 1385–401.

Cowan, P. (1987) 'Patient Satisfaction With an Office Visit for the Common Cold.' *Journal of Family Practice* 24: 412–13.

Crawford, R. (1980) 'Healthism and the Medicalisation of Everyday Life.' *International Journal of Health Services* 10 (3): 365–90.

Crawford, R. (2000) 'The Ritual of Health Promotion.' In *Health, Medicine and Society: Key Theories, Future Agendas*, edited by S. Williams. London: Routledge.

Crombie, A. (1994) *Styles of Scientific Thinking in the European Tradition*, 3 vols. London: Duckworth.

Crook, S., Pakulski, J. and Waters, M. (1992) *Postmodernization: Change in Advanced Society*. London: Sage.

Crossley, M. (1998) 'Sick Role or Empowerment – The Ambiguities of Life with an HIV Positive Diagnosis.' *Sociology of Health and Illness* 20: 507–31.

Crowley, H. and Himmelweit, S. (eds) (1992) *Knowing Women: Feminism and Knowledge*. London: Polity Press.

Curry, J. and Stabile, M. (2004) 'Child Mental Health and Human Capital Accumulation: The Case of ADHD.' *Journal of Health Economics* 25 (6): 1094–118.

Darity, W., Guilkey, D. and Winfrey, W. (1995) 'Ethnicity, Race and Earnings.' *Economic Letters* 47: 401–8.

Darmon, N. and Drewnowski, A. (2008) 'Does Social Class Predict Diet Quality?' *American Journal of Clinical Nutrition* 87: 1107–17.

Davis, P. (1994) 'A Socio-Cultural Critique of Transition Theory.' In *Social Dimensions of Health and Disease*, edited by J. Spicer, A. Trlin and J. Walton. Palmerston North: Dunmore Press.

Davis, P. and Lee, R. (1990) 'Patterns of Care and Professional Decision Making in a New Zealand General Practice Sample.' *New Zealand Medical Journal* 103: 309–12.

Davis-Floyd, R. (1994) 'The Technocratic Body: American Childbirth as Cultural Expression.' *Social Science and Medicine* 38: 1125–40.

Davison, C., Macintyre, S. and Smith, G. (1994) 'The Potential Impact of Predictive Genetic Screening for Susceptibility to Common Chronic Disease: A Review and Proposed Research Agenda.' *Sociology of Health and Illness* 16: 340–71.

Day, P., Lancaster, P. and Smith, G. (1997) *Australia's Mothers and Babies 1995*. Sydney: Australian Institute of Health and Welfare.

de Beauvoir, S. (1953) *The Second Sex*. London: Harmondsworth.

de Carnargo, K. (2002) 'The Thought Style of Physicians: Strategies for Keeping up with Medical Knowledge.' *Social Studies of Science* 23 (5–6): 827–55.

de la Barra, X. (1998) 'Poverty: The Main Cause of Ill Health in Urban Children.' *Health Education and Behaviour* 25: 45–59.

de Swaan, A. (1981) 'The Politics of Agoraphobia: On Changes in Emotional Management.' *Theory and Society* 10: 359–85.

Delaporte, F. (1986) *Disease and Civilisation: The Cholera in Paris, 1832*. Cambridge, MA: MIT Press.

Denny, E. (1994) 'Liberation or Oppression? Radical Feminism and In Vitro Fertilisation.' *Sociology of Health and Illness* 16 (1): 62–80.

Denny, E. (1996) 'New Reproductive Technologies: The Views of Women Undergoing Treatment in Modern Medicine.' In *Modern Medicine: Lay Perspectives and Experiences*, edited by S. Williams and M. Calnan. London: University College London.

Department of Health and Ageing (2005) 'Australian Health Care Agreements: Do Age and Gender Make a Difference?' *Australian Government Department of Health and Ageing Website*, http://www.health.gov.au (accessed 25 July 2007).

Department of Health and Human Services, Australian Medical Association, and Royal College of General Practitioners (1992) *The Future of General Practice: A Strategy for the Nineties and Beyond*. Canberra: Department of Community Services and Health.

Department of Health and Social Security (1980) 'Inequalities in Health.' In *Inequalities in Health: The Black Report and the Health Divide*, edited by P. Townsend and N. Davidson. Harmondsworth: Penguin.

Diamond, S. and Solomon, G. (1999) *The Practicing Physician's Approach to Headache*, 6th edn. Philadelphia: W.B. Saunders.

Dilhuydy, M. and Barreau, B. (1997) 'The Debate Over Mass Mammography: Is it Beneficial for Women?' *European Journal of Radiology* 24 (2): 86–93.

Doessel, D. (1990) 'Editor's Introduction.' In *Towards Evaluation in General Practice: A Workshop on Vocational Registration*, edited by D. Doessel. Canberra: Department of Community Services and Health.

Doll, R. (1988) 'Epidemiological Evidence of the Effects of Behavior and the Environment on the Risk of Human Cancer.' *Recent Results in Cancer Research* 154: 3–21.

Domhoff, W. (2006) 'Wealth, Income, Power.' *Who Rules America?*, University of California. http://sociology.ucsc.edu/whorulesamerica/power/wealth.html (accessed 25 July 2007).

Dooley, D. and Catalano, R. (1984) 'Why the Economy Predicts Help-seeking: A Test of Competing Explanations.' *Journal of Health and Social Behaviour* 25: 160–76.

Douglas, M. (1973) *Natural Symbols*. Harmondsworth: Penguin.

Doyal, L. and Pennell, I. (1979) *The Political Economy of Health*. London: Pluto Press.

Doyle, S., Skoner, W., Rabin, B. and Gwaltney, J. (1997) 'Social Ties and Susceptibility to the Common Cold.' *Journal of the American Medical Association* 277: 1940–4.

Draper, E. (1991) *Risky Business: Genetic Testing and Exclusionary Practices in the Hazardous Work Place*. Cambridge: Cambridge University Press.

Dressler, W. (1991) 'Social Class, Skin Colour, and Arterial Blood Pressure in Two Societies.' *Discourse Analysis* 1: 60–77.

Dubos, R. (1959) *Mirage of Health*. New York: Harper & Row.

Durkheim, E. (1915) *The Elementary Forms of the Religious Life*. New York: Free Press.

Durkheim, E. (1933) *The Division of Labor in Society*. New York: Free Press.

Durkheim, E. (1966) *Suicide: A Study in Sociology*. New York: Free Press.

Durkheim, E. and Mauss, M. (1963) *Primitive Classifications*. Chicago: Chicago University Press.

Dussault, G. and Sheiham, A. (1982) 'Medical Theories and Professional Development.' *Social Science and Medicine* 16: 1405–12.

Edwards, S. (1993) 'Selling the Body, Keeping the Soul: Sexuality, Power and the Theories and Realities of Prostitution.' In *Body Matters*, edited by S. Scott and D. Morgan. London: Falmer Press.

Egbert, L., Battit, G., Welch, C. and Bartlett, M. (1978) 'Reduction of Postoperative Pain by Encouragement and Instruction of Patients: A Study of Doctor–Patient Rapport.' In *Basic Readings In Medical Sociology*, edited by D. Tuckett and J. Kaufert. London: Tavistock.

eHealth (2015) 'Healthcare Providers FAQs: General Questions.' http://www.ehealth.gov.au/internet/ehealth/publishing.nsf/Content/faqs-hcp-gen (accessed 25 June 2015).

Ehrenreich, B. and English, D. (1978) *For Her Own Good: 150 Years of the Experts' Advice to Women*. London: Pluto Press.

Elias, N. (1971) 'Sociology of Knowledge: New Perspectives Part 1.' *Sociology* 5: 149–69.

Elias, N. (1978) *The Civilising Process*, 2 vols. Oxford: Basil Blackwell.

Elias, N. (1985) *The Loneliness of the Dying*. Oxford: Basil Blackwell.

Elstad, J. (1998) 'The Psycho-social Perspective on Social Inequalities in Health.' *Sociology of Health and Illness* 20: 598–618.

Eng, P., Rimm, E., Fitzmaurice, G. and Kawachi, I. (2002) 'Social Ties and Change in Social Ties in Relation to Subsequent Total and Cause-specific Mortality and Coronary Heart Disease Incidence in Men.' *American Journal of Epidemiology* 155 (8): 700–9.

Engel, G. L. (1981) 'The Need for a New Medical Model: A Challenge for Biomedicine.' In *Concepts of Health and Disease*, edited by A. Caplan, H. Englehardt and J. McCartney. Reading, MA: Addison-Wesley.

Engels, F. (1948 [1884]) *The Origins of the Family, Private Property and the State*. Moscow: Progress Publishers.

Engels, F. (1974) *The Condition of the Working Class in England*. Moscow: Progress Publishers.

Englehardt, H. T. (1981) 'The Disease of Masturbation: Values and the Concept of Disease.' In *Concepts of Health and Disease*, edited by A. Caplan, H. Englehardt and J. McCartney. Reading, MA: Addison-Wesley.

Epstein, S. and Swartz, J. (1981) 'Fallacies of Life Style Related Cancer Theories.' *Nature* 289: 127–30.

Erchak, G. and Rosenfeld, R. (1989) 'Learning Disabilities, Dyslexia, and the Medicalisation of the Classroom.' In *Images of Issues: Contemporary Social Problems*, edited by J. Best. New York: Aldine.

Esping-Andersen, G. (ed.) (1993) *Changing Classes*. London: Sage.

Ettling, J. (1981) *The Germ of Laziness: Rockefeller Philanthropy and Public Health in the New South*. Cambridge, MA: Harvard University Press.

Evans, R. and Stoddart, G. (1990) 'Producing Health, Consuming Health Care.' *Social Science and Medicine* 31: 1347–63.

Eysenck, H. (1971) *The IQ Argument: Race, Intelligence, Education.* New York: Library Press.

Farley, R. (1984) *Blacks and Whites: Narrowing the Gap.* Cambridge, MA: Harvard University Press.

Feher, M., Naddaff, R. and Tazi, N. (eds) (1989) *Fragments for a History of the Human Body,* 3 vols. New York: Zone.

Fein, O. (1995) 'The Influence of Social Class on Health Status: American and British Research on Health Inequalities.' *Journal of Internal Medicine* 10: 577–86.

Feinstein, J. (1993) 'The Relationship Between Socioeconomic Status and Health: A Review of the Literature.' *The Milbank Quarterly* 71: 279–322.

Felton, B. and Shinn, M. (1992) 'Social Integration and Social Support: Moving "Social Support" Beyond the Individual Level.' *Journal of Community Psychology* 20: 103–15.

Figert, A. (1995) 'The Three Faces of PMS: The Professional, Gendered, and Scientific Structuring of a Psychiatric Disorder.' *Social Problems* 42 (1): 56–73.

Figlio, K. (1978) 'Chlorosis and Chronic Disease in Nineteenth Century Britain: The Social Constitution of Somatic Illness in a Capitalist Society.' *Social History* 3: 167–79.

Figlio, K. (1982) 'How Does Illness Mediate Social Relations?' In *The Problem of Medical Knowledge,* edited by P. Wright and A. Treacher. Edinburgh: Edinburgh University Press.

Firestone, S. (1974) *The Dialectic of Sex: The Case for the Feminist Revolution.* New York: Morrow.

Flax, J. (1987) 'Postmodernism and Gender Relations in Feminist Theory.' In *Feminist Theory and Process,* edited by M. Malson. Chicago: Chicago University Press.

Fleck, L. (1935 [1979]) *The Genesis and Development of a Scientific Fact.* Chicago: Chicago University Press.

Fleck, L. (1935 [1981]) 'On the Question of the Foundations of Medical Knowledge.' *Journal of Medicine and Philosophy* 6: 237–56.

Fletcher, R. (1996) 'Testosterone Poisoning or Terminal Neglect? The Men's Health Issue.' Briefing paper. Canberra: Department of the Parliamentary Library.

Folkman, S. (1984) 'Personal Control and Stress and Coping Processes: A Theoretical Analysis.' *Journal of Personality and Social Psychology* 46: 839–52.

Forde, O. (1998) 'Is Imposing Risk Awareness Cultural Imperialism?' *Social Science and Medicine* 47 (9): 1155–9.

Foreman, T. A. (2003) 'The Social Psychological Costs of Racial Segmentations in the Workplace: A Study of African Americans'. *Journal of Health and Social Behaviour* 44 (3): 332–52.

Forsythe, D. (1996) 'New Bottles, Old Wine: Hidden Cultural Assumptions in a Computerized Explanation System for Migraine Sufferers.' *Medical Anthropology Quarterly* 10 (4): 551–74.

Foster, P. (1989) 'Improving the Doctor/Patient Relationship: A Feminist Perspective.' *Journal of Social Policy* 18: 337–61.

Foucault, M. (1967) *Madness and Civilisation.* London: Tavistock.

Foucault, M. (1973) *The Birth of the Clinic.* London: Routledge.

Foucault, M. (1976) *The History of Sexuality. Volume 1: An Introduction.* Harmondsworth: Penguin.

Foucault, M. (1977a) *Discipline and Punish: The Birth of the Prison.* Harmondsworth: Penguin.

Foucault, M. (1977b) 'Nietzsche, Genealogy and History.' In *Language, Countermemory, Practice,* edited by D. F. Bouchard. Oxford: Blackwell.

Foucault, M. (1982) 'The Subject and Power.' In *Michel Foucault: Beyond Structuralism and Hermeneutics*, edited by H. Dreyfus and P. Rabinow. Chicago: Chicago University Press.

Fox, P. (1989) 'From Senility to Alzheimer's Disease: The Rise of the Alzheimer's Disease Movement.' *The Milbank Quarterly* 67: 58–101.

Fox, R. (1979) 'Medical Evolution.' In *Essays in Medical Sociology*. New York: John Wiley.

Fox, R. (2008) 'Towards an Ethics of Iatrogenesis.' In *Dark Medicine: Rationalising Unethical Medical Research*, edited by W. Lafleur, G. Böhme and S. Shimazono. Bloomington: Indiana University Press.

Fox-Keller, E. (1985) *Reflections on Gender and Science*. New Haven, CT: Yale University Press.

Frank, A. W. (1992) 'Nightmares of the Medical Simulacrum: Jean Baudrillard and David Cronenburg.' In *Jean Baudrillard: The Disappearance of Art and Politics*, edited by W. Stearn and W. Chaloupka. London: Macmillan.

Frank, A. W. (1993) 'The Rhetoric of Self Change: Illness Experience as Narrative.' *The Sociological Quarterly* 34: 39–52.

Frank, A. W. (1995) *The Wounded Story Teller: Body, Illness and Ethics*. Chicago: Chicago University Press.

Freedman, D., Khan, L., Serdula, M., et al. (2005) 'The Relation of Childhood BMI to Adult Adiposity: The Bogalusa Heart Study.' *Paediatrics* 115 (10): 22–7.

Freid, M. (2000) 'Poor Children Subject to Environmental Injustice.' *Journal of the American Medical Association* 283: 3055.

Freidson, E. (1970a) *Profession of Medicine: A Study of the Sociology of Applied Knowledge*. New York: Dodd and Mead.

Freidson, E. (1970b) *Professional Dominance: The Social Structure of Medical Care*. New York: Aldine Publishing Company.

Freund, P. (2004) 'Civilised Bodies Redux: Seams in the Cyborg.' *Social Theory and Health* 2 (3): 273–89.

Fritschi, L. and Driscoll, T. (2006) 'Cancer Due to Occupation in Australia.' *Australian and New Zealand Journal of Public Health* 30 (3): 213–19.

Frohlich, K., Corin, E. and Potvin, L. (2001) 'A Theoretical Proposal for the Relationship Between Context and Disease.' *Sociology of Health and Illness* 23 (6): 776–97.

Gabe, J. and Calnan, M. (1989) 'The Limits of Medicine: Women's Perception of Medical Technology.' *Social Science and Medicine* 28: 223–31.

Gabe, J. and Thorgood, N. (1986) 'Prescribed Drug Use and the Management of Everyday Life: The Experiences of Black and White Working Class Women.' *The Sociological Review* 34: 737–72.

Gamble, V. (1993) 'A Legacy of Distrust: African Americans and Medical Research.' *American Journal of Preventive Medicine* 9: 35–9.

Garfinkel, H. (1972) 'Studies in the Routine Grounds of Everyday Activities.' In *Studies in Social Interaction*, edited by D. Sudnow. New York: Free Press.

Gatens, M. (1992) 'Power, Bodies, and Difference.' In *Destabilising Theory*, edited by M. Barrett and A. Phillips. Cambridge: Polity Press.

Gerald, L., Anderson, A., Johnson, G., et al. (1994) 'Social Class, Social Support and Obesity Risk in Children.' *Childcare Health Development* 20 (3): 145–63.

Germov, J. (ed.) (2005) *Second Opinion: An Introduction to Health Sociology*. Melbourne: Oxford University Press.

Gerth, H. and Mills, C. Wright (1948) *From Max Weber.* London: Routledge and Kegan Paul.

Giddens, A. (1987) *Social Theory and Modern Sociology.* London: Polity Press.

Giddens, A. (1992) *The Consequences of Modernity.* Cambridge: Polity Press.

Gillick, M. (1984) 'Health Promotion, Jogging and the Pursuit of the Moral Life.' *Journal of Health Politics, Policy and Law* 9 (3): 369–87.

Gimenez, M. (1989) 'The Feminization of Poverty: Myth or Reality.' *International Journal of Health Services* 19: 45–61.

Glaser, B. and Strauss, A. (1968a) *The Discovery of Grounded Theory.* London: Weidenfeld and Nicolson.

Glaser, B. and Strauss, A. (1968b) *Time for Dying.* Chicago: Aldine.

Glenn, L., Beck, R. and Burkett, G. (1998) 'Effect of a Transient, Geographically Localised Economic Recovery on Community Health.' *Journal of Epidemiology and Community Health* 52: 749–57.

Glikman, M., Kawachi, I., Hunter, D., Colditz, G., Manson, J., Stampfer, M., et al. (1995) 'Childhood Socioeconomic Status and Risk of Cardiovascular Disease in Middle Aged US Women.' *Journal of Epidemiology and Public Health* 49: 10–15.

Goffman, E. (1961) *Asylums.* New York: Doubleday and Co.

Gold, M. (1977) 'A Crisis of Identity: The Case of Medical Sociology.' *Journal of Health and Social Behaviour* 18: 160–8.

Gordon, C. (1991) 'Governmental Rationality.' In *The Foucault Effect,* edited by G. Burchell, C. Gordon and P. Miller. London: Harvester Wheatsheaf.

Goudsblom, J. (1986) 'Public Health and the Civilising Process.' *The Milbank Quarterly* 64: 161–88.

Gould, S. (1981) 'The Hereditarian Theory of IQ: An American Invention.' In *The Mismeasure of Man,* edited by S. Gould. New York: W. W. Norton.

Graham, H. (2009) 'Introduction: The Challenge of Health Inequalities.' In *Understanding Health Inequalities,* edited by H. Graham. New York: Open University Press.

Graham, J. (1972) 'Cluster Headache.' *Headache* 11 (4): 175–85.

Gray, D. and Saggers, S. (1994) 'Aboriginal Ill Health: The Harvest of Injustice.' In *Just Health,* edited by C. Waddell and A. Petersen. Melbourne: Churchill Livingstone.

Grodsky, E. and Pager, D. (2001) 'The Structure of Disadvantage: Individual and Occupational Determinants of the Black–White? Wage Gap.' *American Sociological Review* 66 (4): 547–67.

Grosz, E. (1988) 'The In(ter)vention of Feminist Knowledge.' In *Crossing Boundaries: Feminism and the Critique of Knowledge,* edited by B. Caine, E. Grosz and M. De Lepervanche. Sydney: Allen and Unwin.

Grosz, E. (1994) *Volatile Bodies: Towards a Corporeal Feminism.* Sydney: Allen and Unwin.

Grosz, E. and De Lepervanche, M. (1988) 'Feminism and Science.' In *Crossing Boundaries: Feminism and the Critique of Knowledge,* edited by B. Caine, E. Grosz and M. De Lepervanche. Sydney: Allen and Unwin.

Gustafson, E. (1972) 'Dying: The Career of the Nursing Home Patient.' *Journal of Health and Social Behaviour* 13: 226–35.

Hacking, I. (1992a) '"Style" for Historians and Philosophers.' *Studies in the History and Philosophy of Science* 23: 1–20.

Hacking, I. (1992b) 'Statistical Language, Statistical Truth, and Statistical Reason: The Self Authentication of a Style of Scientific Reasoning.' In *The Social Dimensions of Science,* edited by E. McMullin. Notre Dame: University of Notre Dame Press.

Hahn, R., Eaker, E., Barker, N., Teutsch, S., Sosniak, W., et al. (1996) 'Poverty and Death in the United States – 1973–1991.' *International Journal of Health Services* 26: 673–90.

Hall, P. and M. Lamont (2013) *Social Resilience in the Neo-liberal Era.* Cambridge: Cambridge University Press.

Hall, S. E., Holman, C. D., Heudrie, D. V. and Spilsbury, K. (2004) 'Unequal Access to Breast-Conserving Surgery in Western Australia 1982–2000.' *ANZ Journal of Surgery* 74 (6): 413–19.

Haller, J. (1971) *Outcasts From Evolution: Scientific Attitudes of Racial Inferiority.* Urbana: University of Illinois Press.

Hamalainen, P., Takala, J. and Saarela, K. (2007) 'Global Estimates of Fatal Work-related Diseases.' *American Journal of Industrial Medicine* 50 (1): 28–41.

Hamilton, V., Broman, C., Hoffman, W. and Renner, D. (1990) 'Hard Times and Vulnerable People: Initial Effects of Plant Closings on Autoworkers' Mental Health.' *Journal of Health and Social Behaviour* 31: 123–40.

Harris, T., Surtees, P. and Bancroft, J. (1991) 'Is Sex Necessarily a Risk Factor to Depression?' *British Journal of Psychiatry* 158: 708–12.

Hart, C., Smith, G. and Blane, D. (1998) 'Social Mobility and 21 Year Mortality in a Cohort of Scottish Men.' *Social Science and Medicine* 47: 112–30.

Harwood, J. (1993) *Styles of Scientific Thought: the German Genetics Community 1900–1933.* Chicago: University of Chicago Press.

Haug, M. (1973) 'Deprofessionalisation: An Alternate Hypothesis for the Future.' *Sociological Review Monograph* 20: 195–211.

Haug, M. (1988) 'A Re-examination of the Hypothesis of Physician Deprofessionalisation.' *Milbank Quarterly* 66 (Suppl. 2): 48–56.

Hawkins, A. H. (1990) 'A Change of Heart: The Paradigm of Regeneration in Medical and Religious Narrative.' *Perspectives in Biology and Medicine* 33: 547–59.

Hawryluk, M. (2015) 'World's First Skull, Scalp Transplant Gives Patient Life-Saving Organs.' SBS. http://www.sbs.com.au/news/article/2015/06/05/worlds-first-skull-scalp-transplant-gives-patient-life-saving-organs (accessed 1 December 2015).

Hayakawa, K. (1992) 'Intrapair Differences of Physical Aging and Longevity in Identical Twins.' *Acta Genetica Medicae Gemellologiae* 41: 177–85.

Hearn, J. (2012) 'Male Bodies, Masculine Bodies, Men's Bodies: The Need for a Concept of Gex.' *Routledge Handbook of Body Studies*, edited by B. S. Turner. London: Routledge.

Heath, I., Haines, A., Glover, J. and Hetzel, D. (2000) 'Open Invitation from International Poverty and Health Network to all Health Care Professionals.' *Medical Journal of Australia* 172: 356–7.

Helman, C. (1985) 'Psyche, Soma, and Society: The Social Construction of Psychosomatic Disorders.' *Culture, Medicine and Society* 9: 1–26.

Helman, C. (1991) *Body Myths.* London: Chatto and Windus.

Henderson, L. J. (1935) 'Physician and Patient as a Social System.' *New England Journal of Medicine* 212: 819–23.

Henderson, L. J. (1936) 'The Practice of Medicine as Applied to Sociology.' *Transactions of the Association of American Physicians* 51: 8–15.

Hennessy, R. (1993) *Materialist Feminism and the Politics of Discourse.* London: Routledge.

Hernstein, R. and Murray, C. (1994) *The Bell Curve: Intelligence and Class Structure in American Life.* New York: The Free Press.

Heyman, B., Henriksen, M. and Maughan, K. (1998) 'Probabilities and Health Risks – A Qualitative Approach.' *Social Science and Medicine* 47: 1295–306.

Higgs, P. and Scambler, G. (1998) 'Explaining Health Inequalities: How Useful are Concepts of Social Class?' In *Modernity, Medicine and Health*, edited by G. Scambler and P. Higgs. London: Routledge.

Hirschkorn, K. (2006) 'Exclusive Versus Everyday Forms of Professional Knowledge: Legitimacy Claims in Conventional and Alternative Medicine.' *Sociology of Health and Illness* 28 (5): 533–57.

Hogle, L. (1995) 'Tales From the Crypt: Technology Meets Organism in Living Cadaver.' In *The Cyborg Handbook*, edited by C. H. Gray. London: Routledge.

Holmes, H. (1980) *Birth Control and Controlling Birth*. Clifton, NJ: Humana Press.

Holmes, T. and Rahe, R. (1967) 'The Social Readjustment Rating Scale.' *Journal of Psychosomatic Research* 11: 213–18.

Holton, R. (1996) 'Has Class Analysis a Future?' In *Conflicts About Class: Debating Inequality in Late Industrialism*, edited by D. Lee and B. S. Turner. London: Longman.

Hopkins, A. (1989) 'The Social Construction of Repetition Strain Injury.' *Australia and New Zealand Journal of Sociology* 25: 239–59.

Hudson, L. (1976) *The Cult of the Fact*. London: Jonathan Cape.

Hughes, D. and Griffiths, L. (1996) '"But If You Look at the Coronary Anatomy …": Risk and Rationing in Cardiac Surgery.' *Sociology of Health and Illness* 18: 172–97.

Hurley, S. and Kaldor, J. (1992) 'The Benefits and Risks of Mammographic Screening for Breast Cancer.' *Epidemiological Reviews* 14: 101–30.

Hyden, L.-C. (1997) 'Illness and Narrative.' *Sociology of Health and Illness* 19: 48–69.

Idler, E. (1979) 'Definitions of Health and Illness and Medical Sociology.' *Social Science and Medicine* 13A: 723–31.

Illich, I. (1975) *Medical Nemesis: The Expropriation of Health*. London: Marion Boyars.

Industry Commission (1996) *Work, Health and Safety: Inquiry into Occupational Health and Safety*. Canberra: Australian Government Printer.

Ivanov, I. and Straif, D. (2006) 'Prevention of Occupational Cancer.' *World Health Organization GOHNET Newsletter* 11: 1–4

James, R. (2014) 'Incandescence, Melancholy, and Feminist Bad Vibes: A Response to Ziarek's *Feminist Aesthetics and the Politics of Modernism*.' *Differences* 25 (2): 116–29.

James, R. (2015) *Resilience and Melancholy: Pop Music, Feminism, Neoliberalism*. London: Zero Books.

Jameson, F. (1991) *Postmodernism, or The Cultural Logic of Late Capitalism*. London: Verso.

Jamous, H. and Pelloile, B. (1970) 'Professions or Self Perpetuating Systems?' In *Professions and Professionalization*, edited by J. A. Jackson. Cambridge: Cambridge University Press.

Jan, S. (1998) 'A Holistic Approach to the Economic Evaluation of Health Programs Using Institutionalist Methodology.' *Social Science and Medicine* 47: 1565–72.

Jenkins, R., Bebbington, P., Brugha, T., et al. (1998) 'British Psychiatry Morbidity Survey.' *British Journal of Psychiatry* 173: 4–7.

Jensen, A. (1969) 'How Much Can We Boost IQ and Scholastic Achievement?' *Harvard Educational Review* 39: 1–123.

Jewson, N. (1976) 'The Disappearance of the Sick Man from Medical Cosmology, 1770–1870.' *Sociology* 10: 225–44.

Johnson, J., Stewart, W., Hall, E., Fredlund, P. and Theorell, T. (1996) 'Longterm Psychosocial Work Environment Exposure and Cardiovascular Mortality Among Swedish Men.' *American Journal of Public Health* 86: 324–331.

Johnson, R., Roter, D., Powe, N. and Cooper, L. (2004) 'Patient Race/Ethnicity and Quality of Patient–Physician Communication During Medical Visits.' *American Journal of Public Health* 94 (12): 2084–90.

Johnson, T. (1977) 'The Profession in the Class Structure.' In *Industrial Society: Class, Cleavage and Control*, edited by R. Scase. London: Allen and Unwin.

Jones, J. (1981) *Bad Blood: The Tuskegee Syphilis Experiment*. New York: The Free Press.

Jones, J. (1992) 'The Tuskegee Legacy: AIDS and the Black Community.' *Hastings Centre Report*, November–December: 38–40.

Kaasik, T., Anderson, R. and Horte, L. (1998) 'The Effects of Political and Economic Transitions on Health and Safety in Estonia – An Estonian–Swedish Comparative Study.' *Social Science and Medicine* 47: 1589–99.

Kamin, L. (1974) *The Science and Politics of IQ*. Potomac: Lawrence Erlbaum.

Kaplan, G., Pamuk, E., Lynch, J., Cohen, R. and Balfour, J. (1996) 'Inequality in Income and Mortality in the United States: An Analysis of Mortality and Potential Pathways.' *British Medical Journal* 312: 999–1003.

Kaptchuk, T., Kelley, J., Conboy, L., Davis, R., Kerr, C., Jacobson, E., et al. (2008) 'Components of Placebo Effect: Randomized Controlled Trial in Patients with Irritable Bowel Syndrome.' *British Medical Journal* 336: 999–1003.

Karasek, R. and Theorell, T. (1990) *Healthy Work: Stress, Productivity and the Reconstruction of Working Life*. New York: Basic Books.

Kardiner, A. (1941) *The Traumatic Neuroses of War*. New York: Paul B. Hoebener.

Karoly, L. (1993) 'The Trend in Inequality Among Families, Individuals and Workers in the United States: A Twenty-five Year Perspective.' In *Uneven Tides: Rising Inequality in America*, edited by S. Danziger and P. Gottschalk. New York: Russell Sage.

Kasper, A. and Ferguson, S. (eds) 2000 *Breast Cancer: Society Shapes an Epidemic*. New York: St Martin's Press.

Kaufert, P. A. (1982) 'Myth and Menopause.' *Sociology of Health and Illness* 4: 141–65.

Kawachi, L., Kennedy, B. P., Lochner, K. and Prothrow-Stith, D. (1997) 'Social Capital, Income Inequality and Mortality.' *American Journal of Public Health* 87: 1491–8.

Kawachi, I., Subramanian, S. and Kim, D. (2008) 'Social Capital and Health: A Decade of Progress and Beyond.' In *Social Capital and Health*. New York: Springer.

Kearsley, J. (1986) 'Mammography in 1986: Keeping Abreast of the Times.' *Medical Journal of Australia* 145: 181–2.

Kelleher, C., Newell, J., MacDonaghwhite, C., Machale, E., et al. (1998) 'Incidence and Occupational Pattern of Leukaemias, Lymphomas and Testicular Tumours in Western Ireland Over an 11 Year Period.' *Journal of Epidemiology and Community Health* 52: 651–6.

Kelly, S., Hertzman, C. and Daniels, M. (1997) 'Searching for the Biological Pathways Between Stress and Health.' *Annual Review of Public Health* 18: 437–62.

Kempner, J. (2006) 'Gendering the Migraine Market: Do Representations of Illness Matter?' *Social Science and Medicine* 63 (8): 1986–97.

Kent, R. (1981) *A History of British Empirical Sociology*. Aldershot: Gower.

Kentikelenis, A., King, L., McKee, M. and Stuckler, D. (2015) 'The International Monetary Fund and the Ebola Outbreak.' *The Lancet Global Health* 3 (2): e69–e70.

Kessler, R., McGonagle, K., Nelson, C., et al. (1994) 'Lifetime and 12 Month Prevalence of DSM-III-R Psychiatric Disorders in the United States.' *Archives of General Psychiatry* 51: 8–19.

Kimsma, G. (1990) 'Frames of Reference and the Growth of Medical Knowledge.' In *The Growth of Medical Knowledge*, edited by H. ten Have. Dordrecht: Kluwer Publishers.

Kleit, A. and Ruiz, J. (2003) 'False Positive Mammograms and Detection Controlled Estimation.' *Health Services Research* 38 (4): 1207–39.

Klepinger, L. (1980) 'The Evolution of Human Disease: New Findings and Problems.' *Journal of Biological and Social Sciences* 12: 481–6.

Know, E. and Gilman, E. (1998) 'Migration Patterns of Children with Cancer in Britain.' *Journal of Epidemiology and Community Health* 52: 716–26.

Kokoska, E., Bird, T., Robbins, J., Smith, S., Corsi, S. and Campbell, B. (2007) 'Racial Disparities in the Management of Pediatric Appendicitis.' *Journal of Surgical Research* 130 (2): 83–8.

Kondilis, K., Elias, G., Gavana, M., et al. (2013) 'Economic Crisis, Restrictive Policies, and the Population's Health and Health Care: The Greek Case.' *American Journal of Public Health* 103 (6): e1–e8.

Koos, E. (1954) *The Health of Regionville*. New York: Columbia University Press.

Koutroulis, G. (1990) 'The Orifice Revisited: Portrayal of Women in Gynaecological Texts.' *Community Health Studies* 24: 73–84.

Krieger, N. (1990) 'Racial and Gender Discrimination: Risk Factors for High Blood Pressure.' *Social Science and Medicine* 30: 1273–81.

Krieger, N., Rowley, D., Herman, A., Avery, B. and Phillips, M. (1993) 'Racism, Sexism, and Social Class: Implications for Studies of Health, Disease and Well Being.' *American Journal of Preventive Medicine* 9 (Suppl.): 82–122.

Kroll-Smith, S., Brown, P. and Gunter, V. J. (eds) (2000) *Illness and the Environment: A Reader in Contested Medicine*. New York: New York University Press.

Kuh, D. J., Power, C., Blane, D. and Bartley, M. (1997) 'Social Pathways Between Childhood and Adult Health.' In *Lifecourse Approach to Chronic Disease Epidemiology*, edited by D. J. Kuh and Y. Ben-Schlomo. Oxford: Oxford University Press.

Kuhn, T. (1962 [1970]) *The Structure of Scientific Revolutions*. Chicago: Chicago University Press.

Kuni, C. (1993) 'Mammography in the 1990s: A Plea for Objective Doctors and Informed Patients.' *American Journal of Preventive Medicine* 9: 185–9.

Labonte, R. (1998) 'World Trade and Investment Agreements: Implications for Public Health.' *Canadian Journal of Public Health* 89: 10–12.

Laing, R. D. (1961) *The Divided Self: An Existential Study in Sanity and Madness*. London: Tavistock.

Laing, R. D. (1964) 'What is Schizophrenia?' *New Left Review* 28: 63–9.

Lance, J. (1982) *Mechanism and Management of Headache*, 4th edn. Sydney: Butterworth Scientific.

Lantz, P., House, J., Mero, R. and Williams, D. (2005) 'Stress, Life Events, and Socioeconomic Disparities in Health: Results from the Americans' Changing Lives Study.' *Journal of Health and Social Behavior* 46 (3): 274–88.

Larson, E. (1998) 'Reframing the Meaning of Disability to Families – The Embrace of Paradox.' *Social Science and Medicine* 47: 865–75.

Lawrence, C. (1985) 'Incommunicable Knowledge: Science, Technology, and the Clinical Art in Britain, 1850–1914.' *Journal of Contemporary History* 20: 503–21.

Laws, S. (1983) 'The Sexual Politics of Premenstrual Tension.' *Women's Studies International Forum* 6: 19–31.

Leeder, S. and McAuley, I. (2005) 'Why Health Insurance is Unsustainable.' *New Matilda*, June. http://www.newmatilda.com (accessed 25 July 2007).

Leeson, J. and Gray, J. (1978) *Women and Medicine*. London: Tavistock.

Leete, R. and Fox, J. (1977) 'Registrar General's Social Classes: Origins and Uses', *Population Trends*, 8: 1–7.

Leibrich, J., Hickling, J. and Pitt, G. (1987) *In Search of Well Being: Exploratory Research into Complementary Therapies*. Wellington: Health Services Research and Development Unit, Department of Health.

Lennane, J. and Lennane, J. (1973) 'Alleged Psychogenic Disorders in Women: A Possible Manifestation of Sexual Prejudice.' *New England Journal of Medicine* 228 (6): 288–92.

Lennon, M. and Rosenfield, S. (1992) 'Women and Mental Health: The Interaction of Job and Family Conditions.' *Journal of Health and Social Behaviour* 33: 316–27.

Lerner, B. (1997) 'From Careless Consumptives to Recalcitrant Patients – The Historical Construction of Noncompliance.' *Social Science and Medicine* 45: 1423–31.

Levintova, M. and Novotny, T. (2004) 'Noncommunicable Disease Mortality in the Russian Federation: From Legislation to Policy.' *Bulletin of the World Health Organization* 82 (11): 875–80.

Lewins, F. (1995) *Transsexualism in Society: A Sociology of Male to Female Transsexuals*. Melbourne: Macmillan.

Lewis, J. and Majoribanks, T. (2003) 'The Impact of Financial Constraints and Incentives on Professional Autonomy.' *International Journal of Health Planning and Management* 18 (1): 49–61.

Lewis, M. (1988) *A Rum State: Alcohol and State Policy in Australia*. Canberra: Australian Government Publishing Services.

Lewontin, R. (1973) 'The Apportionment of Human Diversity.' *Evolutionary Biology* 6: 381–97.

Lewontin, R., Rose, S. and Kamin, L. (1984) *Not in Our Genes: Biology, Ideology and Human Nature*. New York: Pantheon Books.

Link, B. and Phelan, J. (1995) 'Social Conditions as Fundamental Causes of Disease.' *Journal of Health and Social Behavior* Extra Issue: 80–94.

Link, B., Lennon, M. and Dohrenwend, P. (1993) 'Socioeconomic Status and Depression: The Role of Occupations Involving Direction, Control, and Planning.' *American Journal of Sociology* 98: 1351–87.

Little, M., Jorens, C., Paul, K., Montgomery, K. and Philipson, B. (1998) 'Liminality – A Major Category of the Experience of Cancer Illness.' *Social Science and Medicine* 47: 1485–94.

Lomas, J. (1998) 'Social Capital and Health – Implications for Public Health and Epidemiology.' *Social Science and Medicine* 47: 1181–8.

Longbottom, H. (1997) 'Emerging Infectious Diseases.' *Communicable Diseases Intelligence* 21: 89–93.

Loring, M. and Powell, B. (1988) 'Gender, Race and the DSM III: A Study of the Objectivity of Psychiatric Diagnosis Behaviour.' *Journal of Health and Social Behaviour* 29 (1): 1–22.

Lupton, D. (1995) *The Imperative of Health: Public Health and the Regulated Body.* London: Sage.

Lupton, D. (2013) 'Quantifying the Body: Monitoring and Measuring Health in the Age of Health Technologies.' *Critical Public Health* 23 (4): 393–403.

Lupton, D. (2016) *The Quantified Self: A Sociology of Self Tracking.* Cambridge: Polity Press.

Lynch, J., Kaplan, G., Pamuk, E., Cohen, R., Heck, K., Balfour, J. and Yen, I. (1998) 'Income Inequality and Mortality in Metropolitan Areas of the United States.' *American Journal of Public Health* 88: 1074–80.

Lynd, R. and Lynd, H. (1931) *Middletown in Transition.* London: Constable and Co.

MacDonald, R. (2005) 'Mammography Screening for Breast Cancer – Does it Reduce the Mortality Rate? A Review of the Literature.' *Vision* 13 (1): 8–12.

Macintyre, S. (1986) 'The Patterning of Health by Social Position in Contemporary Britain.' *Social Science and Medicine* 23: 393–413.

McAuley, I. (2005) 'Private Health Insurance: Still Muddling Through.' *Agenda* 12 (2): 159–78.

McClelland, A. and Scotton, R. (1998) 'Poverty and Health.' In *Australian Poverty Then and Now*, edited by A. McClelland and R. Scotton. Melbourne: Melbourne University Press.

McKeown, T. (1965) *Medicine and Modern Society.* London: Routledge and Kegan Paul.

McKeown, T. (1979) *The Role of Medicine.* Princeton, NJ: Princeton University Press.

McKevitt, C. and Morgan, M. (1997) 'Anomalous Patients – The Experience of Doctors with an Illness.' *Sociology of Health and Illness* 19: 644–67.

McKie, L. (1995) 'The Art of Surveillance or Reasonable Prevention – The Case of Cervical Screening.' *Sociology of Health and Illness* 17: 441–57.

McKinlay, J. (1981) 'From Promising Report to Standard Procedure: Seven Stages in the Career of a Medical Innovation.' *Milbank Quarterly* 59: 374–411.

McKinlay, J. and McKinlay, S. (1977) 'The Questionable Effect of Medical Measures on the Decline of Mortality in the United States in the Twentieth Century.' *Milbank Memorial Fund Quarterly* 55: 405–28.

McKinlay, J. and McKinlay, S. (1989) 'A Review of the Evidence Concerning the Impact of Medical Measures on Recent Mortality and Morbidity in the United States.' *International Journal of Health Services* 19: 181–208.

McKinlay, J. and Marceau, L. (2002) 'The End of the Golden Age of Doctoring.' *International Journal of Health Services* 32: 379–416.

McLaren, I. (2007) 'Socioeconomic Status and Obesity', *Epidemiological Review* 29: 29–48.

McLoone, P. and Boddy, F. (1994) 'Deprivation and Mortality in Scotland, 1981 and 1991.' *British Medical Journal* 309: 1465–70.

McMahon, S. (1998) 'Professional Purpose and Academic Legitimacy: Ross's Social Control and the Founding of American Sociology.' *The American Sociologist* 29: 9–26.

McNay, L. (1991) 'The Foucauldian Body and the Exclusion of Experience.' *Hypatia* 6: 125–39.

McNay, L. (1994) *Foucault: A Critical Introduction.* London: Polity Press.

Maienschein, J. (1988) 'Whitman at Chicago: Establishing a Chicago Style of Biology?' In *The American Development of Biology*, edited by R. Rainger, K. Benson and J. Maienschein. Philadelphia: University of Pennsylvania Press.

Maienschein, J. (1991a) 'Epistemic Styles in German and American Embryology.' *Science in Context* 4: 407–27.

Maienschein, J. (1991b) *Transforming Traditions in American Biology, 1880–1915*. Baltimore: Johns Hopkins University Press.

Mann, C. (1993) *Unequal Justice: A Question of Race*. Bloomington: Indiana University Press.

Mannheim, K. (1936 [1972]) *Ideology and Utopia*. London: Routledge and Kegan Paul.

Mansfield, A. and McGinn, B. (1993) 'Pumping Irony: The Muscular and the Feminine.' In *Body Matters*, edited by S. Scott and D. Morgan. London: Falmer Press.

Manzoni, G. and Torelli, P. (2005) 'Behavior During Cluster Headache.' *Current Pain and Headache Reports* 9: 113–19.

Margolis, J. (1976) 'The Concept of Disease.' *Journal of Medicine and Philosophy* 1: 238–55.

Markle, G. and Chubin, D. (1987) 'Consensus Development in Biomedicine: The Liver Transplant Controversy.' *The Milbank Quarterly* 65: 1–23.

Markova, I. and Farr, R. (eds) (1995) *Representations of Health, Illness and Handicap*. Chur, Switzerland: Harwood.

Marmot, M. (1998) 'Contribution of Psychosocial Factors to Socioeconomic Differences in Health.' *The Milbank Quarterly* 76: 403–33.

Marmot, M. (2004) *Status Syndrome: How Your Social Standing Directly Affects Your Health and Life Expectancy*. Oxford: Bloomsbury.

Marmot, M. and Wilkinson, R. G. (eds) (1999) *Social Determinants of Health*. Oxford: Oxford University Press.

Marmot, M., Rose, G., Shipley, M. and Hamilton, P. (1978) 'Employment Grade and Coronary Heart Disease in British Civil Servants.' *Journal of Epidemiology and Community Health* 3: 244–9.

Marmot, M., Davey-Smith, G., Stansfeld, S., Patel, C., North, F. and Head, J. (1991) 'Health Inequalities Among British Civil Servants: The Whitehall Study.' *The Lancet* 337: 1387–93.

Marmot, M., Bosma, H., Hemingway, H., Brunner, E. and Stansfeld, S. (1997) 'Contribution of Job Control and Other Risk Factors to Social Variations in Coronary Heart Disease.' *The Lancet* 350: 235–40.

Marshall, T. H. (1963) *Sociology at the Crossroads*. London: Heinemann.

Marteau, T. and Richards, M. (eds) (1996) *The Troubled Helix: Social and Psychological Aspects of the New Human Genetics*. Cambridge: Cambridge University Press.

Martin, B. and Richards, E. (1995) 'Scientific Knowledge, Controversy and Public Decision Making.' In *Handbook of Science and Technology Studies*, edited by S. Jasanoff, G. Markle, J. Petersen and T. Pinch. London: Sage.

Martin, E. (1987) *The Woman in the Body: A Cultural Analysis of Reproduction*. Boston: Beacon Press.

Martin, L. (1989) *Technologies of the Self*. Amherst, MA: MIT Press.

Masia, R., Pena, A., Marrugat, J., Sala, J., Vila, J., Pavesi, M., et al. (1998) 'High Prevalence of Cardiovascular Risk Factors in Gerona, Spain.' *Journal of Epidemiology and Community Health* 52: 707–15.

Mathers, C., Vos, T. and Stevenson, C. (1999) *The Burden of Disease and Injury in Australia – Summary*. Canberra: Australian Institute of Health and Welfare.

Mauss, M. (1935 [1973]) 'Techniques of the Body.' *Economy and Society* 2: 71–88.

Mayer, W. and McWhorter, W. (1989) 'Black/White Differences in Non-Treatment of Bladder Cancer Patients and Implications for Survival.' *American Journal of Public Health* 79: 772–4.

Mechanic, D. (1981) *Medical Sociology*. New York: The Free Press.

Meltzer, H., Baljit, G., Peticrew, M. and Hinds, K. (1995) *The Prevalence of Psychiatric Morbidity Among Adults Living in Private Households*. London: HMSO.

Merton, R. (1957) *The Student Physician: Studies in the Sociology of Medical Education*. Cambridge, MA: Harvard University Press.

Merton, R. (1973) *The Sociology of Science: Theoretical and Empirical Investigations*. Chicago: Chicago University Press.

Meyer, R. (1996) 'The Disease Called Addiction: Emerging Evidence in a Two Hundred Year Debate.' *The Lancet* 347: 162–6.

Miles, R. (1982) *Racism and Migrant Labour*. London: Routledge and Kegan Paul.

Milewa, T., Valentine, J. and Calnan, M. (1998) 'Managerialism and Active Citizenship in Britain's Reformed Health Service – Power and Community in an Era of Decentralisation.' *Social Science and Medicine* 47: 507–17.

Miller, A. (1993) 'The Costs and Benefits of Breast Cancer Screening.' *American Journal of Preventive Medicine* 9: 175–84.

Miller, G., Stark, R. and Valenti, L. (2007) 'Management of Migraine in Australian General Practice.' *Medical Journal of Australia* 187 (3): 142–6.

Mills, C. Wright (1940) 'Situated Actions and Vocabularies of Motive.' *American Sociological Review* 5: 904–13.

Mills, C. Wright (1959) *The Sociological Imagination*. New York: Oxford University Press.

Miniño, A., Heron, M. and Smith, B. (2004) 'Deaths: Preliminary Data for 2004.' *National Vital Statistics Report* 54 (19): 1–50.

Miniño, A., Xu, J. and Kochanek, K. (2010) 'Deaths: Preliminary Data for 2008.' *National Vital Statistics Reports* 59 (2): 1–51.

Mirowsky, J. and Ross, C. (1989) *Social Causes of Psychological Distress*. New York: Aldine de Gruyter.

Mitchell, K. (1987) 'Organised Mammographic Screening Programmes: Benign or Malignant Neglect?' *Medical Journal of Australia* 146: 87–90.

Moerman, D. (1981) 'General Medical Effectiveness and Human Biology: Placebo Effects in the Treatment of Ulcer Disease.' *Medical Anthropology Quarterly* 14: 14–16.

Molinari, C., Ahern, M. and Hendryx, H. (1998) 'The Relationship of Community Quality to the Health of Women and Men.' *Social Science and Medicine* 47: 113–20.

Montgomery, R. (1974) 'A Cross-cultural Study of Menstruation, Menstrual Taboos and Related Social Variables.' *Ethos* 2: 139–70.

Montgomery, S., Cook, D., Bartley, M. and Wadsworth, M. (1998) 'Unemployment, Cigarette Smoking, Alcohol Consumption and Body Weight in Young British Men.' *European Journal of Public Health* 8: 21–7.

Mooney, G. (1998) 'Communitarian Claims as an Ethical Basis for Allocating Health Care Resources.' *Social Science and Medicine* 47: 1171–80.

Morgan, D. (1992) *Discovering Masculinities*. London: Routledge.

Morton, W. and Ungs, T. (1979) 'Cancer Mortality in the Major Cottage Industry.' *Women and Health* 4: 345–54.

Multiple Risk Factor Intervention Trial (1982) 'The Multiple Risk Factor Intervention Group – Risk Factor Changes and Mortality Results.' *Journal of the American Medical Association* 248: 1465–76.

Myers, S. (1993) 'Measuring and Detecting Discrimination in the Post-Civil Rights Era.' In *Race and Ethnicity in Research Methods*, edited by J. Stanfield and R. Dennis. Newbury Park, CA: Sage.

Navarro, V. (1976) *Medicine Under Capitalism*. New York: Prodist.

Navarro, V. (1980) 'Work, Ideology and Medicine.' *International Journal of Health Services* 10: 523–50.

Navarro, V. (1983) 'Radicalism, Marxism, and Medicine.' *International Journal of Health Services* 13: 179–202.

Nazroo, J., Edwards, A. and Brown, G. (1997) 'Gender Differences in the Onset of Depression Following a Shared Life Event: A Study of Couples.' *Psychological Medicine* 27: 9–19.

Nazroo, J., Edwards, A. and Brown, G. (1998) 'Gender Differences in the Prevalence of Depression: Artefact, Alternative Disorders, Biology or Roles.' *Sociology of Health and Illness* 20: 312–30.

Nettleton, S. (1985) 'Protecting a Vulnerable Margin.' *Sociology of Health and Illness* 10: 156–69.

Neubauer, D. and Pratt, R. (1981) 'The Second Public Health Revolution: A Critical Appraisal.' *Journal of Health Politics Policy and Law* 6: 205–28.

Newman, J. (1984) 'Sex Differences.' *Journal of Health and Social Behaviour* 25: 136–59.

Nicolson, M. and McLaughlin, C. (1988) 'Social Constructionism and Medical Sociology: A Study of the Vascular Theory of Multiple-sclerosis.' *Sociology of Health and Illness* 10: 234–61.

Oakley, A. (1984) *The Captured Womb*. Oxford: Basil Blackwell.

O'Connor, J. (1984) *Accumulation Crisis*. New York: St Martin's Press.

Offman, A. and Kleinplatz, P. (2004) 'Does PMDD Belong in the DSM? Challenging the Medicalization of Women's Bodies.' *Canadian Journal of Human Sexuality* 13 (1): 17–27.

Ogburn, W. F. (1922) *Social Change with Respect to Culture and Original Nature*. New York: Huebsch.

Ogden, C., Carroll, M., Curtin, L., et al. (2010) 'Prevalence of High Body Mass Index in US Children and Adolescents, 2007–2008.' *Journal of the American Medical Association* 30 (3): 242–9.

Omran, A. (1971) 'The Epidemiologic Transition.' *The Milbank Quarterly* 40: 509–38.

O'Neill, Y. (1980) *Speech and Speech Disorders in Western Thought Before 1600*. Westport, CT: Greenwood Press.

Open University (1985) *The Health of Nations*. Milton Keynes: Open University Press.

Opie, A. (1991) *Caring Alone: Looking After the Confused Elderly at Home*. Wellington: Daphne Brassell Associates.

Opie, A. (1992) *There's Nobody There: Community Care of Confused Older People*. Auckland: Oxford University Press.

Otten, M., Teutsch, S., Williamson, D. and Marks, J. (1990) 'The Effect of Known Risk Factors on the Excess Mortality of Black Adults in the United States.' *Journal of the American Medical Association* 263: 845–50.

Palosuo, H., Uutela, A., Zhuravleva, I. and Lakomova, N. (1998) 'Social Patterning of Ill Health in Helsinski and Moscow – Results From a Comparative Survey in 1991.' *Social Science and Medicine* 46: 1121–36.

Pan American Health Organization (1994) *Health Conditions in the Americas*. Washington, DC: PAHO.

Parsons, T. (1950) *The Social System*. Glencoe, IL: Free Press.

Parsons, T. (1954) *Essays in Sociological Theory*. Chicago: Free Press.

Parsons, T. (1958) 'The Definitions of Health and Illness in the Light of American Values and Social Structure.' In *Patients, Physicians and Illness*, edited by E. Jaco. Chicago: Free Press.

Parsons, T. (1964) *Social Structure and Personality*. New York: Free Press.

Parsons, T. (1978) *Action Theory and the Human Condition*. London: Free Press.

Paterson, K. (1981) 'Theoretical Perspectives in Epidemiology – A Critical Appraisal.' *Radical Community Medicine* 2: 23–33.

Patrick, D. L. and Wickizer, T. M. (1995) 'Community and Health.' In *Society and Health*, edited by B. C. Amick, S. Levine, R. Tarlov and C. D. Walsh. New York: Oxford University Press.

Pearlin, L. (1989) 'The Sociological Study of Stress.' *Journal of Health and Social Behaviour* 30: 241–56.

Pearlin, L., Schieman, S., Fazio, E. and Meersman, S. (2005) 'Stress, Health, and the Life Course: Some Conceptual Perspectives.' *Journal of Health and Social Behavior* 46: 205–19.

Peck, M. and Denney, M. (2012) 'Disparities in the Conduct of the Medical Encounter: The Effects of Physician and Patient Race and Gender'. *Sage Open* 2 (3). http://sgo.sagepub.com/content/2/3/2158244012459193

Pena, G. (2011) 'The Epistemology of Ludwik Fleck and the Classification of Renal Allograft Pathology.' *American Journal of Transplantation* 11 (5): 907–10.

Peter, R., Alfredson, N., Hammar, N., et al. (1998) 'High Effort, Low Reward and Cardiovascular Risk Factors in Employed Swedish Men and Women.' *Journal of Epidemiology and Community Health* 52: 540–7.

Peterson, C. (1999) *Stress at Work: A Sociological Approach*. New York: Baywood.

Pezzullo, P. (2003) 'Resisting "National Breast Cancer Awareness Month": The Rhetoric of Counterpublics and their Cultural Performances.' *Quarterly Journal of Speech* 89 (4): 345–65.

Pfeffer, N. (1985) 'The Hidden Pathology of the Male Reproductive System.' *The Sexual Politics of Reproduction*, edited by H. Homans. Aldershot: Gower.

Phelan, S. (1990) 'Foucault and Feminism.' *American Journal of Political Science* 34: 421–40.

Phillimore, P., Beattie, A. and Townsend, P. (1994) 'Widening Inequality of Health in Northern England, 1981–91.' *British Medical Journal* 308: 1125–8.

Phillips, J. (1983) *Mothers Matter Too*. Wellington: A. H. and A. W. Read.

Pomare, E. (1988) 'Groups with Special Health Care Needs.' *New Zealand Medical Journal* 101: 297–308.

Popay, J., Williams, G., Thomas, C. and Gatrell, T. (1998) 'Theorising Inequalities in Health.' *Sociology of Health and Illness* 20: 619–44.

Poulantzas, N. (1975) *Classes in Contemporary Capitalism*. London: New Left Books.

Power, C. and Matthews, S. (1997) 'Origins of Health Inequalities in a National Population Sample.' *The Lancet* 350: 1584–9.

Power, P. and Aloizos, J. (2000) 'The Operating Environment of General Practice.' *General Practice in Australia*. Canberra: Department of Health and Aged Care.

Price, L. (1984) 'Art, Science, Faith and Medicine: The Implications of the Placebo Effect.' *Sociology of Health and Illness* 61 (1): 61–73.

Prout, A. (1988) 'Off School Sick: Mothers' Accounts of School Sickness Absence.' *The Sociological Review* 36: 765–89.

Public Health Services (1985) *Women's Health: Report of the PHS Task Force on Women's Health Issues.* Washington, DC: US Department of Health and Human Services.

Puhl, B. and Heur, C. (2010) 'Obesity Stigma: Important Considerations for Public Health.' *American Journal of Public Health* 100 (6): 1019–28.

Purdue, M., Hutchings, S., Rushton, L., et al. (2015) 'The Proportion of Cancer Attributable to Occupational Exposure.' *Annals of Epidemiology* 25 (3): 188–92.

Putnam, R. D. (1995) 'Tuning In, Tuning Out: The Strange Disappearance of Social Capital in America.' *Political Science and Politics* December: 664–83.

Rabinbach, A. (1990) *The Human Motor: Energy, Fatigue and the Origins of Modernity.* New York: Basic Books.

Ramazanoglu, C. (1989) *Feminism and the Contradictions of Oppression.* London: Routledge and Kegan Paul.

Reay, D. (2006) 'Doing the Dirty Work of Social Class? Mothers' Work in Support of their Children's Schooling.' *The Sociological Review* 53: 104–16.

Redman, S., Webb, G., Hennrikus, D., Gordon, J. and Sanson-Fisher, R. (1991) 'The Effects of Gender on Diagnosis of Psychological Disturbance.' *Journal of Behavioural Medicine* 14 (5): 527–40.

Reid, B., Hagan, B. and Coppleson, M. (1979) 'Homogeneous Heterosapiens.' *Medical Journal of Australia* 5 May: 377–80.

Relman, A. (1980) 'The New Medical-Industrial Complex.' *New England Journal of Medicine* 303: 963–70.

Renaud, M. (1975) 'On the Structural Constraints to State Intervention in Health.' *International Journal of Health Services* 5: 559–72.

Rich, A. (1992) *Of Woman Born.* London: Virago.

Richards, E. (1991) *Vitamin C and Cancer: Medicine or Politics?* London: Macmillan.

Richards, M. (1993) 'The New Genetics: Some Issues for Social Scientists.' *Sociology of Health and Illness* 15: 567–86.

Riessman, C. K. (1983) 'Women and Medicalisation.' *Social Policy* 14: 3–18.

Robertson, A. (1998) 'Critical Reflections on the Politics of Need – Implications for Public Health.' *Social Science and Medicine* 47: 1419–30.

Robinson, J. (1987) 'Trends in Racial Inequality and Exposure to Work-Related Hazards.' *Milbank Quarterly* 65: 404–20.

Rodberg, L. and Stevenson, G. (1979) 'The Health Care Industry in Advanced Capitalism.' *Review of Radical Political Economy* 9: 104–15.

Roepstorff, A. (2002) 'Transforming Subjectivity into Objectivity: An Ethnography of Knowledge in a Brain Imaging Laboratory.' *Folk: Journal of the Danish Ethnographic Society* 44: 145–69.

Romanucci-Ross, L. and Moerman, D. (1988) 'The Extraneous Factor in Western Medicine.' *Ethos* 16: 146–66.

Rook, K. (1992) 'Detrimental Aspects of Social Relationships: Taking Stock of an Emerging Literature.' In *The Meaning and Measurement of Social Support,* edited by H. Veiel and U. Baumann. New York: Hemisphere.

Rose, G. and Marmot, M. (1981) 'Social Class and Coronary Heart Disease.' *British Heart Journal* 45: 13.

Rose, R., Lewontin, R. and Kamin, L. (1984) *Not in Our Genes: Biology, Ideology and Human Nature*. Harmondsworth: Penguin.

Rosenberg, C. (1989) 'Disease in History: Frames and Framers.' *The Milbank Quarterly* 67 (Suppl. 1): 1–15.

Rosenberg, C. and Golden, J. (eds) (1989) 'Framing Disease: The Creation and Negotiation of Explanatory Schemes.' *The Milbank Quarterly* 67: 1–15.

Rosengren, A., Hawken, S., Ounpuu, S., et al. (2004) 'Association of Psychosocial Risk Factors with Risk of Acute Myocardial Infarction in 11,119 Cases and 13,648 Controls from 52 Countries (the INTERHEART Study): Case Control Study.' *The Lancet* 364: 953–62.

Ross, E. (1938) *Principles of Sociology*. New York: D. Appleton Century.

Rossi, A. (1977) 'A Biosocial Perspective on Parenting.' *Daedalus* 106: 1–32.

Roth, J. (1963) *Timetables, Structuring the Passage of Time in Hospital Treatment and Other Careers*. Indianapolis: Bobbs-Merrill.

Rowland, R. (1992) *Living Laboratories: Women and the Reproductive Technologies*. London: Macmillan.

Rubinow, D. and Schmidt, P. (1996) 'Androgens, Brain and Behavior.' *American Journal of Psychiatry* 153: 974–84.

Rushton, J. (1989) 'Population Differences in Susceptibility to AIDS and Evolutionary Analysis.' *Social Science and Medicine* 28: 1211–20.

Sabo, D. and Gordon, F. (1995) *Men's Health and Illness: Gender, Power and the Body*. London: Sage.

Saez, E. and Zucman, G. (2014) 'Wealth Inequality in the United States since 1913: Evidence from Capitalized Income Tax Data.' CEPR discussion paper 10227, October.

Safe Work Australia (2014) *Key Work Health and Safety Statistics, Australia*. Canberra: Safe Work Australia.

Safran, D., Rogers, W., Tarlov, A., et al. (1997) 'Gender Differences in Medical Treatment – The Case of Physician-Prescribed Activity Restrictions.' *Social Science and Medicine* 15: 711–22.

Saguy, A. C. and Almeling, R. (2008) 'Fat in the Fire? Science, the News Media, and the "Obesity Epidemic".' *Sociological Forum* 23 (1): 53–83.

Sayer, G. and Britt, H. (1997) 'Sex Differences in Prescribed Medications – Another Case of Discrimination in General Practice.' *Social Science and Medicine* 15: 1581–7.

Schilder, P. (1950) *The Image and Appearance of the Human Body*. New York: International Universities Press.

Schrijvers, C. and Mackenbach, J. (1994) 'Cancer Patient Survival by Socioeconomic Status in Seven Countries – A Review for Six Common Cancer Sites.' *Journal of Epidemiology and Community Health* 48: 554–5.

Seaman, B. (1987) 'The Dangers of Oral Contraception.' In *Seizing our Bodies*, edited by C. Dreifus. New York: Vintage.

Secretary of State for Health (1988) *Our Healthier Nation: A Contract For Health*. London: HMSO.

Senese, L., Almeida, N., Fath, A., et al. (2009) 'Associations between Childhood Socioeconomic Position and Adult Obesity.' *Epidemiological Review* 31: 21–51.

Sheldon, T. and Parker, H. (1992) 'For Debate: Race and Ethnicity in Health Research.' *Journal of Public Health Medicine* 14: 104–11.

Shi, L. (1994) 'Primary Care, Speciality Care and Life Chances.' *International Journal of Health Services* 24: 431–58.

Shkolnikov, V., Leon, D., Adamets, S., et al. (1998) 'Educational Level and Adult Mortality in Russia – An Analysis of Routine Data 1979–1994.' *Social Science and Medicine* 47: 357–69.

Shuman, S. (1977) *Psychosurgery and the Medical Control of Deviance.* Detroit: Wayne State University Press.

Silverman, D. (1981) 'The Child as Social Object: Down's Syndrome Children in a Cardiology Clinic.' *Sociology of Health and Illness* 3: 254–75.

Silverman, D. (1983) 'The Clinical Subject: Adolescents in a Cleft Palate Clinic.' *Sociology of Health and Illness* 5: 253–75.

Silverman, D. (1987) *Communication and Medical Practice: Social Relations in the Clinic.* London: Sage.

Sinclair, B. (1989) 'Strategies for Reducing the Drug Bill.' *New Zealand Medical Journal* 102: 165–7.

Singer, M. (1984) 'Hypoglycemia: A Controversial Illness in US Society.' *Medical Anthropology* 8: 1–36.

Singh, G. and Siahpush, M. (2006) 'Widening Socioeconomic Inequalities in US Life Expectancy, 1980–2000.' *International Journal of Epidemiology* 35: 969–79.

Skrabanek, P. (1988) 'The Debate Over Mass Mammography in Britain: The Case Against.' *British Medical Journal* 297: 971–2.

Smaje, C. (1996) 'The Ethnic Patterning of Health: New Directions for Theory and Research.' *Sociology of Health and Illness* 18: 139–71.

Smith, A. (1985) 'The Epidemiological Basis of Community Medicine.' In *Recent Advances in Community Medicine 3*, edited by A. Smith. Edinburgh: Churchill Livingstone.

Smith, D. (1995) *The Conceptual Practices of Power: A Feminist Sociology of Knowledge.* Toronto: University of Toronto Press.

Smith, J. (1988) 'Can New Zealand Afford Nonrestricted Antibiotic Prescribing?' *New Zealand Medical Journal* 101: 213.

Smith, R. (1981) *Trial by Medicine: Insanity and Responsibility in Victorian Trials.* Edinburgh: Edinburgh University Press.

Snow, J. (1936) *On Cholera.* New York: Commonwealth Fund.

Sontag, S. (1978) *Illness as Metaphor.* New York: Farrar, Straus and Giroux.

State and Territory Health Ministers (2007) *Caring for our Health: A Report Card on the Australian Government's Performance on Health Care.* Governments of the Australian Capital Territory, New South Wales, Northern Territory, Queensland, South Australia, Tasmania, Victoria and Western Australia.

Steinberg, D. (1990) 'The Depersonalisation of Women through the Administration of "In Vitro Fertilisation".' In *The New Reproductive Technologies*, edited by M. McNeil, I. Varcoe and S. Yearley. London: Macmillan.

Stephenson, J. (2000) 'Exposure to Home Pesticides Linked to Parkinson's Disease.' *Journal of the American Medical Association* 283: 3055.

Stern, B. (1927) *Social Factors in Medical Progress.* New York: AMS Press.

Stimson, G. (1976) 'Doctor–Patient Interaction in Some Problems for Prescribing.' *Journal of the Royal College of General Practitioners* 26: 88–96.

Storch, E., Milsom, V., Debraganza, N., et al. (2007) 'Peer Victimization, Psychosocial Adjustment, and Physical Activity in Overweight and At-Risk-for-Overweight Youth.' *Journal of Paediatric Psychology* 32 (1): 80–9.

Stovner, L., Hagen, K., Jensen, R., Katsarava, Z., Lipton, R. Z., Scher, A., Steiner, T. and Zwart, J. (2007) 'The Global Burden of Headache: A Documentation of Headache Prevalence and Disability Worldwide.' *Cephalalgia* 27: 193–210.

Sudnow, D. (1967) *The Social Organization of Dying*. New York: Prentice Hall.

Svensson, C. (1989) 'Representation of American Blacks in Clinical Trials of New Drugs.' *Journal of the American Medical Association* 261: 263–5.

Syme, S. (1996) 'Rethinking Disease: Where Do We Go from Here?' *Annals of Epidemiology* 6: 463–8.

Szasz, T. (1971) *The Manufacture of Madness: A Comparative Study of the Inquisition and the Mental Health Movement*. London: Routledge and Kegan Paul.

Szeto, A. and Dobson, K. (2013) 'Mental Disorders and their Association with Perceived Work Stress: An Investigation of the 2010 Canadian Community Health Survey.' *Journal of Occupational Health Psychology* 18: 191–7.

Szreter, S. (1988) 'The Importance of Social Intervention in Britain's Mortality Decline c. 1850–1914.' *Social History of Medicine* 1: 1–37.

Taylor, F. K. and Scadding, J. (1980) 'The Concepts of Disease.' *Psychological Medicine* 10: 419–24.

ten Have, H. (2001) 'Genetics and Culture: The Geneticization Thesis.' *Medicine, Health Care and Philosophy* 4: 295–304.

Terris, M. (1996) 'The Development and Prevention of Cardiovascular Disease Risk Factors: Socioenvironmental Influences.' *Journal of Public Health Policy* 17: 426–41.

Terris, M. (1998) 'Epidemiology and Health Policy in the Americas: Meeting the Neoliberal Challenge.' *Journal of Public Health Policy* 19: 15–24.

Tesh, S. (1988) *Hidden Arguments*. New Brunswick, NJ: Rutgers University Press.

Thoits, P. (1995) 'Stress, Coping and Social Support Processes: Where Are We? What Next?' *Journal of Health and Social Behaviour* Extra Issue: 53–79.

Thomas, K., Nicholl, J. and Fall, M. (2001) 'Access to Complementary Medicine via General Practice.' *British Journal of General Practice* 51 (462): 25–30.

Thomas, W. I. (1923) *The Unadjusted Girl with Cases and Standpoint for Behavior Analysis*. Montclair, NJ: Patterson Smith.

Thomson, A. (1988) 'Workloads in Auckland General Practice 1981/82 to 1984/85.' *New Zealand Medical Journal* 101: 763–5.

Thomson, J., Lin, M., Halliday, L., et al. (1998) 'Australia's Notifiable Disease Status, 1998.' *Communicable Diseases Intelligence* 23: 277–305.

Toon, P. (1981) 'Defining Disease: Classification Must be Distinguished from Evaluation.' *Journal of Medical Ethics* 7: 197–201.

Townsend, J. and Carbone, C. (1980) 'Menopausal Syndrome: Illness or Social Role – A Transcultural Analysis.' *Culture, Medicine, and Psychiatry* 4: 229–48.

Townsend, P. and Davidson, N. (eds) (1988) *Inequalities in Health: The Black Report and the Health Divide*. Harmondsworth: Penguin.

Tukuitonga, C. and Bindman, A. (2002) 'Ethnic and Gender Differences in the Use of Coronary Artery Revascularisation Procedures in New Zealand.' *New Zealand Medical Journal* 115 (1152): 179–82.

Turner, B. S. (1984) *The Body and Society*. London: Basil Blackwell.

Turner, B. S. (1986a) *Citizenship and Capitalism: The Debate Over Reformism*. London: Allen and Unwin.

Turner, B. S. (1986b) 'Sickness and Social Structure: Parsons' Contribution to Medical Sociology.' In *Talcott Parsons on Economy and Society*, edited by R. J. Holton and B. S. Turner. London: Routledge and Kegan Paul.

Turner, B. S. (1992) *Regulating Bodies*. London: Routledge.

Turner, R. and Marino, F. (1994) 'Social Support and Social Structure: A Descriptive Epidemiology.' *Journal of Health and Social Support* 35: 193–212.

Turner, R. and Roszell, P. (1994) 'Psychosocial Resources and the Stress Process.' In *Stress and Mental Health*, edited by W. R. Avison and I. H. Gotlib. New York: Plenum.

Turner, T. (1980) 'The Social Skin.' In *Not Work Alone*, edited by J. Cherfas and R. Lewin. London: Sage.

Turrell, G. and Mathers, C. (2001) 'Socioeconomic Inequalities in All-Cause and Specific-Cause Mortality in Australia 1985–1987 and 1995–1997.' *International Journal of Epidemiology* 30: 231–39.

Twaddle, A. C. (1982) 'From Medical Sociology to the Sociology of Health: Some Changing Concerns in the Sociological Study of Sickness and Treatment.' In *Sociology: The State of the Art*, edited by T. Bottomore, M. Sokolowska and S. Nowak. London: Sage.

Ussher, J. (1991) *Women's Madness: Misogyny or Mental Illness*. London: Harvester Wheatsheaf.

Veale, B. and Douglas, R. (1992) *Money Matters in General Practice*. Canberra: National Centre for Epidemiology and Public Health.

Verbrugge, L. (1989) 'The Twain Meet: Empirical Explanations of Sex Differences in Health and Mortality.' *Journal of Health and Social Behavior* 30: 282–304.

Vertianen, E., Pekkanen, J. and Koskinen, J. (1998) 'Do Changes in Cardiovascular Risk Factors Explain the Increasing Socioeconomic Differences in Mortality from Ischaemic Heart Disease in Finland?' *Journal of Epidemiology and Community Health* 52: 416–19.

Volin, I. (1983) 'Health Professionals as Stigmatisers and De-stigmatisers of Disease: Alcoholism and Leprosy.' *Social Science and Medicine* 17: 385–93.

Wagner, M. (1998) 'The Public Health versus Clinical Approaches to Maternity Services: The Emperor Has No Clothes.' *Journal of Public Health Policy* 19: 25–35.

Wagner, P. (1994) *A Sociology of Modernity: Liberty and Discipline*. London: Routledge.

Wainwright, D. (2008) 'Illness Behaviour and the Discourse of Health.' In *A Sociology of Health*, edited by D. Wainwright. London: Sage.

Waitzkin, H. (1981) 'A Marxist Analysis of the Health Care Systems of Advanced Capitalist Societies.' In *The Relevance of Social Science for Medicine*, edited by L. Eisenberg and A. Kleinmann. Dordrecht: D. Riedel.

Waitzkin, H. (1986) 'A Marxian Interpretation of the Growth and Development of Coronary Care Technology.' In *The Sociology of Health and Illness*, edited by P. Conrad and R. Kern. New York: St Martin's Press.

Waitzkin, H. (1989) 'A Critical Theory of Medical Discourse: Ideology, Social Control and the Processing of Social Context in Medical Encounters. *Journal of Health and Social Behavior* 30: 220–39.

Waitzkin, H. (1991) *The Politics of Medical Encounters*. New Haven, CT: Yale University Press.

Waitzkin, H. (2000) *The Second Sickness: Contradictions of Capitalist Health Care*. Lanham, MD: Rowman and Littlefield.

Walker, M., Shaper, A. and Wannamethee, G. (1988) 'Height and Social Class in Middle-Aged British Men.' *Journal of Epidemiology and Community Health* 42: 299–303.

Wardwell, W. (1952) 'A Marginal Professional Role: The Chiropractor.' *Social Forces* 30: 339–48.

Waterhouse, R. (1993) 'The Inverted Gaze.' In *Body Matters*, edited by S. Scott and D. Morgan. London: Falmer Press.

Watkins, C., Harvey, I., Carthy, P., Moore, L., Robinson, E. and Brawn, R. (2003) 'Attitudes and Behaviour of General Practitioners and their Prescribing Costs: A National Cross-Sectional Survey.' *Quality and Safety in Health Care* 12 (1): 29–35.

Watson, P. (1995) 'Explaining Rising Mortality Among Men in Eastern Europe.' *Social Science and Medicine* 41: 923–34.

Weber, M. (1968) *Economy and Society*. Berkeley: University of California Press.

Weitz, R. (2010) 'The Social Sources of Illness.' In *The Sociology of Health, Illness, and Health Care: A Critical Approach*. Boston: Wadsworth Cengage Learning.

Wennberg, J., Barnes, B. and Zubkoff, M. (1982) 'Professional Uncertainty and the Problem of Supplier-Induced Demand.' *Social Science and Medicine* 16: 811–24.

Wertz, D. (1980) 'Man, Midwifery, and the Rise of Technology.' In *Birth Control and Controlling Birth: Women-Centered Perspectives*, edited by H. Hoskins and M. Gross. Boston: Beacon Press.

Wertz, D. (1992) 'Ethical and Legal Implications of the New Genetics: Issues for Discussion.' *Social Science and Medicine* 35: 495–505.

White, K. (1988) 'The Sociology of Knowledge and Medical Sociology.' *Explorations in Knowledge* 6 (1): 31–65.

White, K. (1991a) 'Sociological Perspectives on Disease.' *Explorations in Knowledge* 8 (1): 27–38.

White, K. (1991b) 'The Sociology of Health and Illness.' *Current Sociology* 39: 1–134.

White, K. (1992) 'Towards a Sociology of Disease.' In *New Directions in the Philosophy of Science*, edited by D. Lamb. London: Avebury Gower.

White, K. (1993) 'Ludwik Fleck and the Foundations of the Sociology of Medical Knowledge.' *Explorations in Knowledge* 10 (2): 1–21.

White, K. (1994) 'Social Construction of Medicine and Health.' In *Social Dimensions of Health and Disease*, edited by J. Spicer, A. Trlin and J. Walton. Palmerston North: Dunmore Press.

White, K. (1996) 'The Social Origins of Illness and the Development of the Sociology of Health.' In *Health in Australia: Sociological Concepts and Issues*, edited by C. Grbich. Sydney: Prentice Hall

White, K. (1999) 'Negotiating Science and Liberalism: Medicine in Nineteenth-Century South Australia.' *Medical History* 43: 173–91.

White, K. (2000a) 'The State, the Market, and General Practice: The Australian Case.' *International Journal of Sociology* 30 (2): 285–308.

White, K. (2000b) 'Health and Illness.' In *Sociology: Australian Connections*, edited by R. Jureidini and M. Poole. Sydney: Allen and Unwin.

White, K. (ed.) (2001) *The Early Sociology of Health*, 6 vols. London: Routledge.

White, K. (2015) 'Ludwik Fleck, the Sociology of Knowledge and the Sociology of Medical Knowledge.' In *The Palgrave Handbook of Social Theory in Health, Illness and Medicine*, edited by F. Collyer. Basingstoke: Palgrave Macmillan.

White, K. and Collyer, F. (1998) 'Health Care Markets in Australia: Ownership of the Private Hospital Sector.' *International Journal of Health Services* 28: 487–510.

Whitehead, M. (1987) *The Health Divide: Inequalities in Health in the 1980s*. London: Health Education Council.

Whiteis, D. (1998) 'Third World Medicine in First World Cities: Capital Accumulation, Uneven Development and Public Health.' *Social Science and Medicine* 47: 795–808.

Wilkinson, R. (1995) 'Socioeconomic Determinants of Health: Health Inequalities: Relative or Absolute Material Standards?' *British Medical Journal* 311: 1285–7.

Wilkinson, R. (1999) 'Health, Hierarchy and Social Anxiety.' *Annals of the New York Academy of Sciences* 896: 48–63.

Wilkinson, R. and Marmot, M. (eds) (1998) *Social Determinants of Health – The Solid Facts*. Copenhagen: World Health Organization.

Wilkinson, R. and Pickett, K. (2006) 'Income Inequality and Population Health: A Review and Explanation of the Evidence.' *Social Science and Medicine* 62 (7): 1768–84.

Wilkinson, R., Kawachi, I. and Kennedy, B. (1998) 'Mortality, the Social Environment, Crime and Violence.' *Sociology of Health and Illness* 20: 578–97.

Wilkinson, R. G. (1996) *Unhealthy Societies: The Afflictions of Inequality*. London: Routledge.

Wilkinson, S. and Kitzinger, C. (eds) (1994) 'Towards a Feminist Approach to Breast Cancer.' *Women and Health: Feminist Perspectives*. Bristol: Taylor and Francis.

Williams, F., Florey, C., Ogston, S. D., Patel, N., Howie, P. and Tindall, V. (1998) 'UK Study of Intrapartum Care for Low Risk Primagravidas – A Survey of Interventions.' *Journal of Epidemiology and Community Health* 52: 494–500.

Williams, L. and Germov, J. (2005) 'The Social Appetite: A Sociological Approach to Food and Nutrition.' In *Second Opinion: An Introduction to Health Sociology*, edited by J. Germov. Melbourne: Oxford University Press.

Williams, S. (1995) 'Theorising Class, Health and Lifestyle: Can Bourdieu Help Us?' *Sociology of Health and Illness* 17: 577–604.

Williams, S. (1997) 'Modern Medicine and the "Uncertain" Body: From Corporeality to Hyperreality.' *Social Science and Medicine* 45: 1041–9.

Willis, E. (1989) *Medical Dominance*. Sydney: Allen and Unwin.

Willis, E. (1996) 'The Political Economy of Genes.' *Journal of Australian Political Economy* 36: 104–14.

Wirth, L. (1931) 'Clinical Sociology.' *American Journal of Sociology* 37: 49–66.

Wohlfarth, T. and Vandenbrink, W. (1998) 'Social Class and Substance Abuse Disorders – The Value of Social Class as Distinct from Socio-economic Status.' *Social Science and Medicine* 47: 51–8.

Wolff, E. (1995) *Top Heavy: A Study of the Increasing Inequality of Wealth in America*. New York: Twentieth Century Fund Press.

World Health Organization (2004) 'Headache Disorders.' http://www.who.int/mediacentre/factsheets/fs277/en/ (accessed 27 April 2011).

World Health Organization (2008) 'Australia's Disturbing Health Disparities Set Aboriginals Apart'. *Bulletin Of the World Health Organization* 86 (4): 241.

World Health Organization (2009) *Women and Health: Today's Evidence, Tomorrow's Agenda*. Geneva: WHO Press.

Wright, E. (2000) *Class Counts: Student Edition*. Cambridge: Cambridge University Press.

Wright, E. O., Hachen, D., Costello, C., et al. (1982) 'The American Class Structure.' *American Sociological Review* 47: 709–26.

Wright, P. and Treacher, A. (eds) (1982) *The Problem of Medical Knowledge: Examining the Social Construction of Medicine*. Edinburgh: Edinburgh University Press.

Yen, L. (1995) 'From Alma Ata to Asda – and Beyond: A Commentary on the Transition in Health Promotion Services in Primary Care from Commodity to Control.' In *The Sociology of Health Promotion: Critical Analyses of Consumption, Lifestyle and Risk*, edited by R. Bunton, S. Nettleton and R. Burrows. New York: Routledge.

Young, A. (1995) *The Harmony of Illusions: Inventing Post-Traumatic Stress Disorder*. Princeton, NJ: Princeton University Press.

Young, F. and Bacadayan, A. (1965) 'Menstrual Taboos and Social Rigidity.' *Ethnology* 4: 225–41.

Young, I. (1990) *Throwing Like a Girl and Other Essays in Feminist Philosophy and Social Theory*. Bloomington: Indiana University Press.

Youngson, A. (1979) *The Scientific Revolution in Victorian Medicine*. London: Croom Helm.

Zaretsky, E. (1976) *Capitalism, the Family and Personal Life*. London: Pluto Press.

Zavestoski, S., Brown, P., Linder, M., McCormick , S. and Mayer, B. (2002) 'Science, Policy, Activism, and War: Defining the Health of Gulf War Veterans.' *Science, Technology and Human Values* 2 (2): 171–205.

Zhang, Q and Wang, Y. (2004) 'Trends in the Association between Obesity and Socioeconomic Status in US Adults: 1971–2000.' *Obesity Research* 12 (10): 1622–32.

Zheng, H. (2015) 'Losing Confidence in Medicine in an Era of Medical Expansion?' *Social Science Research* 52: 701–15.

Zinsser, F. (1935) *Rats, Lice and History*. Boston: Little Brown.

Zola, I. (1972) 'Medicine as an Institution of Social Control.' *American Sociological Review* 20: 487–504.

INDEX